Gender, Politics, and Poetry
in Twentieth-Century Argentina

Gender, Politics, and Poetry
in Twentieth-Century Argentina

〖

Jill S. Kuhnheim

UNIVERSITY PRESS OF FLORIDA

Gainesville Tallahassee Tampa Boca Raton
Pensacola Orlando Miami Jacksonville

01 00 99 98 97 96   6 5 4 3 2 1

Library of Congress Cataloging-in-Publication Data

Kuhnheim, Jill S.
  Gender, politics, and poetry in twentieth-century Argentina/ Jill S. Kuhnheim.
    p.   cm.
  Includes bibliographical references and index.
  ISBN 0-8130-1393-3 (cloth: alk. paper)
  1. Argentine poetry—Women authors—History and criticism.
  2. Argentine poetry—20th century—History and criticism.
  3. Literature and society—Argentina. 4. Subjectivity in literature.
  I. Title
PQ7633.K84   1996   95-20489
861–dc20

The interview with Olga Orozco is published with her permission. The following poems
and poetry extracts are reprinted by permission: Inés Aráoz, "Estampar los intersticiales
. . . ," from *Los intersticiales*. Courtesy of El imaginero, Poetry and Criticism Notebooks,
Buenos Aires, Argentina. /Oliverio Girondo, "Aridandantemente," from *En la Masmédula*.
Courtesy of the Estate of Oliverio Girondo. /Liliana Lukin, "Si yo hubiera . . . ," from
Cortar por lo sano. Courtesy of Liliana Lukin. /Olga Orozco, "Densos velos te cubren,"
from *Mutaciones de la Realidad, 1979*. Copyright by Editorial Sudamericana S.A., Buenos
Aires, Argentina. /Cristina Piña, "Oficio de máscaras," from *Oficio de máscaras*. Courtesy
of Cristina Piña. /Alejandra Pizarnik, "has construído tu casa," "silencio," and "sólo la
sed," from *Extracción de la piedra de la locura 1968*. Copyright by Editorial Sudamericana
S.A., Buenos Aires, Argentina.

The University Press of Florida is the scholarly publishing agency for the State University
System of Florida, comprised of Florida A & M University, Florida Atlantic University,
Florida International University, Florida State University, University of Central Florida,
University of Florida, University of North Florida, University of South Florida, and
University of West Florida.

University Press of Florida
15 Northwest 15th Street
Gainesville, FL 32611

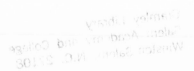

This book is for my father,
E. James Kuhnheim

Contents

Preface

This book began from a desire to examine the separation between social and aesthetic concerns characteristic of the analysis of twentieth-century Latin American poetry. I wanted to reconnect the aesthetist strand, founded in modernism, that viewed the poem as an artistic construct, distant from the world, to the social thread that came to fruition in the late vanguard emphasis on literature's role in social transformation. With this theoretical problem in mind, I also sought an answer to a question frequently posed to me by my students: Why read poetry today? This study combines these problems and attempts an answer via the specific case of Argentina. I suggest that twentieth-century Argentina may offer us an instance in which lyric poetry's increasing marginality from mainstream social discourse and from an escalating attention to narrative has allowed it to work against hegemonic discourse and to open a space for the construction of different subjectivities.

Highlighting the work of female poets, but not reading them in isolation, I also wanted to bring some part of the Spanish American women's tradition to an English-speaking audience. To do so I construct a lyrical overview by reading a constellation of voices that lead us to comprehend this poetry historically, in terms of literary, social, and political changes. In the process it becomes clear that while gender differences are always a factor to be considered, the construction of a gendered subjectivity is not monolithic—in every case it is necessary to speak in the plural, of subjectiv*ies*. Adding to the growing corpus of feminist scholarship in the Latin American realm, this study should interest scholars of the region, those who work in comparative literature, and readers attentive to contemporary theoretical approaches to the lyric.

My work on Argentine poetry began at the University of California, San Diego, and I am indebted to Jaime Concha, Susan Kirkpatrick, and Rosaura Sánchez for their generous interest in and comments on my early work. I have received helpful feedback from Linda Krumholz, Kathryn McKnight, and Alberto Moreiras, who each read and reflected on sections of this project, and from Margarita Zamora, who responded to an earlier version of the manuscript. I am also appreciative of the careful and perceptive remarks of Francine Masiello and the other anonymous readers of the manuscript. I am grateful to the Tinker Foundation of the University of California–San Diego for a grant to travel to Argentina in 1988 and to the Graduate School of the University of Wisconsin-Madison for summer support, enabling me to revise and expand my manuscript. Olga Orozco generously lent me materials during my stay in Buenos Aires and met with me on several occasions, and I am indebted to her for her participation in my project. Myriam Osorio's detailed attention to the nuances of her native tongue are apparent in the translations with which she assisted me; any missteps in this realm, however, are my own responsibility for I had the final word. Thanks to Luanne Ransley and Bruno Browning for their help with the electronic elements of the book's appearance and to Melissa McNeill, my friends, and my family for their continual encouragement.

Chapter 2 originally appeared, in a modified form, in *Confluencia* 5, no. 1 (Fall 1989) and part of chapter 4 in *Monographic Review/Revista Monográfica* 1, no. 6 (Spring 1991); I am grateful to these journals for permission to republish these pieces. I would also like to thank the following publishers and individuals for permission to reproduce copyrighted material: Editorial Sudamericana, S.A. (for material from Pizarnik's *Extracción de la piedra de la locura* and Orozco's *Mutaciones de la realidad*), and Cristina Piña (from her own *Oficio de máscaras*), the editors of El imaginero (from Aráoz's *Los intersticiales*), Liliana Lukin (from her book *Cortar por lo sano*), Susana Lange (from Girondo's *En la masmédula*), and Olga Orozco for permission to print the text of our interview in Buenos Aires.

CHAPTER 1

Defining the Subject

[]

Questioning the construction of subjectivity in literature and cultural criticism has become an accepted, even popular, practice. This interrogation has been stimulated by post-structuralist consciousness of the constructedness of speaking positions, by the "death of the author" as heralded by Barthes, Foucault, and others, and by a generalized trend toward historicization which has to some degree denaturalized certain concepts by identifying the specificity of their practice. Feminist, "post"-colonial, non-European voices are receiving increasing critical attention, competing for subject positions while challenging accepted notions of subjectivity. We have learned to examine the social construction of subject positions, to ask who can occupy them and how.

In a Latin American context, the problem of the subject in Argentina caught the interest of many cultural critics in the 1980s. This attention may be in part due to a strong tradition of literary self-referentiality in Argentina (begun in the nineteenth century with writers such as Domingo Faustino Sarmiento, Esteban Echeverría, and José Hernández, and continued into the twentieth by Martínez Estrada and Jorge Luis Borges, among others); it may be due to the clear twentieth-century interest in Lacanian theory, which depends upon a notion of the Law of the Father and intersects with the continual presence of strong authoritarian figures in the national culture (both discursive—as exemplified by authors such as Leopoldo Lugones—and literal, as seen through Juan Manuel Rosas, Juan Domingo Perón, and the military *junta*). It may also be linked to readers' fascination with contemporary Argentine narrative—the work of authors such as Borges, Cortázar, Puig, and Valenzuela—which has led to a reexamination of earlier sectors and periods in Argentine literature. After a hushed 1970s, recent attention has been fixed on post-dictatorship cultural production in Argentina, as critics search for seeds of cultural change in the nation's reconciliation with the horrors of its recent history. We find examples of this in Ana María Amar Sánchez's treatment of the testimonial form in *El relato de los hechos*, a consideration of the work of Rodolfo Walsh, and in the metacritical elements of Ricardo Piglia's 1980 novel, *Respiración artificial*.

One part of the effort to come to terms with the present has necessarily entailed an exploration of the past. Reconsiderations of turn-of-the-century Modernism and the Vanguard of the 1920s, such as Gwen Kirkpatrick's *The Dissonant Legacy of Modernismo*, Beatriz Sarlo's *La modernidad periférica*, and Francine Masiello's *Lenguaje e Ideología: las escuelas argentinas de vanguardia*, have focused on evidence of dissonance present in hegemonic authors and movements (Kirkpatrick, Masiello) or examine previously marginalized perspectives in an attempt to reaffirm the plurality of speaking positions present in Argentina's early twentieth-century cultural production (Sarlo, Masiello). Several other critics return to nineteenth-century literature and politics; Josefina Ludmer explores the gaucho in his double inflection as both Argentine and Other in *El género gauchesco: Un tratado sobre la patria* and Adolfo Prieto and Nicholas Shumway (in *El discurso criollista en la formación de la Argentina moderna* and *The Invention of Argentina*, respectively) scrutinize the country's early discursive disparities and "guiding fictions," in order to uncover the ideological underpinnings of present day contradiction in Argentine thought. Each of these studies in some way touches upon the conflictive construction of national identity and the disaccord produced by the continued call for a homogeneous social subject, a demand which has often been controlled by authoritarian means in Argentine history.

This study adds yet another perspective to the collective rereading of Argentina's literary legacy; by approaching the problem from the other side, tracing the construction of subjectivity in a genre and a poet whose texts distance themselves from historical events, we will find that the struggle for (or against) a cohesive social subject can be observed at every level of cultural production in Argentina, not only those which most overtly address it. Evidence of a fragmented identity is deeply embedded in the lyric poetry we will examine, even though many of these texts appear to be far removed from social realities. This very distancing can be read historically; for the "lost generation" of the forties it is an elementary mode of survival, of perpetuating a role for the poet in an increasingly hostile society, and a way of disguising certain "transgressive" differences in the positions and demands imposed upon particular poets (most notably, differences in gender, class, and, in some instances, sexual orientation). Argentina, Olga Orozco, the forties generation, and the other poets considered in this study provide specific examples of a larger problem; a problem that Svetlana Boym has articulated as "the tension and interdependence of literature and life," which, she asserts, "constitutes the central aporia of modernity" (9). It is a tension that has been very apparent in Spanish America, as different nations contend with the often irreconcilable ideas and realities of "modernity." It has also been at the center of the struggle between conflicting ideas about twentieth-century Spanish American poetry, a struggle between a valuation of literary autonomy and the effort to relate literature to the world.

Reading the Receding 1940s

Olga Orozco, born in Toay, Las Pampas, in 1920, has produced more than nine volumes of poetry, a play, and a narrative work. She published her first book of poems, *Desde lejos* [From afar], in 1946. This date places the beginning of her career in something of a literary interstice; between the vanguard of the 1920s and the more political poetry of the 1960s and, in narrative, between the 1920s and 1930s *novelas de la tierra,* their urban counterparts, and the later, overshadowing boom in narrative. Historically, Orozco's entrance into the literary scene coincides neatly with the advent of *peronismo;* she continued to publish through the turbulent fifties and sixties, during the recent years of Argentina's dictatorship and the "dirty war" until the present (her most recent work, published in 1994, is *Con esta boca en este mundo* [With this mouth in this world]). The connection between Orozco's aesthetic production and her particular context is not immediately apparent; her lyric style creates another linguistically defined dimension that seems independent of constraining social conditions. Still, starting from the assertion that "all uses of language are interpretations of reality" (Fish 1023), we will see that Orozco's work is crossed by a number of discourses that situate it in terms of its historical, social, and aesthetic positions. Subjective, metaphysical, cosmopolitan traits seem to dominate Orozco's poetry and are augmented by a rigorous formal construction. But these are only some of her text's most obvious characteristics. Rereading her work with a Bakhtinian notion of intertextuality, using his concept of the "'literary word' as an intersection of textual surfaces rather than a point (a fixed meaning)" (*Kristeva Reader* 36), will disclose other strands. Orozco responds to earlier and contemporary poets in language that does not release her from reality but places her in her society and marks a particular historical moment. Orozco's work has a specific relation to the symbolic realm, a relation that indicates a gendered, regional identity as well as a degree of alienation from society. In spite of the continual erasure of specific times and places in her poetry, Orozco's language frequently discloses a speaker who is both female and Argentine. At the same time this poetry fits into a broader modern Latin American tradition of negation, taking its place as a part of a larger ideological struggle.

In Argentine literary history, Orozco is sometimes included as a late member of the *Generación del 40,* a categorization which would define her as a neoromantic poet. Carlos Giordano, in *El 40,* situates this generation as publishing between 1935 and 1945, in conjunction with the appearance of the journal *Canto,* and the later *revista, El 40* (1951–53). In an anti-romantic vein, however, Orozco frequently decentralizes the speaker of her poems and concentrates instead on language itself. For these traits, Orozco is called a surrealist. The poet acknowledges her use of surrealist techniques:

> Aunque no sea una surrealista ortodoxa, creo que hay elementos en común: el predominio de lo imaginario, búsquedas subconscientes, el fluir de las imágenes, la inmersión en lo onírico y en el fondo de sí mismo como cantera de la sabiduría, la creencia en una realidad sin límites, más allá de toda apariencia y de toda superficie, y la avidez de captar esa realidad por entero, en todos sus planos. (*Páginas* 277)

> [Although not an orthodox surrealist, I believe that my work has some surrealist elements: the predominance of the imaginary realm, unconscious searches, the flow of images, the immersion in the oneiric and in the depths of the self as the source of wisdom, the belief in an unlimited reality, beyond appearances and surface, and the desire to capture this reality completely, in all of its dimensions.][1]

But her use of language is not strictly surrealistic either; this author still creates a coherent symbolic structure that can be interpreted in the course of her work; meaning is not solely associational. In fact, her poetry shows traits of both these movements and contradictions as well. As with her chronological position, Orozco does not fit precisely into any category.

Orozco writes from a strong Argentine poetic tradition marked by polemics. Each twentieth-century literary generation or movement takes its place in opposition to any apparent predecessor or concurrent formation, beginning with turn-of-the-century modernism synonymous with the poet Leopoldo Lugones in Argentina. Eclipsing Rubén Darío, Lugones *is* the modernist tradition in Argentina and, as such, serves as the point of departure for later poetic developments. Yet Lugones's work also marks a significant detour from mainstream modernism; implementing what might be called an "excessive" modernism, the Argentine takes its practice to parodic levels, interrogating the conventions of the modernist movement.[2] Another Argentine response to modernism was posed by the ultraist movement of the 1920s, which cited modernism's use of a "poetic" vocabulary as a collection of clichés, and advocated free verse, seeking to condense poetry to its primary element—a revitalized metaphor (Running 23). Jorge Luis Borges is the principal figure of *ultraísmo*, which he "brought" from Spain and subsequently abandoned. Not, however, without larger effects, for ultraism marks the beginning of Argentina's avant-garde. Predating surrealism in Argentina, ultraism was important to Orozco's poetic development because its technical innovations, its loosening of poetic possibilities, its use of free verse, and its concept of "negative creation" (destroying its predecessors to create something new) set the stage for later experimentation.

As a response to dominant poetic practices, ultraism resembled the European avant-garde. Its cosmopolitan leanings and its notoriety as a primarily aesthetic movement are exemplified by the "Grupo Florida" (which included such authors as Borges, Girondo, Lange, Marechal).[3] At the same time, ultra exhibited contrasting democratic, urban, and nationalistic traits. For example, its first publication, *Prisma* (1921), was presented in poster form in order to allow mass access to poetry (Running 24). The following titles of works by the Florida group also signal a national consciousness: Borges' *Fervor de Buenos Aires* (1923), Marechal's *Adan Buenosayres* (1948), and *Prisma*'s successor, the periodical *Martín Fierro,* named after the gaucho hero. As *Ultraísmo* primarily defined itself against its modernist predecessor, it was able to incorporate heterogeneous strains elaborated by members of the *Grupo Boedo,* a leftist, socially conscious group, against Florida's aestheticism. Yet in spite of their differences, members of Boedo (such as Arlt, Castelnuovo, and Mariani) still published and contributed to the ultraist dialogue in *Martín Fierro.* As Beatriz Sarlo describes it,

El movimiento de renovación estética no había cristalizado todavía en posiciones ideológicas irreductibles. Por el contrario, en esta primera mitad de la década del veinte, el conjunto de "los jóvenes" estaba enfrentado con el conjunto de los intelectuales tradicionales y establecidos. Se trataba aún de una empresa generacional. Finalmente estas mezclas . . . indican un campo intelectual relativamente reducido, donde las fracciones de "izquierda" y "derecha" son, por el momento, menos importantes, como principio de división, que el eje de "lo viejo" y "lo nuevo." Existe un continuum ideológico-experiencial animado por el proyecto de conquistar a la sociedad y cambiar la estética moral o políticamente. (Sarlo 111)

[The movement of aesthetic renovation had not yet crystallized into irreducible ideological positions. On the contrary, in this first half of the twentieth century the group of "young ones" found itself face to face with the traditional, established intellectual group. It [the movement] was still a generational enterprise. Finally, these mixtures . . . indicate a relatively reduced intellectual field, where "left" and "right" factions are, in this moment, less important than the axis "old" and "new." An experiential-ideological continuum existed, animated by the shared project of conquering society and changing the aesthetic, either morally or politically.]

Within ultraism, nationalism coexisted with universal or cosmopolitan desires. Aestheticism, emphasizing formal innovation, prospered along with socialist realist literary aims. Ultraism's novelty allowed it to incorporate long-standing opposition in Argentine society, previously characterized as between civilization and barbarism, Europe and America (opposition epitomized in Sarmiento's 1845 *Facundo*). This apparent balance of differences did not last; in the thirties and forties previously ultra poets turned to surrealism, neoromanticism, or *invencionismo* and the Argentine *vanguardia* fractured into different elements. In relation to these literary movements, the difficulty we began to observe in attempting to classify Orozco's work can now be seen as an aspect of a more generalized confusion of artistic schools. No longer a unity of differences, the Argentine literary scene of the forties was composed of an amalgam of styles representative of individual poets. The ironic efforts of the avant-garde of the twenties and thirties to integrate itself as a group into the institutional structure of Art (through its manifestos, its "public"

policies, its counterreaction to modernism), while questioning the valid-
ity of the institution itself, had failed (a victim, perhaps, of its own contradictory impulses). The succeeding generation comes to be described in
terms of its lack of cohesion; as referred to by a later critic, Noe Jitrik, it
is represented by the "desaparecidos poetas del 40" [disappeared or
absent poets of the forties] (*Escritores argentinos* 14).

Significantly, this shift occurs as Argentina's period of modern liberal-
ism ends. Hipólito Yrigoyen of the Unión Cívica Radical, was elected
president of Argentina in 1916. During the years of *yrigoyenismo*, Argentina prospered financially and enjoyed a substantial period of democratic
stability. In 1930, however, faced with the world economic crisis and
pressures from the still existent national oligarchy, Yrigoyen ceded his
power to the 1930 so-called "revolution," the restoration of Argentina's
constitutional regime.[4] The Yrigoyen government was succeeded by
several years of the conservative military rule of Agusto B. Justo, then
the election of Dr. Ortiz in 1937. Ortiz seemed to promise a return to
democracy but, dying before the end of his term, he was replaced by his
ultraconservative vice president, Castillo. Throughout these years, Argentina (as much of the world) experienced increased economic strain,
producing stress and cynicism that were augmented by fascist victories in
Europe. On the literary scene, this situation was complicated by the
ideological impact of the social tensions represented by the Spanish Civil
War. The late thirties brought a new wave of Spanish immigration to
Argentina, and many of the exiled writers exemplified a strong link
between literature and life. The high degree of writers' support for the
Republican cause and the Republic's subsequent defeat resulted in a more
generalized pessimism about literature's potential to influence reality. In
this atmosphere of circumscribed possibilities produced by the "infamous
decade," as the thirties came to be known, Argentina waited out World
War II with President Castillo, who controlled Argentine politics until the
1943 coup that preceded the 1946 victory of Juan Perón. Thus the end of
yrigoyenismo marks the end of a period of social and economic strength
in Argentina and signals the beginning of the vacillation between conservative and reformist governments, between *peronismo* and a series of
anti-Peronist military juntas, that would culminate in the 1976 coup and
subsequent dictatorship.

In the dialectic between literary and social processes we can observe
some corollaries; the consolidation of literature into nationalistic and
heterogeneous avant-garde movements corresponds to the social stability

and self-assurance of *yrigoyenismo*.[5] While ultraism and the surrealism that followed can be read as social protests, their social commentary and the reaction against modernism's elitism is based upon confidence in the possibility of creating an alternative. Later, when literary schools separate and lose their unity, Argentine society is fluctuating between periods of repression and resistance and entering into a long struggle for economic independence. The nation, increasingly torn apart, is losing what was its fragile center. The phenomenon of *peronismo* is a testimony to this confluence of apparently diverse interests as the party (in its early manifestation) supported workers, was anti-imperialist in its rhetoric, yet had strong ties to the old oligarchy and fascism. Contradictory philosophies such as fascism and communism were present within the same party "not as polar opposites, but as rival aspects of the same redemptive movement of the twentieth century: the struggle against capitalist-imperialism and its political counterpart, liberal democracy" (Hodges 126). Peronism would come to represent many things but in its initial stages it separated itself from the literary aristocracy, implementing mass culture as its vehicle and increasing the distance between high and popular cultural forms. With this change, literature's primary function was no longer to support an intellectual elite; instead, it became an arm of *peronismo* through this movement's control of mass media and publications. Narrative and essay forms predominated as Argentine literary production took part in an expanded international market, emphasized nationalist goals, and experienced a twentieth-century "rise of the novel." In these circumstances, poetry became increasingly marginalized, *angustiada* and *ensimismada* [anguished and self-involved].

Faced with a crisis in self-definition stemming (broadly) from turn-of-the-century immigration, the global and economic shift of the thirties, and concurrent change in neocolonial powers, Argentine poetic production appears to retreat. Poets of the forties in Argentina are generally noted for the "elegiac" quality of their work, as if in response to the present they seek to memorialize the past. Traditional verse forms such as the sonnet and the *silva* reappear to coexist with free verse forms. It appears to be a regressive move or, as Giordano, Becco, and Romano qualify it, this poetry is "una prueba reiterada de impotencia" [reiterated proof of powerlessness] (75). But even the anguish of this generation is open to a variety of interpretations; while observers such as Giordano and Romano read it as self-absorption, others, such as León Benarós, see in it different possibilities. In the series of manifestos of *El 40,* Benarós states that his generation, faced with a decaying world, will not be satisfied with more rhetoric in the style of the Martín Fierrist generation. Instead they search for the "essential" in their poetry as "hoy *decir algo* significa *compro-meterse,* estar situado dinámicamente en el tiempo. Antes el hombre de letras podía evadirse; en la actualidad le es cada vez más difícil la fuga ideal pues su época está hecha para él y él está hecho para ella" [Today, to say something means to commit oneself, situating oneself dynamically in time. Before, the man of letters could be evasive; now the idealist retreat is more difficult because the epoch is made for him and he is made for the epoch] (75). Benarós's perspective would suggest that the forties poets, rather than being *ensimismados* in a private sense, turn inward in order to interrogate the human condition, a step in their search for more global connections.[6]

The work of the writers who began to publish in the forties, like their very classification—a temporal relation instead of a thematic or political one—may not appear to be as socially committed when compared with earlier ultraism and the *vanguardia.* Certainly it does not operate in the same way and perhaps it is this comparison with the avant-garde that disguises the post-vanguard's less conformist elements. Later readers looking for similar strategies (i.e., collective efforts, surrealism's deconstruction of European colonial mentality, as per Aimé Césaire's definition) will not find them present to the same degree. Return to "traditional" forms or themes, however, does not always hold the same meaning. As always, it is context specific; what is radical or traditional in one time or context may be articulated quite differently in another, as is true of any artistic movement. For example, in *After the Great Divide,* Andreas Huyssen historicizes the avant-garde of the early twentieth century observing that until the 1930s the term "avant-garde" denoted political as well as artistic radicalism. Huyssen argues that we must examine how the art-life question was articulated then in contrast to the present for otherwise there is a tendency to canonize the movement and sever the "vital dialectic between the avantgarde and mass culture" (4). Later in his study Huyssen observes that while aestheticism separated art from life in modernism, the avant-garde attempted to reintegrate the two; both intents are ultimately based on the same art-life opposition (32). This is pertinent to our discussion of Orozco in that this poet reacts against modernism and the avant-garde while incorporating elements of both, providing us with another manifestation of the art/society dichotomy. In this instance, the changes we observe are to some extent dependent upon how we read, our expectations, the possibilities we uncover in the practice of "decoding."

The lyric form depends upon certain conventions of reading. Poetry constructs readers who read with a specific set of assumptions about meaning; for example, in poetry the reader looks for symbols, for figures of speech, for other, noncommunicative relations between words. Readers assume that, as Yuri Lotman describes it, "a poem is complexly constructed meaning" (35). The lyric demands an attention to form that has provoked self-contained, self-referential, New Critical readings of poetry as well as the post-structuralist turn of reading poems as language problems. Both of these habits of reading detach lyric poetry from its more worldly functions. Yet even with its emphasis on form, poetic discourse is not self-enclosed and can be used to different ends; it can, at times, "attack the symbolic foundations of society" (Harlow 65). There are some constants in our expectations of the lyric and some variables because our assumptions about reading poetry are historically specific. Anthony Easthope explains that our conventions of reading poetry are "both autonomous and historically relative. On one side poetry is a distinct and concrete practice with its own independence, conforming to its own laws and effects. . . . On the other and at the same time, poetry is always a poetic discourse, part of a social formation defined historically" (21).[7] A consciousness of the historicity of poetic production is necessary in order to observe transformations in the genre, changes in what poetry requires of its readers. Its apparent "autonomy" and "universality" are an effect of our reading practices. One of the often presumed "constants" that shifts in the case of Orozco (and perhaps other poets of "el 40"), is the construction of the poetic subject. Just as the creation of a collective subject is problematic in twentieth-century Argentina, so is an apparently individual subject. In my study of Orozco's and the other poets' work we will observe a pervasive problem in the positioning of the poetic speaker, a problem that will lead us back to the author's context and his or her position in twentieth-century Argentina.

Lyrical Subjectivities

New questions about subjectivity arise early in the twentieth century. Assumptions based on a romantic construction of the poetic subject as an individual consciousness that reflects the infinite are challenged by changing circumstances. The once-new, apparently unified European bourgeois subject essential to the rise of nineteenth-century capitalism is increasingly obscured by its alienated components, the subjects that this monolithic construct does not represent. Lyric poetry, however, continues to be read as the subjective expression of an individual voice in twentieth-century modernism, but it is a voice that is increasingly opposed to or separated from society. We see evidence of this perceived gap between art and society in Theodor Adorno's 1957 article, "Lyric Poetry and Society." In this essay, Adorno asserts that the experienced "individuality" of the lyric voice in fact demonstrates the extent of alienation in our atomistic twentieth-century society. For Adorno, the apparent absence of the world and presence of the individual voice in lyric poetry is socially significant. The distance that the poetic subject must take from society indicates the restrictive conditions of that society. The social is present in lyric poetry in its degree of resistance to community, in its seeming autonomy. Significantly, what makes it impossible for the individual poet/speaker to remove him- or herself from the social realm is poetry's materiality. Adorno explains that "lyric poetry, therefore, shows itself most thoroughly integrated into society at those points where it does not repeat what society says—where it conveys no pronouncements—but rather where the speaking subject (who succeeds in his expression) comes to full accord with the language itself, i.e., with what the language seeks by its own inner tendency" (62). It is in the individual's lack of awareness of language as an ideological construct that he or she becomes a social subject. Language mediates the subject's entrance into the realm of public meanings or, in Lacanian terms, the symbolic order. Adorno's work, rather than mask the importance of language, demonstrates a consciousness of form and writing indicative of the transition from early modernism to later twentieth-century movements—the avant-garde, postmodernism—in which poetry focuses more attention on the limitations of its own medium.

Adorno's attention to language can be read as a reaction to modern linguistic theories concerning the formation of subjectivity. In the work of theorists such as Benveniste or Derrida, subjectivity was shown to be a fundamental property of language instead of a tool by means of which a speaker might constitute him- or herself. In the successive step, Adorno proposes an interdependency between language and the subject. The determining function of language, the idea that there is no subject outside of language, arises as a characteristic of modernity. The psychological-linguistic component of this shift appears in the theories of Lacan, who, as Fredric Jameson puts it, disengaged the "linguistic theory which was implicit in Freud's practice but for which he did not yet have the appropriate conceptual instruments" ("Imaginary and Symbolic" 386). By linking psychological and social realms through his concept of the symbolic, Lacan arrives at a paradigm for the construction of the subject.

Lacan's model of how subjectivity is produced stresses that our sense of ourselves as subjects is not natural, given, but constructed. Lacanian psychoanalysis offers one set of theories to explain the creation of subjectivity in language; it is an important starting point as Lacanian thought and terminology provides a basis for both Louis Althusser's and Julia Kristeva's theoretical formulations. Both these theorists broaden Lacan's focus on the individual to a more social and historical perspective. Althusser adds the essential ideological function to Lacan's notion of subjectivity and Kristeva adds elements that arise in part from her study of Mikhail Bakhtin to suggest possibilities for change, ruptures, a refusal of the signifying system's regulation of desires. In an early article on Bakhtin ("Word, Dialogue and Novel" 1966), Kristeva calls attention to the importance of Bakhtin's replacement of the term "intersubjectivity" with "intertextuality," thereby situating the text in a social relation to other texts that communicate as well as create subjects (39). Bakhtin also examines the disruptive aspects of Menippean discourse and the carnivalesque that challenge past writing—a concept that has a similar function but precedes Kristeva's notion of the "semiotic," representing possible strategies of resistance (54). Kristeva combines social aspects of Bakhtin's intertextuality with psychoanalytic theories of the individual subject to produce a picture of the subject in social relations to others. I will trace the development of and connections between these theories of the subject in order to use them later as analytical tools to show how Orozco produces an unstable, transgressive subject in her poetry.

In Lacan's psychoanalytic theory, the production of subjectivity takes part through an interaction among three categories—the Imaginary, the Symbolic, and the Real—that exist in an interdependent and dialectical relation to one another. No single concept exists without the others. This relation destabilizes the subject as it shifts between the different registers, making the construction of subjectivity a process and undoing rigid notions of an individual, autonomous subject that have governed occidental philosophy for so long. Diana Fuss has pointed out the important fact that Lacan "always speaks in terms of the *place* of the subject" (29–30). This focus on positionality rather than identity undermines the apparent unity of more conventional psychoanalytic notions of the ego. However, while the Lacanian subject may be less constrained as it shifts between orders, his theory has certain limitations for it does not include a variety of other elements that determine discourse and subjectivity. Sexuality is acknowledged as a construct but Lacan invariably privileges the male subject in his theories, making it clear that it is the *son* who will inherit the place and name of the father. Using the patriarchal western bourgeois family as his model, Lacan naturalizes it, ignoring possibly conflicting class, gender, and cultural differences. Lacan's formulation of subjectivity is superseded by theories that attempt a more social and historical explanation for the creation of the subject, taking into account a broader number of social relations, expanding beyond the binary or tripartite interactions of the Freudian nuclear family.

Fredric Jameson elaborates Lacan's categories, explaining that the Real is, in Marxist terms, history (or in structuralist terms, the referent).[8] It is the clarification of this third category of the Real (perhaps better thought of as "that which is beyond textualization") which allows Jameson to relate the material aspects of both Lacanian psychoanalysis and Marxism. Both theories work as "master" texts (employing sexuality, the Oedipus conflict, or class struggle, social history) to provide readings of the Real (384). As reread by Jameson, in the case of both Marxism and psychoanalysis, there is an awareness of the composition of the subject and reference to the idea that subjectivity is a socially and historically determined construct.

Louis Althusser also uses apparently Lacanian terminology when he defines ideology as a "representation of the imaginary relationship of individuals to their real conditions of existence" ("Ideology" 162). "Representation" would, of course, refer to the Symbolic order, while he directly uses the terms "imaginary" and "real." Althusser redefines these three categories to demonstrate that the subject produced in language has specific ideological functions. In his 1977 article, "Ideology and Ideological State Apparatuses," Althusser goes on to explain that "the category of the subject is constitutive of all ideology but at the same time and immediately I add that the category of the subject is only constitutive of all ideology insofar as all ideology has the function (which defines it) of 'constituting' concrete individuals as subjects" (171). Ideology creates subjects and subjects uphold ideology. Althusser and Lacan share the idea that subjects are produced and held in place by discourse. Applying this concept, we can come to see the nineteenth- and twentieth-century subject as a specific historical construct. In the late eighteenth and early nineteenth century, the dominant subject constructed in lyrical poetry functions to support an ideology of individualism by positioning itself as a transcendental ego (Easthope 28). Jameson and other critics mark the end of this bourgeois, "universal" subject with the advent of the era of late monopoly capitalism.[9] Now the subject we observe in texts is often a "decentered" one, more relative, "postmodern," fragmented, Lacanian. Through this theoretical development we come to see the subject as constructed in language (not previous to it) and recognize that the ego-centered position is only a temporary point in a dialectic between the Imaginary and the Symbolic (Easthope 45). A particular subject might imagine he or she can control meaning but language and history ensure that meaning remains outside an individual's determination.

For this reason, I alternate between the singular and the plural terms ("subject" and "subjects") when describing subject positions in particular texts throughout this study. In doing so, I am attempting to maintain a tension between my argument that the subject is a process or a series of positions interpellated in discourse and the historical fact of the presence of a writing subject. To focus only on the textual subjects would lead us to a philosophical/linguistic dead end, creating a fragmented subject with little real power in the world and, perhaps, ahistorically deny the existence of an actual (however nonunified and contradictory) subject.

In the chapters that follow, we will see how these Argentine poets correspond to, yet differ from, these particular, often male, European patterns in terms of the subjectivities present in their creation. Images in Orozco's poetry curiously coincide with Lacanian (and, we will see later, Kristevan) terms, a characteristic which may be due to Lacan's popularity in Argentina.[10] There is the recurring element of a "lost object" in Orozco's poetry, a ceaseless motif of desire and lack, which provides further evidence that psychoanalysis may be an influencing narrative. In signaling this coincidence with Lacan, I am not proposing that Orozco is self-consciously psychoanalytic but, rather, that she is structured by the presence and power of this discourse in her society. Similarly, the author is not necessarily conscious of the transformation of subject positions that takes place in her writing, the decentering and possible disaccord between the writing subject and the written subject. There are numerous factors influencing her discourse for, as Anthony Easthope reminds us, discourse is "cohesive and determined simultaneously in three respects:

materially, ideologically, subjectively" (47). These three categories can be doubled when the reader's role is taken into account. It is our reading practices that will uncover the process of production of changing subjectivities in Argentine poetry.

The concept of the decentered subject is especially tricky when applied to lyric poetry that rests on a long tradition of a represented speaker. Orozco uses this convention too; we see it in her lyric "I," which is sometimes a "you" that easily slips into an "I": "Sí, tú, mi otra yo misma en la forma hechizada de otra piel ceñida al memorial del rito y la pereza" [Yes, you my other I myself in the bewitched form of another skin gripped to the memorial of ritual and laziness] (*Obra Poética* 174). Orozco's poetic subject presents itself in apparent unity, similar to a universalist, transcendent subject, but in fact, features of subjectivity as represented in her poetry subvert some of the standard features of a modernist poetic subject. Her speaker is not as ego-centered, not as stable or complacent as it may first appear, and in this exploration of her poetry, we will find that we cannot identify with one fixed position. In this shifting subject position Orozco reveals an element of her *in*subordination to authority; while in many ways conforming to tradition, this poet still manages to undermine dominant signifying practices.

Julia Kristeva's theories, building on Lacan's, create a model of subjectivity that comes closer to describing this characteristic of Orozco's work. The Kristevan subject speaks from the margins of discourse and its presence undermines the hegemony of an ostensibly universal voice. It is one subject located among others as Kristeva combines social and psychoanalytical theories to see literary creation as the interplay of voices. While linked to Bakhtinian intertextuality, Kristeva's formulation of the subject adds the element of gender, one of the products of the creation of the subject, to specify the "feminine" as it occurs in recent Western culture.[11] Reading poetry with a consciousness of the poetic subjects' constructed nature that these theories develop allows us to see its nonconformity. This more provisional subjectivity leads me to my methodology in this exposition of Orozco's work—a series of intertextual readings—while these readings should, in turn, increase attention to the relative nature of her poetry.

Combining Kristevan theories of subjectivity with Bakhtinian intertextuality unites two complementary perspectives.[12] In Bakhtin's terms the social relation of the subject is implied in every utterance: "Discourse comes upon the discourse of the other on all the roads that lead to its object, and it cannot but enter into intense and lively interaction with it" (Todorov 62). Bakhtin's subject comes into existence within a broader set of relations—other texts. One author's writing is always also a *reading*, determined by the existence of prior texts. Orozco's poetic subject, in Bakhtinian style, is consistently positioned relationally; not dominating but in interaction with other subjects, in motion, displaced, decentered, and produced in contrast to other texts.[13] There are both direct and indirect references to other authors in her work. Reading Orozco intertextually highlights a variety of comparative elements: contrasts in terms of history, nationality or internationality, gender, and form, as well as subjectivity.

This study begins by situating Olga Orozco and rereading her early works in relation to the "female tradition" in Spanish American letters. We find links to *posmodernismo* through her relation to the Uruguayan poet, Delmira Agustini. Distance is a theme these two poets share, a theme which is enacted, perhaps, in Orozco's relation to T. S. Eliot. This comparison provides us with an international component and a means to judge this Argentinean's distance from North American modernism, for all of the "fathers" she mentions are either North American or European. Orozco's work makes overt reference to Eliot's; he is quoted in her poem "Crónica entre dos ríos" [Chronicle between two rivers] from *Mutaciones de la realidad,* her *Cantos a Berenice* honors cats in true Eliot fashion, and in an interview Orozco notes similarities she has observed in their concept of time (see Appendix). Eliot is also a figure of institutionalized modernism in North America and his influence in 1930s and 1940s Argentina was not particular to Orozco, but general as evidenced by his recurring prominence in Victoria Ocampo's *Sur.*[14] The North American poet seemed to represent the aristocratic aesthetic values of a select group of intellectuals in Argentina. When we compare poems of each author we will see that they share the themes of language; both attempt a self-conscious examination of poetry's forms and possibilities. These features link Orozco to North American modernism while her changing subject, specific experimentations with language, and indications of a gendered, regional identity situate her in another time and place.

The dream-like, irrational qualities of Orozco's work often stimulate comparisons to surrealism. Chapter 3 explores the coincidences and incongruities in this relationship by juxtaposing Orozco's work to that of her Argentine precursor and contemporary, Oliverio Girondo. While

Orozco's and Girondo's poetry are not similar in technique, he, like Eliot, is a major figure, a voice to which later poetic production must respond. Girondo is an important representative of the national tradition; he is an Argentine who uses the tools of European culture to assert his nationality, his difference. His poetry also presents a refusal, a challenge to dominant European culture, and instead of denying a relation between Girondo and those who came later, seeing him as an anomaly or an isolated instance, I seek out connections between Girondo and Orozco in this chapter. These two poets temporally overlap, and their poetry shares evidence of a cultural identity crisis. Through Girondo's work I will relate Orozco to the avant-garde; the poetry of these two authors, which appears to be very different, upon closer examination shows some significant correspondences.

Alejandra Pizarnik is another contemporary of Orozco but slightly younger, a member of the *generación del 60* in Argentina. These two poets share biographical traits of nationality and gender, and in the poetry of both there are gestures of refusal, themes of doubleness, death, silence. Each of these poets writes of her experience of alienation, either directly or by strategically refusing an authoritative speaking position. The two were friends, and Orozco wrote the introduction to Pizarnik's *Los trabajos y las noches* [Works and nights] and dedicated a poem to Pizarnik, "Pavana para una infanta difunta" [Pavane for a dead princess] (*La noche a la deriva*). Pizarnik has reciprocally dedicated two poems from her book, *Extracción de la piedra de la locura* [Extraction from the stone of madness] to Orozco, creating a literal dialogue between authors. Orozco and Pizarnik are more frequently mentioned in relation to one another, perhaps because of their actual relationship and because they are both female poets—a trait that in some respects links their poetry but that each poet textualizes differently. The counterposition of Orozco and Pizarnik's work in chapter 4, as in all my comparisons, will allow us to see the specificity of Orozco's work. It provides another example of how her poetic subjectivity evolves relationally.

This methodology of comparative readings will also allow me to situate Olga Orozco historically, to see how her poetry creates a more relative, "postmodern" subject. To do this, I will focus my study primarily on her more recent work, *Mutaciones de la realidad* (1979), *La noche a la deriva* (1984), and *En el revés del cielo* (1987). There is a progression in her *obra,* an increasing focus on the poetic subject which becomes more subtly problematic in its construction in these later volumes. In each case, we find that the relation between Orozco's work and that of another author alters our understanding of the works in question, expanding our conclusions beyond the bounds of a single author or movement. This exploration of the representation of subjectivity in Orozco's poetry, then, is an integral step toward our understanding of the social and political processes of this time period in Argentina. For while the decentering of subjectivity is not subversive always and everywhere, in mid-twentieth-century Argentina, with its increasing demand for a homogeneous social subject, these signs of marginalization in an ostensibly conventional poet are disruptive. I read them as cracks in the culture—they are indications of distress.

This historical approach leads us to speculate about the role of poetry in Argentina in the transition from dictatorship to democracy. What happens to lyric poetry, which creates a seemingly "private" space, in an atmosphere where the private is dangerous? In not choosing the alternatives of silence or exile, Orozco is not able to construct a clearly alternative vision in her poetic production but is, perhaps, saving a space for one. We see its legacy in chapter 5, which examines how many of the strategies we have uncovered in Orozco's work are reworked by female poets in present-day Argentina. Considering the work of Cristina Piña, Liliana Lukin, Diana Bellessi, and Inés Aráoz, members of the generation that is awarded prizes in competitions judged by now "canonical" authors such as Orozco, we find that their lyric voices create still another relation to contemporary society. Tying together divergent strands, the work of these younger poets demonstrates the coexistence of "social" poetry and the influence of the neoromantic, metaphysical line.

Finally, I return to the problem of the creation of the subject in a nonpoetic context. Reading against idealist notions supporting the individuality of the author I end this study by analyzing the author-as-subject created in the text of a literary interview. Examining the text of this interview with Orozco calls attention to the relations between the biographical subject, the professional author subject, and her textual personae or poetic subjects. With its built-in dialogic qualities, the interview is a less controlled situation for the author, who may attempt to present a unified self but who is inevitably subjected by conflicting discourses and identities. The text reveals disjunctions between the exigencies of different subject positions and exposes the ideological elements behind their construction. The contradictions among Orozco's roles as author, poet, Argentine, woman, and interview subject (among others), are more apparent in this textual representation of self than in her poetic discourse. This analysis problematizes our access to the biographical subject and, in the process, uncovers some of the author's and the reader's assumptions about the interpretative act.

All these readings are based on the understanding that poetry is not separate from history or everyday life but engaged with it. Examining the dialogue between poets of different generations and countries revitalizes the lyric and calls attention to shifts in the relationship between individuality and the lyric voice. We find that no subject exists in isolation, truly apart from the world. These changes in our reading of the lyric recall the necessity of poetry in any society, for as Julio Cortázar reminds us, "Un poema de amor, un relato puramente imaginario, son la más hermosa prueba de que no hay dictadura ni represión que detenga ya ese profundo enlace que existe entre nuestros mejores escritores y la realidad de sus pueblos, esa realidad que necesita la belleza como necesita la verdad y la justicia" [A love poem, a purely imaginary story, are the most beautiful proof that no dictatorship or repression exists which can stop this deep connection that exists between our best writers and their people's reality, this reality that needs beauty just as it needs truth and justice] (*Argentina* 120).

CHAPTER 2

From a Distance
Posmodernismo and Other Modernisms

[]

In her poetry Olga Orozco reworks the relation between her texts and those of other authors. Critic Juan Liscano has noted that with Rilke she shares "oracular" qualities and the desire to "sondear las profundidades" [explore the depths] (30). She positions herself in the visionary tradition in several interviews, linking her role to that of Rimbaud in his desire to use poetry as a tool to discover the unknown. This evocation of the magical, ritual, almost religious power of the poetic word is characteristic of Orozco, for she uses language to lift us away from ordinary life. The titles of her books evidence many of her primary, constantly recurring motifs: distance, separation, and obstacles in *Desde lejos* [From afar, 1946], death, life, transcendence, artistic creation in *Las muertes* [The dead ones, 1952] and *Cantos a Berenice* [Songs to Berenice, 1977], ritual and change in *Los juegos peligrosos* [Dangerous games, 1962], solitary, minute self-examination via the body in *Museo salvaje* [Wild museum, 1974]. *Mutaciones de la realidad* [Reality's mutations, 1979], *La noche a la deriva* [Night adrift, 1983], *En el revés del cielo* [The other side of the sky, 1987], and *Con esta boca en este mundo* [With this mouth in this world, 1994] address these same issues as well as considering memory, metaphysical travel between different worlds, silence, language, and poetry itself. Her work is frequently read in terms of separation, division, all struggles condensed in the partial, fragmentary nature of the lyric itself.

Orozco's poetry continues what might be defined as a modernist emphasis on language, verbal perfection, the power of the imagination, and it is a style that has a certain authority in Argentina. We can see this in the national recognition that Olga Orozco has maintained throughout almost 50 years—as evidenced by the regular publication of her books, by her participation in literary competitions (winning prizes and, more recently, judging younger poets), by her presence on official commissions (such as the Advisory Committee of the "Fundación Argentina para la Poesía"). Yet her formalism does not remove her poetry from the world for, as John Hollander has put it, "poems talk to, and of, themselves, not to evade discourse about the rest of the world . . . but to enable it" (15). Orozco's poetry is emblematic of a lyrical style which repeatedly distances the historical world, but rather than repress it, history appears in other ways. Her work is distinctive yet representative of a larger yearning to sustain aesthetic values, a desire with its roots in Spanish American modernism. In this chapter, through contrasts with the work of Delmira Agustini and T. S. Eliot, we will see how Orozco's poetry responds to some of the principal movements of the early twentieth century, North American modernism and Latin America's *posmodernismo*.

I use the term *posmodernismo* in Spanish in order to distinguish this movement, occurring between late modernism (roughly, 1905, the date of publication of Darío's *Cantos de vida y esperanza*) and the vanguard movements in the Hispanic tradition, from the later twentieth-century use of the term "postmodern." Whether *posmodernismo* exists as a separate movement or is an extension of modernism is still debated (see, for example, José Emilio Pacheco's "Introduction" to *Poesía modernista*). I apply it here to denote the expansion or shifting of modernist characteristics in nonvanguard poetry written between approximately 1905 and 1930. This poetry is markedly more intimate, often situated in local, rural, rather than urban, cosmopolitan settings, and includes the group of now-canonical female poets—Agustini, Ibarbourou, Storni, and Mistral—who often treat atypical modernist themes such as the body, desire, and specifically gendered relations. *Posmodernismo* is a reaction to modernism, articulating perspectives marginalized by modernism's hegemony. For this reason it also marks the beginning of the strong tradition of female poets in Spanish America, a legacy present in Orozco's work as well.

Desde lejos is the title of Orozco's first collection, published in 1946. The title signals a relational position but it does not specify who or what happens from this distance and so does not greatly limit interpretative possibilities. "Desde lejos" could indicate a temporal separation from the past, for Orozco has suggested that these poems nostalgically evoke her childhood in Toay, La Pampa (*Páginas* 274); it could indicate a physical distance from us, her audience, or it could signify aloofness from the world and the present and a concomitant entrance into poetry. Or it could mark the inverse trajectory, reminding us that the speaker is always remote, unable to completely penetrate the lyrical space she creates (the space we are about to enter). The title sets up a spatial model that, as Yuri Lotman has explained, becomes the organizing element in the text, an element around which all the nonspatial characteristics are arranged (*La structure du texte artistique* 313). This distancing move evokes a kind of "absent presence," both limiting and expanding the speaker's terrain in a paradox that we will see is typical of Orozco's lyric production. She speaks to us "desde lejos"; her own distance always conditions the text, making us focus on her contradictory self-exile from and desire for inclusion in a poetic tradition.

The poetry in *Desde lejos* does not appear to be anchored in any familiar region but drifts in an atmosphere filled with *niebla, ecos, rumores, seres indefinidos* [fog, echoes, noises, undefined beings]. The poems themselves are loaded with ironic deictic references usually elaborated in adjectival phrases which, instead of situating us more precisely, only serve to increase the reader's distance or sense of dislocation. In "Quienes rondan la noche" [Those who watch the night] for example, the speaker is "aquí, junto a la niebla" [here, near the fog] or "allá, donde el pájaro de la piedad canta sin cesar sobre la indiferencia del que duerme" [there, where the bird of pity sings without stopping about the indifference of the sleeper]. The lack or postponement of verbs adds to the almost static, drifting quality for we move otherwise here—propelled from image to image, turning with the impetus of the metaphors rather than at line's end. Comparisons frequently do not elaborate, they complicate. Language is made to function in nonlinguistic modes, it is disarticulated in a way that draws the reader more completely in for there is clearly no referent outside the poetry itself. Temporal distinctions collapse and the past is juxtaposed to present and future, which all exist in the same realm. There is no need for metaphysical transcendence here as there doesn't seem to be a solid world to escape; it is already fragmented and we are already unanchored in a space that is clearly textual. *Desde lejos* is a consciously aesthetic product.

The title of the volume echoes that of a poem by Delmira Agustini (from *El libro blanco* [The white book], 1907), one of her female literary antecedents, and this intertextual reference invites us to look for associations. At first glance, Orozco's book does not appear to have much in common with Agustini's love sonnet in which the poetic speaker addresses an absent "tú"; Orozco's *yo poético* is most often descriptive, a perceiving presence that speaks in free verse form. Both poets spatialize time and share a number of themes: distance, absence, separation, all of which possess a certain "negativity" (a term that I use not in the value-laden sense of negating or denying but, as it appears so often in relation to contemporary poetry, in the sense of confronting or indicating constraints); but each poet handles the resulting limitations differently. In Agustini's poem the speaker overcomes or recuperates the temporal and spatial dislocation of a loved one by achieving a transcendent union: "Mi alma es frente a tu alma como el mar frente al cielo" [My soul faces your soul like the sea faces the sky]. She breaks physical constraints by proposing a metaphysical union, and although Agustini does not actively call attention to her role in making it so, it is a meeting that the *poet* makes possible, for it can only transpire in imagination or writing. In this characteristic, Agustini, as *posmodernista*, demonstrates her difference from Orozco's postvanguard production, for while the later poet is also concerned with overcoming physical and temporal boundaries, rather than transcend her space, the topos for her struggle becomes poetry itself. Orozco's poetry does not evidence a desire to remove the speaking subjects from constraints but to map out new territory in the midst of language's limitations. In this trait, she is more comparable to some of her modernist rather than *posmodernista* predecessors.

With Agustini, Orozco does share a conflictive relation to her poetic tradition. We see this in the tension in Agustini's work between sadistic and masochistic, masculine and feminine perspectives, between the violent activity of the vampire and a fear of sculptural immobility—of being the art object rather than the artist. Agustini's 1913 collection, *Los cálices vacíos* [The empty chalices], provides various examples of the poetic speakers' vacillating roles. Poems such as "El vampiro," in which the speaker *is* the sadistic and traitorous vampire who drinks blood, appear to be diametrically opposed to "Otra estirpe" [Another origin], whose submissive speaker masochistically offers herself to the vultures. "Fiera de amor" presents an intriguing intersection of culturally constructed masculine and feminine traits in the poetic speaker who characterizes herself as both a "fiera" (female wild beast) with a "hunger for hearts," and at the same time, a vine that crawls up and entangles itself around the statue (with verbs that suggest a masculine sexuality: "crecí," "ascendió mi deseo" [I grew, my desire rose]), a lifeless captive. In this poem the statue is of the "antiguo emperador" [the old emperor], an inert and powerless masculine figure.

The poem marks a transformation in the image of the statue in Agustini's work, for it is most often an incarnation of beauty, frequently a feminine aesthetic object. There are other poetic speakers in *Los cálices vacíos*, however, who undermine the power of this object's customary formal beauty in different ways; rather than transforming the object they draw attention to its empty, static, sepulchral qualities. This critical perspective is present in "Plegaria" [Supplication], in which the speaker asks Eros, "¿acaso no sentiste nunca / piedad de las estatuas?" [perhaps you never felt / pity for statues?] (54), a sentiment continued in the poem "La estatua": "¡Moved ese cuerpo, dadle un alma!" [move that body / give it a soul!] (106). Agustini's speakers' relations to the statue are important because they are emblematic of a more extended activity— recreating inherited forms, the author remakes and reclaims them. In order to participate in poetic production she must respond to patriarchal tradition, at the same time using and loosening her "fathers'" constructs. This double move is analogous to Orozco's "paradoxical positioning" that we will discover in the course of this chapter, a process by which she situates herself as both outcast from and participant in a predominantly male-defined poetic heritage.

In Orozco's production one poem may be read as an instance of the concerns of an entire volume and her poetry stands in a similar relation to that of other poets. There is a constant tension between a fragment and its absorption into the whole, between individuation and the poet's identity as one-among-others, her social role. Orozco's work presents the poet as visionary in twentieth-century modernist or symbolist style, but her poet-seer is dependent upon a public and a past for her position. While aware of her particularity, Orozco also situates her poetry rela-tionally; she is conscious of her work's interaction with other texts. We see this through her use of epigraphs, dedications, mentions and citations of specific authors in her poetry and interviews, and perhaps most obvi-ously, in her 1952 book, *Las muertes*. This is a series of poems that come together like moments in a conversation, in which the poetic speaker blends her voice with that of another author's characters. She rewrites these fictive speakers from a different perspective, extends them, answers them, or provides them with a more intimate voice. This sense of "dia-logue" continues throughout Orozco's poetic production and forms a part of the internal compositional system which gives her work its continuity. Olga Orozco invites an intertextual approach to her work.

Even when Orozco's emphasis is self-examination, as it is in *Mutaciones de la realidad* (1979), we find that the breadth of her themes and her method of constructing her poetic speaker place her in contact with other authors. In this book, the poet most consistently looks at her own poetic production and finds it frustrating and paradoxical. The titles in this work suggest struggle, disappointment, confrontation: "Rehenes de otro mundo" [Hostages of another world], "Los reflejos infieles" [Unfaithful reflections], "La imaginación abre sus vertiginosas trampas" [Imagination opens her vertiginous traps], "Densos velos te cubren poesía" [Thick veils cover you, poetry]. In this last poem heightened self-scrutiny leads to a poem about poetry, an instance in which the poet's self-consciousness of her work is generalized through a consideration of the limitations of genre. Through a close reading of this poem we will see how Orozco constructs a relative place for her speaker as both author and her poetic personae struggle with language. Her poem is at once subversive of and subject to the limits of discourse, a situation that makes us read her "negative" conclusion in a different light.

As Orozco poses herself against tradition, so will I, placing her in relation to T. S. Eliot, one of her acknowledged influences. Examining his poem "Little Gidding" (1942), the last of the "Four Quartets," we will find a prefiguration of Orozco's concerns: a heraclitean notion of time and history, the importance of the metaphysical, access to which is conditioned by the problematic physicality of language. Reading Orozco against Eliot will show both her roots as a poet, in the "high art" form exemplified by T. S. Eliot's brand of modernism, and the distance she takes from her predecessor. Eliot represents a particular strain of modernism, one of many modernisms that, while specific to different regions and traditions, at the same time share certain traits. One characteristic common to all modernisms that is also shared by Eliot and Orozco is the reformulation of the role of the artist. Speaking of European and North American modernisms, Andreas Huyssen separates the Mallarmé–Lautréamont–Joyce axis from the Flaubert–Thomas Mann–Eliot axis, indicating that the latter are examples of high modernism characterized by their intent to salvage art from the encroachment of mass culture while the former group has greater ties to the avant-garde's antitraditionalism (49). Like Eliot's, Olga Orozco's poetry separates itself from mass culture, which manifested itself through the Peronist movement in 1940s

Argentina, and reinforces the autonomy of her artistic production. This feature combined with her cosmopolitanism also links Orozco to the Latin American modernists, but in terms of more technical traits of the movement as characterized by Darío—its lexical transformations, musicality, classical allusions, versification—Orozco does not follow suit. In these aspects the Argentine is once more closer to Eliot, who strives to intensify perception through poetry, to demonstrate order through linguistic creation. Eliot utilizes free verse and, as Marjorie Perloff has convincingly demonstrated, a speech-based poetics, seeking to refine natural speech based on rhythms inherent in the language (52). Orozco also uses a free verse form and her poetry maintains a quality of ceremonial orality, making it a kind of ritualization of speech.

Reading Orozco in terms of Eliot highlights the strength of his influence in Argentina, his work's role as cultural capital imported from the North. I am not reading in terms of another modernist tradition in an attempt to codify her work, to absorb the unfamiliar into the familiar but, rather, as a way to see how she reformulates, both brings herself closer to and distances herself from her powerful predecessor. Orozco encourages us to set her in an international scene; almost all of the "fathers" she mentions (either directly, in interviews and texts such as those collected in *Páginas,* or indirectly, through epigraphs, quotes, and dedications in her poetry) are either European or North American. Even in this respect Eliot provides an interesting corollary to Orozco: an American who inserted himself into the British tradition, he is "radical" as a modernist poet while he is clearly reactionary in his life. These two poets demonstrate the conflicts of their positions in relation to tradition, both identifying with it and differentiating themselves from it (a situation analogous to their conflictive connection to the languages they use). But they arrive at different solutions to their respective conflicts: Eliot opting for closure achieved through faith in God, while Orozco concludes in an impasse, a "failure" full of possibilities, which distinguishes her from North American modernism. Orozco's negativity is an opening, an opportunity to hear the unspoken, the marginalized, the voice "del otro lado."

The title of Orozco's poem, "Densos velos te cubren, poesía," immediately calls our attention to several levels of meaning. "Velos," defined in its most common usage as hiding "lo que por respeto o veneración no se quiere que esté comunmente a la vista" [something which for respect or veneration is not commonly revealed] (*Diccionario de la Real Academia Española*) is secondarily explained as "una prenda femenina" [a feminine garment]. The poet plays with the meanings of *velos* and poetry, which both hide and reveal. Poetry is venerated for its procedures, its emphasis on the connotative, its polysemy, which make access to meaning difficult—it offers a pleasure in veiling. As feminine garments, "velos" perform a similar function, hiding gender while calling attention to it. The speaker makes a kind of sisterly transfer of a feminine item to poetry, raising the possibility of her identification with the position of poetry.

The speaker can identify with an object as she endows it with life through her address. Using apostrophe, Orozco invokes a formal poetic trope that indicates communication. As communication can generally only occur between two subjects, by addressing "poetry," Orozco makes it another subject within the confines of the poem. As Jonathan Culler points out, apostrophe is "the pure embodiment of poetic pretension," and by calling attention to itself, it shifts attention from the referential aspect of language to the "poetic event" (Culler 143–44). There is not much pretense of referentiality in the address "Densos velos te cubren, poesía," which is precisely what is called for in a self-reflective poem on poetry. Poetry is the subject and the discursive event. Through apostrophe the speaker grants subjectivity to an object but not only this—Paul de Man calls attention to another of apostrophe's operations. The figure can also be read as an indirect expression of the speaker's subjectivity; it "creates a pseudo-dialectic between pseudo-subjects" (de Man 34). In this case, rather than augmenting subjectivity, apostrophe provides an additional voice or mask ("velo") that the speaker places between him- or herself and the audience. Orozco evokes a dual paradox in her address, simultaneously speaking, asserting her presence, and concealing herself behind language. This paradox between presence and absence is the subject of her poem.

The speaker begins with negative statements, telling us where poetry isn't:

No es en este volcán que hay debajo de mi lengua falaz
donde te busco,
ni en esta espuma azul que hierve y cristaliza en mi
cabeza. (*Mutaciones* 89)

[It isn't in this volcano that exists under my treacherous tongue
where I look for you
nor in this blue foam that boils and crystallizes in my
head.]

She opens with a characteristic onslaught of paired images, *volcán-lengua falaz, espuma azul-cabeza*, groupings that signal the conjunction of interior and exterior, of self and world. Rather than the romantic projection of self into Nature, Nature is present *in* the speaker. The natural world is also the material or corporeal world here and so concepts of body and world are allied. *Poesía*, however, does not partake of this physical presence. It is not "in" a place (*está*), it is an event (*es*), an activity. It occurs not in the head,

> sino en esas regiones que cambian de lugar cuando se
> nombran,
> como el secreto yo
> y las indescifrables colonias de otro mundo. (89)

> [but in these regions which change places when
> they are named,
> like the secret I
> and the indecipherable colonies of another world.]

These poetic spaces are illegible (as they are unnameable), accessible only metaphorically; they are like the shifting places of another world, like the speaker's secret self. Lacking materiality, "poetry" always exists somewhere else, in another unspecifiable form. But poetry is also here—in the poet's use of images, in the sonorous combinations within this first stanza: assonant o's (*busco, como, yo, colonias de otro mundo*), repeated s's and z's (*falaz, azul, cristaliza, cabeza*), and alliterative c's and e's. It is present as well in the rhythm Orozco creates through her strategic placement of *palabras agudas*, which add pauses to the already present punctuation in her long lines.

The opening "No" is echoed in the start of the second verse in "Noches y días" [Nights and days] which places the speaker back in the world, unblinking under the flickering sun. Now the external world is humanized, is more changeable than the unwavering perceiver who seeks a signal. The sun in this poem is not the Platonic source of truth, enlightenment, or transcendence; it gives the observer nothing. She searches Nature for signs to decipher, "la sombra de un eclipse" [the shadow of an eclipse], "una fisura blanca" [a white fissure], but all are "sílabas dispersas de un código/perdido" [dispersed syllables of a lost code]. What she seeks is the ability to read "en estas piedras mi costado invisible" [my invisible side in these stones], to find herself in Nature, to uncover the invisible, and to make Nature speak. But Nature has lost its subjectivity; as it is no longer a part of her, it cannot communicate. The movement of the second verse marks in part the return to a romantic dualism, a division between self and Nature not present in stanza one. The *yo poético* moves in and out of her role as speaking subject; not a part of Nature, she is its scrutinizer.

Orozco's word choices in this verse add a spiritual dimension to her quest. It is *Dios* who writes on the world and *costado* refers to the body part while synecdochically recalling Christ's suffering and the creation of Eve from Adam's side. Does she long for an old allegorical meaning for Nature? In this instance, though, it is *mi costado;* she is, perhaps, martyr to her own physicality. Her allusion to Christ, the spirit made flesh, draws attention again to the paradoxical materiality of the words that refer to something beyond themselves. Christ overcame physical limitations the poet cannot. The reader, too, is made aware of the physical presence of language; as we wend our way through the rocky terrain of the poem images bump up against one another and their referent remains just out of reach.

There is no divine intervention, no descent of the holy spirit, we learn in the next shortened stanza. Instead, "humo" [smoke], "tinieblas" [darkness], "máscaras" [masks], and "meteoros innominados" [unnamed meteors] obscure perception and meaning or understanding escapes "entre un batir de puertas" [a slamming of doors]. The speaker's sensual perceptions are reduced; she can hear but she cannot see. "Puertas" resonate with meanings accumulated in the course of *Mutaciones de la realidad.* In "Rehenes del otro mundo," they are the passages to death: "y unas puertas que se abren cuando ruedan los últimos dado /de la muerte" [and some doors that open when the final dice of death roll] (31), and in "La realidad y el deseo" [Reality and desire] they are "las puertas del deseo" [desire's doors] (35). Their plurality signals that there is not just one exit but a more generalized transition to "otherness" (*muerte, deseo, lo innominado* in this instance). What is left after the passage through the *puertas* is sound. Through sound Orozco makes reference to one characteristic of language, her vehicle for communication, which preserves its sonorous aspect if not its meaning. Directing our attention to this phonic level of words, she calls attention to poetry.

Orozco repeats "Noches y días" in the fourth stanza but this time the observer is not open to receive some external sign but is closed, looking inward:

Noches y días fortificada en la clausura de esta piel,
escarbando en la sangre como un topo,
removiendo en los huesos las fundaciones y las lápidas,
en busca de un indicio como un talismán que me
revierta la división y la caída.
¿Dónde fue sepultada la semilla de mi pequeño verbo
Aún sin formular?
¿En qué Delfos perdido en la corriente
suben como el vapor las voces desasidas que reclaman
mi voz para manifestarse?
¿Y cómo asir el signo a la deriva
—ese y no cualquier otro—
en que debe encarnar cada fragmento de este inmenso
silencio?

[Days and nights fortified in the sanctum of this skin
scratching in blood like a mole
removing the groundworks, the gravestones, in the bones,
in search of a sign as a talisman that would return to me the division
    and the fall.
Where was the still unformulated seed of my little verb buried?
In what Delphos, lost in the current, do the freed voices rise like steam
    demanding that my voice be heard?
And how to grasp the drifting sign
—this one and not any other—
which should embody each fragment of this immense silence?]

Interiority involves the same obstacles as the outward search; with its *fundaciones* and *lápidas* the body is cluttered with meaningless things. The body is like the world in a pejorative sense; it is an indecipherable object. Mourning her separation, fragmentation, the speaker questions her fall from Edenic union with God, the loss of transcendental meaning, the lack of communion with other voices in oracular faith, and the distance of her own words from a referent. Poetry exemplifies all of Orozco's concerns and it is but one manifestation of a wider disunity or separation. It is a tool, she cries out, that does not work. "No hay respuesta" [there is no answer], only pieces, signs of her failure, "astillas de palabras y guijarros que se disuelven en la / insoluble nada!" [shards of words and pebbles which dissolve in the / insoluble nothingness], solid elements that disintegrate.

Words, like *guijarros,* accumulate:

> Sin embargo
> ahora mismo
> o alguna vez
> no sé
> quién sabe
> puede ser
> a través.

> [However
> right now
> or sometime
> I don't know
> who knows
> it could be
> through.]

This is a series of conjunctions and possible answers loosened from their referential-connective functions. Here their value is compositional, and Orozco plays with the varied stress patterns (alternating them) and joins the words through their sounds, the repeating s or z:

> sín embárgo
> ahóra mísmo
> ó algúna véz
> nó sé
> quién sábe
> puéde sér
> á través.

These words are the play of material presence, the answers to her questions relieved of their meanings. The poet for a moment lets go of her desire for resolution and poetry still exists in form. "A través" returns to functionality working double-duty to bridge the string of conjunctions to the complete sentences that follow and regain meaning as it is,

a través de las dobles espesuras que cierran la salida
o acaso suspendida por un error de siglos en la red del
instante
creí verte surgir como una isla
quizás como una barca entre las nubes o un castillo en
el que alguien canta
o una gruta que avanza tormentosa con todos los
sobrenaturales fuegos encendidos.

[through the double thicknesses that seal the exit
or perhaps suspended by an age-old mistake in the instant's net
I thought I saw you appear like an island
maybe like a ship among the clouds or a castle in
which someone sings
or a cave which advances turbulently with all of its supernatural fires lit.]

The active first person voice returns in this final stanza (it disappears after "te busco" of the second line and becomes the object of actions in most of the poem), although its assertions here are quite tentative. "No sé" and "creí": the preterit tells us the moment has passed when poetry, like an *isla, barca, gruta* with other worldly fires (recalling pentecostal fires) or the song emanating from *un castillo,* allowed the speaker a possible perception. Once more poetry is accessible only metaphorically and each comparative image is quickly replaced by another. All work to no avail as the *yo poético* is unable to apprehend, "Ah las manos cortadas, / los ojos que encandilan y el oído que atruena!" [Oh the amputated hands / the eyes that dazzle and the ear that thunders]. Her senses drained, she ends lamenting the futility of her efforts, "¡Un puñado de polvo, mis vocablos!" [a handful of dust, my words].

Closing on a note of failure is a constant in *Mutaciones de la realidad.* Every poem is an attempt at some kind of union or conjunction, each time unachieved. "Densos velos . . ." is the penultimate poem in this collection and reading it as part of the whole (as it must be read) the reader sees that the problem it describes has, by this point, gathered a variety of meanings. Orozco's continual concern with language takes many forms that elaborate a similar relationship. Words are *alhajas, señales, signos, decoraciones* [jewels, signals, signs, decorations], that are governed by *ceremonias, leyes, oráculos, juegos, prohibiciones, agonías litúrgicas* [ceremonies, laws, oracles, games, prohibitions, liturgical agonies], and once united they form *muros, piel, tejidos, vestuarios, fronteras* [walls, skin, weavings, costumes, frontiers] to *encubrirse* or *reforzar* [cover up or reinforce] boundaries that both protect us and against which we must struggle. The poet's battle with words expands as she continually renames her endeavor. We can more precisely characterize it as a multi-faceted tension between unity and dispersal. In terms of language, Orozco contrasts the word as an isolated element to its relational position in language which produces meaning—just as each poem reads as part of the whole. Temporally, we see the tension between the instant and centuries or eternity and personally, between the poet's individual voice and a collective one.[1]

Reading the poems in this framework undoes the meaning of the speaker's failure. Poetry always triumphs here as it unites oppositional concepts through their formal representation; rhythm, internal rhyme and imagistic accumulation bring them together in each poem. It does not resolve the inherent tension between elements, however, but instead highlights their paradoxical relationships through their juxtaposition. Poetic form is both salvation and damnation for Orozco. Choosing the negative path to arrive at a recognition of the constructed and incomplete nature of language brings us closer to "something else" and places Orozco within Spanish mystical tradition as well (with San Juan de la Cruz, for example). It also returns us to the idea of the title and the dialectical position of *velos* which at once indicate a meaning and obstruct our perception of it. "Densos velos . . ." is a poem whose process is its own deconstruction.

This concept of process is essential as Orozco's poetry has a performative function; we arrive at meaning through this struggle with language, the struggle forms a marker (a figure for conflict). As a marker, "Densos velos . . ." gains an elegiac aspect. Its long hesitating verses lament the distance between the speaker and poetry; it is a meditation on a loss (evoked as death too through the terms *otro mundo, sepultada* [other world, buried]), and the elaboration of this lack momentarily bridges the gap, revivifies the dead form by uniting the lyric voice with poetry. The elegiac quality comes from the whole *poemario*, which includes two funeral elegies, "Crónica entre dos ríos" and "Pávana para una infanta difunta," designating specific absences in a book whose overall tone is that of memorialization. The poems are little rituals, momentary apertures through which an idea or a person might emerge, or as Orozco expresses it, they are "mecanismos de revelación" (revelatory mechanisms) (*Páginas* 63). By stressing the discontinuous elements of language, time, subjectivity, and poetry itself, Orozco creates a gap that permits her readers an intense perception of the problem she describes.

T. S. Eliot's poetry also emphasizes language as a process, but in Eliot's poetry it performs a different function. Rather than crack open language, Eliot uses it to mediate. It is an instrument for transport, and as such, it maintains a strong link with its lyrical origins. We see this in Eliot's choice of a musical form for his "Four Quartets." Each one of the quartets in this long poem is composed of five movements and each follows a similar pattern; the poet poses the problem in the first movement (a paradoxical union of opposites as in Orozco), develops it in discursive, lyrical, and descriptive sections (2,3,4), and concludes in the fifth movement with a self-referential examination of poetry and a resolution of the initial problem. With his alternation between free verse and rhymed couplets, Eliot emphasizes his break with tradition. He chooses lyrical discontinuity as if to remind us of what he is not doing. But at the same time, his poem follows a linear narrative development that contrasts with the postsurrealistic cumulative effect Orozco will employ. Eliot, as a North American modernist, poses himself against the English poetic tradition in a self-conscious manner. Orozco, writing 35 years later, uses Eliot as one of her starting points; by 1979, he is a part of the tradition she expands and supersedes, incorporating elements of his style into her own.

"Little Gidding," the last of the "Four Quartets," like "Densos velos" is a search for "something else"—what isn't present, the unnameable other side—it is a search that is also a spiritual quest. The poem begins with a concrete reference to time that in fact situates the speaker outside of time:

> Midwinter spring is its own season
> Sempiternal though sodden towards sundown,
> Suspended in time, between pole and tropic. (I, ll. 1–3)

Not spring or winter, we are suspended between seasons, in and out of time. The image recalls Orozco's "instantanea eternidad" [instantaneous eternity] or "el vacío inmenso entre dos horas" [immense space between two hours] (from "Variaciones sobre el tiempo" 93 [Variations on Time]), but Eliot's midwinter spring is more connected, earth-bound, less conceptual. We are between the paradoxical union of opposites—summer/ winter, hot/cold, melting/freezing, fire/water—in transition. Pentecostal

fire *is* present in Eliot's poem and "stirs the dumb spirit." There is a
divine presence or meaning but it is caught amid elements. What is
longed for in "Little Gidding" is an impossible union: "Where is the
summer, the unimaginable / zero summer?" (I, ll 19–20). It is unimaginable yet imagined in the poet's query. Opposites come together in the
poem and in the clear referent with its blossoms of snow. This poem,
grounded in the seasons, is inspired by a specific place. Little Gidding, the
site of a church and the historic site of a seventeenth-century Protestant
community, is "now and in England" (I, l 40).

While Orozco cannot find (or name) the space where her poetry
occurs, Eliot is much more historically precise. Language is problematic
for the modernist poet but the difficulty with meaning has not been
shifted entirely onto language yet. Language is one tool among many:

And what you thought you came for
Is only a shell, a husk of meaning
From which the purpose breaks only when it is fulfilled
If at all. Either you had no purpose
Or the purpose is beyond the end you figured
And is altered in the fulfillment. (I, ll. 31–36)

As in Orozco, process is crucial to Eliot because it is through using
language that one comes to discard it as a covering for its true content—
faith. Words are useless in themselves but provide a structure which
might lead the devout speaker to another kind of communication. This is
how prayer works beyond language:

You are not here to verify,
Instruct yourself, or inform curiosity
Or carry report. You are here to kneel
Where prayer has been valid. And prayer is more
Than an order of words, the conscious occupation
Of the praying mind, or the sound of the voice praying.
And what the dead had no speech for, when living,
They can tell you, being dead: communication
Of the dead is tongued with fire beyond the language of the
Living. (I, ll. 45–54)

We must use words but not believe in words and so might come to
communicate through pentecostal fire—achieve an epiphany. In this way
we can converse with the dead, with the past, breaking the constraints of

time, space, and language. Discarding language as we use it, we reach the timeless moment that "is England and nowhere. Never and always" (I, l 56). Prayer can transport the speaker beyond words, tear the *velos* of poetry Orozco describes.

In this first movement of "Little Gidding" there are no first person verbs or direct references to the speaker as we observed in the "yo" and "mi" of "Densos velos. . . ." Yet the presence of the lyric subject is stronger here. Orozco retracts herself in the moment she speaks through her negativity ("No es . . .") and by situating her poem as overheard speech. Eliot's speech is directed; while contemplating Nature at Little Gidding the speaker tells us what we will find. He narrates his discovery of the place, creating a self more within the romantic tradition than Orozco's.[2] Eliot's speaker is a male subject observing Nature, the object, while Orozco's speaker, in a more conflictive relation, slips between observing and identifying herself with Nature.

The speaker does surface as an "I" in "Little Gidding's" second movement. Although this part begins with a definitively lyric section (rhymed couplets), it is still narrative, telling us of the death of the elements, earth, air, fire, and water. While Eliot generalizes in speaking of the elements, the images he employs are rooted and localized. Eliot does have a referent from which he departs, and after this lyric prelude we get there—to World War II London. The speaker encounters a "stranger," "some dead master" (II, l. 38–39), and speaks to him. Since the poet can communicate with the dead, he is answered by a fellow poet:

> Since our concern was speech, and speech impelled us
> To purify the dialect of the tribe
> And urge the mind to aftersight and foresight,
> Let me disclose the gifts reserved for age
> To set a crown upon your lifetime's effort. (II, ll. 73–77)

The stranger bears some relation to Mallarmé ("to purify the dialect . . .") but is not specifically or solely Mallarmé. He is clearly a "master," who lists for the poet-listener the gifts of age if he is "restored by that refining fire / where you must move in measure like a dancer" (II, ll. 92–93). This stranger, like the speaker, is also directive. Both poets acknowledge language's power; its redemptive capabilities suggest the possibility of poetic transcendence.

Poetry as an instrument to arrive at something else is a concept that

Orozco confronts, too. But her relation to it, like her relation to Nature, to language, and to her poetic masters, is structured differently. Eliot's poet appropriates another poet's words in order to define himself as a member of a tradition of fellow creators; he is like Mallarmé, Dante, or Yeats, like an older poetic authority. Orozco also consciously uses prior texts, but rather than identify with their authors, her voice merges with that of their characters. In the title poem of the collection *Las muertes*, she explains her identification with her subject (other authors' objects): "Por eso es que sus muertes son los exasperados rostros / de nuestra vida" [For this reason their deaths are the exasperated faces / of our life] (*Poesía antología* 17). They are us, literary recreations of one subject. When Orozco speaks with Miss Havisham, Maldoror, et al., she speaks to them and they speak from her. The pronouns alternate between *tú* and *yo,* a shifting which culminates in the last poem, "Olga Orozco," in which she speaks to and from a divided self: "Yo, Olga Orozco, desde tu corazón digo a todos que / muero" [I, Olga Orozco, from your heart say to everyone that / I am dying] (*Poesía antología* 25).³ Rereading "Densos velos" then, we see that her voice is that of both poet and poetry, subject and object. Orozco fuses with her subject; figurally, her relation is metonymical, one of contiguity. For example in her poem, "Gail Hightower," we first encounter the voice of Faulkner's character from *Light in August* (translated into Spanish) in the epigraph, "No quería más que paz y pagué sin regatear el precio que me pidieron" [I only wanted peace and I paid without bargaining the price that was asked]. Then Orozco's poetic voice reincarnates the character's, "Yo fui Gail Hightower, / Pastor y alucinado, / para todos los hombres un maldito / y para Dios !quién sabe!" [I was Gail Hightower / pastor and deceived one / cursed in the view of mankind / and in God's view, who knows!] (*Poesía antología* 18). Orozco links herself to Faulkner by uniting herself with his creation; she achieves fusion at the expense of self-definition. T. S. Eliot's relation to tradition is metaphorical; he is similar to his masters, in them he sees himself.

Orozco displaces her identification from literary subject (author) to literary object (their creations). In doing so she indicates that recognizing herself in these past masters is unacceptable or impossible. She calls attention to her problematic relation to the symbolic realm—as an Argentine woman she is in some ways outside of it. Orozco enters into her dialogues with Dickens, Faulkner, and Lautréamont indirectly. Eliot makes more direct contact with his literary antecedents. With no lack of literary egoism he figures himself as another Dante, guided by more modern Virgils. Yet in his relation to history Eliot is more humble; closer to Orozco, he qualifies his individual role.

In the third section of "Little Gidding," Eliot elaborates his concept of self and his relation to history.

> There are three conditions which often look alike
> Yet differ completely, flourish in the same hedgerow:
> Attachment to self and to things and to persons, detachment
> From self and from things and from persons; and, growing
> between them, indifference
> Which resembles the others as death resembles life,
> Being between two lives—unflowering, between
> The live and the dead nettle. This is the use of memory:
> For liberation—not less of love but expanding
> Of love beyond desire, and so liberation
> From the future as well as the past. (III, ll. 1–11)

In this didactic tone the speaker tells us what he has learned about history's double bind: it is both servitude and freedom. He has learned this through self-examination; contemplating attachment, detachment, and indifference to the world, he concludes that the last is as death is to life. Life is embodied in the two "nettles" of attachment and detachment, one is now living, the other dead, but either is preferable to indifference (Reibetanz 169). One passes through attachment and detachment to the world as one uses memory to pass from past to future or to transcend the self that is "renewed, transfigured in another pattern" (III, l. 17), reminiscent of poetry. This concept of the self as one moving among many is more like Orozco's. Meaning is not static here but circulates, like self, memory, and time, between poles. Eliot uses a heraclitean notion of time, making the present a moment in constant transformation, incomplete without a relation to the past. Orozco echoes this concept and in her prose tells us that "la memoria es una actualidad de mil caras" [memory is a present moment with a thousand faces] (*Páginas* 62). The past is continually remade in the present. Orozco, however, seldom makes reference to a specific time or place, whereas Eliot repeatedly fixes this poem in England's wartime present and refers to British history.

History reassures Eliot, providing him with symbols—"the spectre of a Rose," the Royal Rose (III, l. 37)—and the knowledge that all things pass. We observe the latter in the poet's repetition of a medieval British mystic's words, "Sin is Behovely, but / All shall be well, and / All manner of thing shall be well" (III, ll. 19–21). This affirmation occurs at the beginning and the end of the third part, enclosing England's present and past strife within an encompassing faith. Divine love is explicitly the answer in the fourth lyric movement, and our only choice is no choice; we must suffer life "consumed by either fire or fire" (IV, l. 14). The poet plays on the paradoxical, creative, and destructive functions of purgatorial, pentecostal, or London's fires. The key symbols in "Little Gidding," rose and fire, are clear before we reach the final section. Both are conventions of contradiction and both lead us back to the place: England.

The assertion that the beginning and the end are interchangeable is an idea that Eliot repeats in each poem of the "Four Quartets." It is an antinomy that keeps the focus on process, and the first person plural voice informs us that it is a group venture. The process in which we are engaged is the creation of meaning:

> The end is where we start from. And every phrase
> And sentence that is right (where every word is at home,
> Taking its place to support the others,
> The word is neither diffident nor ostentatious,
> An easy commerce of the old and the new,
> The common word exact without vulgarity,
> The formal word precise but not pedantic,
> The complete consort dancing together)
> Every phrase and every sentence is an end and a beginning,
> Every poem an epitaph. (V, ll. 3–12)

The fifth movement of every poem in *Four Quartets* confronts the problem of the function of language in poetry. In "Little Gidding" the consideration is parenthetical—what becomes a theme in Orozco's poem is an aside here. Eliot's technique for his metapoetic commentaries, like Orozco's, is indirection. Parentheses separate this portion of the text; it seems at once incidental and elevated in its importance in relation to the rest of the poem. Eliot continues to be indirect as he explains how words work: they are *neither* this *nor* that, they are exact *without*, precise *but not*. . . . Words produce meaning relationally, they indicate the space between and can only be referred to negatively as they move (dance). There is no stasis in language. The concept of every poem as an epitaph challenges our assumptions about endings. Epitaphs, like poems, are formal, ceremonial objects or markers, of a transition from this life to the next (in Eliot's Christian framework), of a loss. They express our separation, our inability to return to a past moment, place, or person while paradoxically revivifying that person, moment, place through language. Orozco's elegiac poems also offer a figural opportunity to transcend, though she comes down more firmly on the negative side ("Un puñado de polvo mis vocablos!").

> And any action
> Is a step to the block, to the fire, down the sea's throat
> Or to an illegible stone: and that is where we start. (V, ll. 12–14)

All actions are a defiance of death, as is by implication the act of confronting the illegible stone. Is it a stone that should bear an epitaph? Or Moses' stone, God's word impossible to read? Or does it represent the poet's desire to mark on Nature, to gain some kind of immortality by creating an objective reminder of himself? "Para poder leer en estas piedras mi costado invisible"; Orozco uses the same image of an illegible stone, and she too wants the impossible—to read an unseen part of herself there. Eliot continues to play upon this sense of the impossible, elaborating a series of fantastic unions: birth-death, history-timelessness, the rose and the yew tree. These last two images are symbols that have cumulative meanings in the "Four Quartets." The yew tree recurs as a symbol for death—a metaphysical death in "Burnt Norton," a literal one in the preceding poem, "The Dry Salvages." The rose gathers more metaphysical meanings in relation to the other poems; it is an image of life and "an emblem of the ecstatic and visionary way of ascent into the light" (Reibetanz 180). Julia Maniates Reibetanz explains the rose–yew tree juncture as the meeting of the two paths to God (through grace or suffering). Essential to Eliot is the idea that both negative and positive moments lead to the same end: divine enlightenment.

Eliot's object is enlightenment, and in the course of "Little Gidding" we learn that illumination comes through process and is in constant flux:

> With the drawing of this Love and the voice of this Calling
> We shall not cease from exploration
> And the end of our exploring
> Will be to arrive where we started
> And know the place for the first time. (V, ll. 25–29)

God's word is given material form (drawn) and sound (voice) by the poet. He succeeds in naming the unnameable by not allowing us to rest long with each reconciliation of opposites before moving to the next. Eliot presents a union of moments: history, now, eternity; and a union of places: beginning, middle, and end of the river. Significantly, as Reibetanz has observed, we cannot see the unity of the river but hear it:

> At the source of the longest river
> The voice of the hidden waterfall
> And the children in the apple-tree
> Not known, because not looked for
> But heard, half-heard, in the stillness
> Between two waves of the sea. (V, ll. 33–38)

Although it remains out of reach, unity is conceivable and we know this through aural evidence. In Orozco's poem the possibility of a conjunction (between meaning-representation, this side and the other) escapes through a "batir de puertas," eluding the listener. In both cases the poets use sound as their means of perception, heightening our awareness of their medium: poetry.

Eliot presents poetry, like faith, as mysterious, but it is a mystery that works to unify opposites. Through the nonsyntactical qualities of language—sound, rhythm, repetition—the poet is able to create unity outside of the signifying process, relations that perhaps bring us closer to the metaphysical (like prayer). We achieve a sense of completion at the end of "Little Gidding":

> And all shall be well and
> All manner of things shall be well
> When the tongues of flame are in-folded
> Into the crowned knot of fire
> And the fire and the rose are one. (V, ll. 42–46)

This third repetition of the mystic's words is a literal enactment of Eliot's structuring idea; they are the same words yet they are different, having changed through repetition, in their new context and as a result of the total meaning of the poem. Meaning and form also converge in the final paradoxical union of fire and rose. The only place where the separate elements can be united while they retain their uniqueness is in language. Fire and rose become one image, demonstrating the idea that poetry is capable of holding things at once together and apart.

The "mystery" in literature, the mobile, rhythmic, musical qualities of the signifying process, are identified by Julia Kristeva as literature's semiotic function. Mallarmé ("father" to both Orozco and Eliot) referred to the semiotic process when he described "Le Mystère dans les lettres." Reading Mallarmé, Kristeva says, "Indifferent to language, enigmatic and feminine, this space underlying the written is rhythmic, unfettered, irreducible to its intelligible verbal translation; it is musical, anterior to judgement, but restrained by a single guarantee: syntax" (97). The semiotic and the symbolic are inseparably linked; syntax makes the semiotic intelligible, ordering it, while the semiotic exists as a transgression, in constant struggle against order. All language has these two elements in different proportions (Kristeva 92). Eliot masterfully manages the semiotic to demonstrate the limitations of language. Words can only indicate "truths" that exist outside of signification, and so we are moved from one symbol or metaphor to the next—no one construction is "right." Yet this process in "Little Gidding" still occurs within a narrative structure. Rather than being destroyed or disintegrating, symbols multiply in meaning but still communicate.

Orozco's more surrealist poetry loosens narrative elements and highlights the semiotic. In "Densos velos" Orozco depends more upon unmediated images. What often appear to be symbols—*puertas, signos*—are drifting, indeterminate. We get a general sense of meaning but can make no connection as clear as yew tree = death = negative way to God. Similarly, she gives us little sense of place. Orozco cannot or does not make bonds between her language and a referent, or if she does, they are deceptive ones (i.e., her *Naturaleza* that shifts in relation to the speaker from interior to exterior). There is no place in "Densos velos" outside of poetry. While she and Eliot share metaphysical concerns and both call attention to language not only as object but as process, Orozco changes how the problem is structured. Her metaphysical dilemmas are formally textualized. Exploiting the semiotic mode, Orozco maintains disjunction; the paradoxical fact of language's material presence and intellectual or emotional function ends not in synthesis but in disunity. In creating meaning Orozco dissolves it, taking advantage of the negativity semiosis introduces into the symbolic order (Kristeva 118). This same process takes place in her positioning of her speaking subject; apostrophe both structures an enunciative position and disguises it, her lyric voice speaks to Nature and is a part of it. She does not remove the *velos* of her title but calls attention to them, dances among them.

Orozco, the later poet, takes Eliot's focus on language as an object and extends it, making her poetic object more dynamic. T. S. Eliot challenged the poetic tradition he inherited when he sought to use language as an object, a formula for expressing experience. His concept of an "objective correlative" is an extension of this idea that poetry can at best be a correlative to emotion; it cannot, as in a romantic notion, directly express the individual's state. Nor is there a place for the romantic ego in Eliot's poetry. As we have observed in "Little Gidding," his lyric I, while indicating the presence of an ego, is less direct, less all-encompassing than that of his romantic predecessors. But while Eliot's focus on language, his attention to how it must objectify emotion, are steps away from tradition, his own ideas become doctrinaire in his time. In his well-known theoretical writings such as "The Social Function of Poetry" (Jones 17–28), Eliot stresses that the first duty of a poet is to language and that language is a sign of cultural strength. Writing "Little Gidding" at the end of World War II, Eliot seeks to shore up civilization, looks for values and order that he finds in traditional Christianity and supports in his poetry. Perhaps this is one reason why "Little Gidding," a late poem, has more visibly romantic traits. Writing at a moment when Europe is questioning its own identity, Eliot, the monarchist attracted to England by its orthodoxy, leans more heavily on tradition. The poem textualizes a deeper conflict between Eliot's self-assured poetic rebellion with its emphasis on the poetic object and the inevitable outcome of his ideas: meaning which is endlessly relational, his inability to objectify consciousness. Eliot finally sidesteps these problems with a leap of faith. Orozco will re-elaborate them and leave them unresolved.

As a poet, Orozco has an obvious interest in language and, in Eliot's terms, therefore a role in preserving her culture. But the question that arises in Orozco's case is, which culture? She continually refers to European and North American literary models; although she obviously admires and writes of Oliverio Girondo in her prose, we see few references to other Latin American precursors such as Darío or Vallejo. Why does she not situate herself against the Latin American modernists? Orozco's work provides evidence of a heightened conflict in her literary identification. When she writes in "Densos velos" of "las indescifrables colonias de otro mundo" [the indecipherable colonies of another world], she writes of herself. Her use of the term "colonias" is not neutral. She is conscious of her position as Latin American and identifies herself with the position of the region in "Continente vampiro" [Vampire continent](*Mutaciones de la realidad*):

No acerté con los pies sobre las huellas de mi ángel guardián.
Yo, que tenía tan bellos ojos en mi estación temprana,
no he sabido esquivar este despeñadero del destino que camina
    conmigo,
que se viste de luz a costa de mi desnudez y mis duelos
y que extiende su reino a fuerza de usurpaciones y rapiñas.

[My feet did not succeed in following the tracks of my guardian angel.
I, who had such beautiful eyes in my early season,
I haven't learned how to avoid this precipice of destiny that walks
    along with me
that dresses itself in light at the expense of my nudity and my
    mournings
and that extends its reign through
the force of usurpations and plunder.]

She cannot faithfully follow the patterns of her masters (*el destino, el continente vampiro*) because she is also the object of their "saqueos" [lootings]. In this poem Orozco's speaker is again figured as both subject and object (noted in "Densos velos" in her relation to Nature), a duality that is never reconciled. Her conflictive identification here is geographical, and conflict is heightened by her position as *mujer*. She is feminine in relation to her dominator's masculinity, "la heroína" [the heroine], "una península raída" [a worn-out peninsula]. This disaccord is also evident in Orozco's reflections on the process of her production. As poet, Orozco both writes and is written on; to her, paper is "una blanca mujer que lee en el pensamiento" [a white woman who reads your thoughts] (*Páginas* 218). Her elevation of the semiotic makes sense in this context; Orozco stresses the dialectical relation Kristeva observes in language by identifying and giving voice to the marginal while attempting to follow in the footsteps of the dominant mode of poetic discourse.

In her poetry, Orozco textualizes her experience of alienation. She cannot "overcome" her marginal position, and so she affirms her experience by maintaining disjunction, making a ritual of it. She tells us as much in the penultimate verse of "Continente vampiro":

No hablo aquí de ganacias y pérdidas,
de victorias fortuitas y derrotas.
No he venido a llorar con agónicos llantos mi desdicha,

mi balance de polvo, sino a afirmar la sede de la negación:
esta vieja cantera de codicias,
este inmenso ventisquero vampiro que se viste de luces con mi duelo.

[I am not speaking here of gains and losses
of fortuitous victories and defeats.
I have not come to lament my misfortune with agonized weeping,
my balance of dust, but to affirm the see of negativity:
this old quarry of greediness,
this immense vampire drift that dresses itself in lights with my grief.]

"Afirmar la sede de la negación": Orozco makes her cultural affirmation when she embraces the contradictions of her position, thereby signaling her resistance.

CHAPTER 3

The Limits of Poetic Discourse
Oliverio Girondo and Olga Orozco

[]

Mutaciones de la realidad is a book dominated by themes of self-examination, by questions; it is an exploration of the poet's role and possibilities. The limits of language that we focused on in chapter 2 are only one aspect of a larger dilemma present in all of Orozco's work. In an interview, she describes her poetic intent as an exploration:

> en las zonas prohibidas, en los deseos inexpresados, en las inmensas canteras del sueño. Procuro destruir las armaduras del olvido, detener el viento y las mareas, vivir otras vidas, crecer entre los muertos. Trato de cambiar las perspectivas, de presenciar la soledad, de reducir las potencias que terminan por reducirme al silencio. (Liscano 87)

> [in prohibited zones, in unexpressed desires, in the immense quarries of dreams. I am able to destroy the framework of forgetfulness, stop the wind and the tides, live other lives, thrive amongst the dead. I try to change perspectives, to witness solitude, to reduce the powers which finally reduce me to silence.]

In *Mutaciones*, Orozco engages in a profound search for a definition in which language becomes an apt metaphor. This move toward definition is protective, defensive, but at the same time the poet is attempting to defy restraints, to struggle against inhibiting orders. In this respect, *Mutaciones* is in many ways a continuation of *Los juegos peligrosos* (1962), but in the later volume, the notion of "peligro," of defiance, overshadows that of "juegos." Orozco's emphasis falls less on the liberating possibilities of ritual or other-worldly formulae, and instead she draws attention to the confines of these devices which she calls "¡tanta alquimía al revés!" [so much backward alchemy!] (*Mutaciones* 64). Conjuring other realities, formulating new modes of access to this one, does not work as there is no access, unity, connection. Interrogation is our only option, and so we are left once more to question: What does poetry do? What is representation, and is it a "mutation" of the "reality" of the work's title? There is a sense of the failure of language, order, and meaning in these poems that leaves the speaker exposed, denuded. We see this in "Presentimientos en traje de ritual," the title suggesting that ritual (like language) is a vestment self-consciously donned to cover, protect, and hide: "Llegan como ladrones en la noche. / Fuerzan las cerraduras / y hacen aparecer esas puertas que se abren en un error del muro / y solamente indican la clausura hacia afuera" [They arrive like thieves in the night, / they force the locks / and conjure doors which open in the wall's defect / and only indicate confinement outside] (*Mutaciones* 15). We can read this passage from a variety of theoretical stances; it could signal a psychoanalytic (re)birth into a hostile world or it might indicate the postmodern end of utopian possibilities. Although the poem has an oneiric quality to it, a reading which takes into account sociohistoric circumstances produces a curious harmony with actual events. In 1979 Argentina under the dictatorship with 30,000 estimated *desaparecidos*,[1] we might speculate about what the reaction was to these first two lines, which work on an axis of "them" against "us" and evoke a nighttime invasion. The poem, while not necessarily a response to specific events, forms an ironic conjunction with history. It marks a moment in a process of disintegration already at work in Orozco's poetry, already present in Argentina.

In her next collection, *La noche a la deriva*, Orozco moves still further from her neoromantic origins. Although these poems are still interrogating, consistent with the thematic and stylistic coherence of her work, there is a shift in tone here and a stronger *yo*. The speaker is more resigned to her role, more accepting of what she *can* do—refuting, undermining, integrating diverse elements—she takes on a kind of Sisyphean task. *La noche*'s more openly defiant voice provides us with another opportunity to examine Orozco's poetic subject. Concentrating on the construction of her poetic speaker in this chapter, I will examine it in relation to her own earlier work and in terms of another poetic antecedent—Oliverio Girondo. An Argentine poet of the generation preceding *los cuarentistas*, Girondo's influence on younger poets is frequently mentioned (as a precursor of surrealism, for example). His direct influence on Orozco's poetry is arguable; what I propose is a more indirect relation. Girondo, after Borges and Lugones, is the best-known and most well regarded of Argentina's early twentieth-century poets. He is obviously an important literary figure to whose texts all successive Argentine poetry must respond, to supersede, reject, or absorb. Like Eliot, he is another of Orozco's literary fathers. While Girondo's work is recognized for its wordplay, its nonsignification, his poetry, like Orozco's, still functions in part as an incantation. His fracture of language, like her *fracaso* [failure], is an attempt to define the limits or test the boundaries of poetic discourse. These two poets are more alike in these terms than it may first appear; they diverge, however, in respect to their poetic subjects. Girondo breaks linguistic boundaries but creates a poetic subject that still dominates (is absolute) while Orozco's takes on a more subversive function.

Oliverio Girondo is known as a literary rebel in the Argentine tradition, a *vanguardista* comparable to Vallejo or Huidobro. Tamara Kamenszain, however, in *El texto silencioso,* sees his work not as a rupture or rebellion but as participating in another movement that she calls a South American "tradition of negation." Speaking of Girondo as one of the "other masters," she says, "Pero si Borges funda la relación con lo extranjero, estos otros maestros, agazapados en los márgenes, encuentran su poder de fundación en estos bordes donde la página queda en blanco" [But if Borges initiates the relationship with the foreign world, these other masters, crouching in the margins, find their foundational power in those blank borders of the page] (12). Girondo's "tradition" is an antitradition, an inverse tradition. In Girondo's work there is a negative progression, an incessant movement toward the "zero" word that would have a new relation to its fellows in his linguistic fantasy. His first works, *Veinte poemas para ser leídos en el tranvía* [Twenty poems to be read on the streetcar, 1922], *Calcomanías* [Transfers, 1925], and *Espantapájaros* [Scarecrow, 1932], while definitely ultra in style retain more of their referentiality than most of his later work. In *En la masmédula* (1954),[2] his last book of poetry, his radical use of language is particularly apparent. Girondo's emphasis on the materiality of language (rather than its referential quality) is obvious; he creates neologisms and relies heavily on onomatopoeia and phonic relations between words. Through sound and the ludic qualities of language, Girondo breaks up the signifier-signified relation. These, combined with his "democratic" interest in the wider distribution of poetry, are Girondo's most radical contributions to the "tradition of negation."

Yet, while Girondo's free play might liberate language from the binary relation of signification, the author reinforces other binarisms. Considered on other than a linguistic level, his poetry is mixed, marked by various interests and practices, some more engaged in preserving the status quo. Examined in this light, Girondo is more easily identified as Orozco's precursor. Her poetry, appearing to be more traditionally lyrical, in fact achieves a different kind of rupture. When the speaker in *La noche a la deriva* invokes her fathers she is not the speaker we examined in *Las muertes,* who metonymically identifies herself more often with the product than the producer. Rather, Orozco uses a surer, more mature voice to speak from many places. Her poetic voice is fragmented, not fixed, and therefore neither subordinated nor dominating. With their contrasting approaches, both these poets participate in the struggle to redefine the nature of poetry and, in the process, change it.

In terms of Girondo's most radical desire, to empty the content from language, *En la masmédula* is the most fully realized of his texts. It is his most "difficult" collection, often cited as the most avant-garde, ahead of its time in its manipulation of language. Altering syntax, making nouns work as verbs, Girondo self-consciously uses words as things. Certain characteristic poems from this volume consistently appear in anthologies or works on Oliverio Girondo and as such can be considered as typical; for example, "Yolleo," the poet's game of subjectivity in which he names and erases his *yo poético* or "El puro no," a multiplication of the monosyllable, expanding its negative powers ("el plurimono"). "Nochetótem," one of the first poems in the collection, is also representative of Girondo's technique and its nocturnal theme provides a link to Orozco's collection, *La noche a la deriva.* The title alone evokes ritual-magic correspondences between the two authors. Uniting the two words *noche* and *tótem,* Girondo begins with an image of the night as a protective force, an elemental being who guards the tribe. At the same time he plays with the classic lyric poetic form, the nocturne—an expressive night ritualized in language. The neologism "nochetótem" announces a poem that does not lack narrative structure (though this may be slight); we can still read the poem as an invocation of the powers of the night and all it represents.

Son los trasfondos otros de la inextremis médium
que es la noche al entreabrir los huesos
las mitoformas otras
aliardidas presencias semimorfas. (*Antología* 123)

[They are the other backgrounds of the in extreme medium
which is the night upon half opening its bones
the other mythoforms
semimorphic, burning-winged presences.]

Customary syntaxis unravels from the start; "son," the first verb,
seems to refer to "los otros." But the grammatical subject really is "los
trasfondos" and "otros" is an adjective, reinforcing the alterity of
trasfondos, or what exists beyond vision. That these *trasfondos* are of the
"inextremis médium" does not clarify their meaning. The oxymoron
expresses the simultaneous connection or communicative function of the
night and the impossibility of any tie. With the phrase "que es la noche"
we arrive at what appears to be the primary subject of this opening
statement and the plurality of "son" is condensed to "es." Almost as
quickly, the night expands again "al entreabrir los huesos," in another
conflictive moment, both outward (*entreabrir*) and inward (because of
the object, *los huesos*) at the same time. Like the title of this collection,
En la masmédula, Girondo steers his readers inside, as we submerge
ourselves in order to excavate some signification in his language, and
outside, as we must correspondingly open and release our hold on
meanings and convention. From the poem's inception, Girondo assaults
us with the difficulty of its form.

"Las mitiformas otras" is the first reference to the possibility of a
physical presence in this poem, but where *are* they? The poem lacks
deictic references, and these "mitiformas otras" float in the *mitonoche,*
creating a tension between presence and absence, being and specter.
Significantly, *otras* in this case is the subject of the line rather than an
adjective as it first appeared; it has literally mutated, the language itself
carrying out the change in form. In their semimorphic presence, these
"others" mimic Girondo's poetic subject, who is both present and absent
in this poem. There is an unidentified voice that invokes the implied
presence of a *nosotros* [we] to counterbalance the *otras,* but it is present
only indirectly. The poetic speaker exists, as almost every element in the
poem does, in a language that cancels itself. Anticipating Derrida, Girondo
might as well have written ~~estoy~~ [I am].

Estar, however, is not poetry. The relationships between the words in Girondo's poem rely more heavily on sonority than meaning. "Alardidas," for example, can be read for sense—a combination of *alas,* wings, and *arder* or consumed (as by fire). This neologism works as an adjective which modifies another subject, *otras.* Supporting this interpretation the assonance of the "a"s and "i"s, combined yet broken by consonants, is playful and musical—a flutter of wings that announces the onomatopoeia of "sotopausas sosoplos" [soft-pauses vapid-puffs] in the next line. Rather than deny meaning in language, Girondo multiplies sense and shifts the poetic function into high gear. His technique recalls Orozco's attention to form rather than meaning in the last part of "Densos velos . . ." when she frees conjunctions from their grammatical duty; yet this focus is but an aspect of Orozco's poetry while in Girondo's poem it is an organizing principle.

Girondo's poetic production is far from automatic writing in surrealist terms. Instead, his word choice is very precise; he creates exact neologisms in order to extract more from his words. His images may seem surrealistic—"suburbanas sangres" [suburban bloods], "atónitos yesos" [amazed plasters], "esmeriles párpados videntes" [emery seeing eyelids]—yet, upon closer inspection, we see that these images follow a pattern, joining the inanimate and animate. The poet uses pseudosurrealistic (almost baroque) techniques to shock his readers, to tear us away from our habitual use of language and syntax. The individual elements in Girondo's poem (words, images, etc.) are related under new conditions that call more attention to the physicality of the words than to their function.

las suburbanas sangres de la ausencia de reman-
sos omóplatos
las agrisomnes dragas hambrientas del ahora
con su limo de nada

[the suburban bloods of the absence of shoulder-bladed
waters
the starved, soursleep dredges of the present
with their slime of nothingness]

These lines seem to refer simultaneously to the temporal and physical decay of the city, the human body, and language itself. Girondo achieves this effect by combining what appear to be dissimilar terms whose relation to one another is more analogous or sonorous than logical. In order to "understand" his poems, we must change our habits of reading. Girondo's work calls for a different reader: more active and with greater literary expertise.

"Nochetótem" is a poem that resists meaning. It is both representational and antirepresentational, and so our attempts at interpretation are always qualified. With this technique, Oliverio Girondo approaches Bakhtin's notion of the carnivalesque. As Bakhtin explains Rabelais's use of carnivalesque language, "all these word-linkages, even those that seem the most absurd in terms of the objects they name, are aimed primarily at destroying every nook and cranny of the habitual picture of the world" (*The Dialogic Imagination* 177). Like Rabelais, Girondo uses language to break with the symbolic; he turns language against itself. Unlike T. S. Eliot's poetry, which still suggests the possibility of lyrical transport, Girondo's proposes another type of "transport"—augmenting the musicality of the lyric over its sense, Girondo's production enters into a semiotic movement. This aspect of poetry, that we observed in chapter 2, is the rebellious, the "feminine" in Kristevan terms. As in Orozco's poetry, there is no "place" as referent here and meaning exists in the text, in the words themselves, and in their relations to one another.

Girondo's use of the semiotic, the carnivalesque possibilities of language, relate his poetry to the experiments of the twenties vanguard movements. The avant-garde distinguishes itself from modernism through its negative, deconstructive characteristics and political values critical of the dominant societies in which the various movements formed (Huyssen 163). Girondo's work shows many of the formal traits of the vanguard but has a qualified relation to politics. Delphina Muschetti, in her 1985 article, "La fractura ideológica en los primeros textos de Oliverio Girondo" [Ideological rupture in the early works of Oliverio Girondo], examines the conflict between elitist and democratic tendencies in Girondo's early work, and signs of this conflicting identity continue in his later poetry. *En la masmédula,* which cultivates a specialized audience, seems to anticipate more the language poetry that has appeared in post-1960s North America. As poet Steve McCaffery describes North American language-centered writing, its features are its "decontextualization," attention to phonological form, which make it "countercommunicative" writing and place different demands upon its readers (McCaffery 160). Girondo's writing was ahead of its time in this respect, but for precisely these qualities *En la masmédula* was not widely read when it first appeared.[3]

Now there is a critical framework in place for understanding Girondo's poetry, and his linguistic games can be read as "deconstructive" poetry. It is seen as "radical" or political by some because of its rejection of convention, but these same techniques limit its sphere of influence.[4] But unlike language poetry, which is so fragmented, often breaking words into parts (graphemes) or absolutely abandoning all connective words, even Girondo's late production still contains a narrative structure; it is not "pure" materiality.

Enrique Medina, one recent critic of *En la masmédula*, cites three characteristic themes around which Girondo constructs his poetry: "la pasión enfrentada a la nada, el rechazo de una realidad degradada y la invocación del amor y la mujer como afirmación vital y acceso, a través de la pasión carnal, a un plano superior del espíritu" [passion confronted with nothingness, the rejection of a degraded reality, and the invocation of love and woman as a vital affirmation and access, through physical passion, to a higher spiritual plane] (20). Medina is not reading Girondo's poetry in linguistic terms but referentially, in terms of more conventional metaphysical dilemmas (in fact, aside from the last theme, they are almost the same problems that critics frequently observe in Orozco's work). His observations suggest that *En la masmédula*, despite its avant-garde qualities, can still sustain this type of reading. Just as we could decipher a slender narrative thread in "Nochetótem," we can also read it as crossed by the conventions of poetic discourse. Girondo employs a verse form, and he uses this form to lend otherwise absent punctuation to his poem. The overall structure of the poem is not in the least chaotic — the repetition of phrases ("Son las . . . ," "que es la noche . . .") provides the framework for a cumulative linear development that he shifts slightly at the end ("también . . . ," "y es la noche . . .") to close the poem. Girondo maintains at least two other structures traditional to poetic discourse: a firmly positioned speaking subject and, in relation to this, holding it in place as it were, an object or other (usually and conventionally female).

There is not a "yo" directly named, however, in "Nochetótem." Instead there is a disembodied voice that speaks of the "others," defining itself in relation to them. This speaking subject that appears (or does not appear) throughout *En la masmédula* is one I will designate Girondo's "no-yo."[5] It is a voice that projects a powerful ordering presence, for all observations emanate from it. As in "Nochetótem," this subject frequently constitutes itself in a Hegelian oppositional dyad in which the speaker maintains its dominant position. Rather than serving as Medina's "means of transport," feminine images are placed in opposition to this subject. Throughout Girondo's poetry female bodies are disarticulated and certain parts fetishized, occasionally in relation to male fetishized body parts. We see this in the scenic description of the earlier poems, for example, "Biarritz" or this extract from "Exvoto":

Al atardecer, todas ellas cuelgan sus pechos sin madurar
del ramaje de hierro de los balcones,
para que sus vestidos se empurpuren al sentirlas
desnudas, y de noche, a remolque de sus mamás
—empavesadas como fragatas—van a pasearse
por la plaza, para que los hombres les eyaculen
palabras por el oído y sus pezones fosforescentes se
enciendan y se apagan como luciérnagas. (*Espantapájaros* 8)

[At dusk, they hang their unripened breasts
from the iron branches of the balconies
so that their dresses will empurple in contact with their
    nakedness, and at night, in their mother's tow
—shielded like frigates—they go for a walk
through the plaza so that men might ejaculate
words in their ears and their phosphorescent nipples
blink on and off like fireflies.]

In later poems, female presence (often synechdochically evoked) most commonly reinforces the male subject's speaking position. The result is a female "present" through her objective description although absent as a subject and a corresponding male appearance of "absence" that is achieved through his structuring presence.

In contrast to the "no-yo," the other speaker of this volume is a kind of super-*yo*, an exaggerated species of transcendent ego run wild. This voice, present in "Yolleo," "Tropos," "El unonones," and "Aridandan-temente," is a subject that speaks incessantly of its presence, of its own subjectivity:

sigo
solo
me sigo
y en otro absorto otro beodo lodo baldío
por neuroyertos rumbos horas opio desfondes

me persigo
junto a tan tantas otras bellas concas corolas erolocas
entre fugaces muertes sin memoria
y a tantos otros otros grasos ceros construdos que me opan
mientras sigo y me sigo
y me recontrasigo
de un extremo a otro estero
aridandantemente
sin estar ya conmigo ni ser un otro otro. (*Antología* 127)

[I follow
alone
I follow myself
and in another absorbed other drunken bare mud
through neurocold roads hours opium breakages
I pursue myself
together with so many other beautiful concave corollas erocrazy
among fleeting deaths without memory
and so many other others greasy builded zeros that opate me
while I follow and I follow myself
and follow myself against myself
from one extreme to another inlet
aridandantly
without being anymore with myself nor being another other.]

In this hyperreflexive poem there is almost nothing but *yo*—a *yo* in pursuit of itself. The "otro" in this case most frequently modifies itself; it is an "otro absorto otro," "otros otros," or "un otro otro" in a double negative indicative of the subject's alienation or lack of identification. In this case, the reflexive "other" ultimately refers back to the speaker.

Comparing Girondo's "no-yo" with his "super-yo" demonstrates that the two poetic subjects are really the same. Either through self-cancellation, a staged rejection of the first person poetic position, or through an overbearing assertion of it, both subjects dominate these poems. They are binary opposites that reinforce each other. In the construction of his split poetic subject, Girondo doesn't escape from language's referential quality, its positing of a subject; instead he inverts it. Girondo brings the relation between language and subjectivity to the forefront and, in doing so, sustains contradiction. He alternates between a series of dualisms, between language and referent, subject and object, male and female in his

structure of antithesis. In composing his work this way, Girondo reinforces the limits of these oppositions rather than breaks out of them.

Orozco and Girondo share a fascination with paradox, language,
limits; both contend with these structures and call upon the semiotic to
undermine language's more symbolic operations. Yet these concerns
produce very different results in each poet. In *En la masmédula*, Girondo
uses humor and disconnects his language from concrete references in
order to create a gesture of defiance, a rupture in the poetic tradition and
with the expectations of his readers. His poetry is confrontational, a
defiant literary creation. Orozco is not confrontational in her poetry or
her prose. Rather, she uses a more lyrical approach in which she includes
deconstructive elements. Unlike Girondo's, Orozco's images do not startle
us but draw us in through their very complexity: "un crisol donde
vuelcan el oro de mis días para acuñar la llave que lo encierra" [a crucible
where the gold of my days is overturned in order to forge the key that
locks it in] ("Presentimientos . . .") or later in the same poem, "Soy la
momia traslúcida de ayer convertida en oráculo" [I am yesterday's trans-
lucent mummy converted into an oracle]. These images are expressive
gestures, designed in a more classical poetic sense to communicate an
emotional state of being.[6] Orozco's is less a rupture with convention and
more a dissolution of it—more subtle, more fluid, her fractures result in
fusion. She does not speak from a traditional controlling ego-centered
position. Mobile rather than static, her speaking subject is more relative
than absolute. This characteristic "permeability" is apparent in the title
of *La noche a la deriva*, a volume cut loose, adrift.

This collection starts with a poem entitled "En su inmensa pupila" [In
your immense pupil] in which the speaker addresses the night (as in
Girondo's poem, returning the reader to the title of the book). Nighttime
is the underside of daytime; the speaker interrogates the night in this
poem in an attempt to communicate with it, to join the secret and
pervasive power of the night. She says in her last lines:

Basta conque me lleves de la mano como a través de un bosque,
noche alfombrada, noche sigilosa,
que aprenda yo lo que *quieres decir*, lo que susurra el viento,
y pueda al fin leer hasta el fondo de mi pequeña noche en tu pupila
    inmensa. (8)

[It is enough that you take me by the hand as through a forest
carpeted night, secret night

that I might learn *what you want to say,* what the wind whispers,
and might at last be able to read to the depth of my little night in your
   immense pupil.]

She wants to read the night, understand it, and she asks the night to
guide her. We see the night's power in its eye—it has a pupil and can see
while the speaker cannot. In this way the poet sets up a "Virgilian"
relation between the speaker and the night who acts as her guide. Orozco's
links to the lyric tradition are much stronger than Girondo's; after
examining his work we're struck by the classic quality of her lines, more
reminiscent of Eliot's. But even in this first poem of *La noche* we see that
the lyric voice has begun to form a particular subject unlike that of either
Eliot or Girondo; it is uncertain, curious, ready to learn, open to experience, and looking for an example. It is developed further in the poem that
follows, "Esbozos frente a un modelo" [Sketches in front of a model], in
which we see a problematic subject, characterized as a sort of hesitant
apprentice, faced with the task of imitation.

The title of the poem, "Esbozos frente a un modelo," refers to the
creative process, to the fine arts, and, as we see in the first lines, specifically to sculpture: the material act of production in front of a literal
model.[7] In a more figurative sense, these lines refer to poetry, another
creative activity. In this way, Orozco refers to her process of production—writing—and the meanings of *modelo* multiply. Her model could
be reality or nature that she attempts to textualize, or it could refer to the
poetic tradition, her poetic antecedents against whom she must define
herself. The tone with which she begins her work (creation) links this
poem to the preceding one; the speaker is reserved, doubtful. "Quizá,"
she says, "tal vez" [maybe, perhaps], and she begins her search "a
tientas" [uncertainly], qualifying this poem as a sketch, *un esbozo.* It is a
tentative gesture that, like the majority of Orozco's efforts, will result in a
state of tension instead of resolution.

Here, as in many of Orozco's poems, the speaker must start blindly, a
condition shared by the reader. Deprived of our sense of sight, we are led
by other clues—in this case by touch that searches for form in a "bloque
de sombras" [block of shadows]. The speaker wants to sculpt, to create
something of substance out of the immaterial, an impossible desire—as
impossible as her desire to achieve "la coincidencia exacta con la imagen
que me impone mi modelo" [the exact correspondence with the image
which my model imposes on me]. This model is not inanimate or passive,

but imposes its desire. It is an "amo implacable que le arrebata" [an implacable master who seduces her], oppressive while overseeing the speakers' attempts. The model is a negative, controlling force with which the speaker forms "un pacto de roca" [a stone pact] in a figure of speech that inverts the raw material of sculpture as the insubstantial (a verbal agreement) is materialized (in rock). *Roca* is qualified as well; gaining an adjective, it is *tiránica roca* in which "debe ser estampada la copia de la ley" [the copy of the law should be stamped]. The word choice evokes an exactitude, a rigidity, and a certain violence which the model imposes but which is impossible to achieve due to the fact that the speaker/sculptor works with a substance that is pliable and therefore equivocal:

> y mi sustancia es dócil pero incierto,
> más errónea que un pájaro atraído por el cristal nocturno,
> que un despertar en sueños en medio de otro sueño. (9)

> [and my substance is docile but uncertain
> more mistaken than a bird attracted by the nocturnal crystal
> than an awakening in dreams in the midst of another dream.]

Changing the referent to poetry, we can read this substance as language; "erróneo" because it can never refer directly to an object (the model, lived experience) but must be indirect, figural, in this case metaphoric.

This speaker's relation to her tools—language, her model—is humble. She positions herself as the artist but she is not in control; she is caught in a hierarchical relation to an authoritarian other. Her goal as an artist is reproduction rather than expression. While Girondo's poetic voice slaps us in the face with its difference, Orozco's appears to conform; she positions herself as student but in the process alters her masters or models. Orozco practices a different style of mastery, as her poetic technique indicates. In the process of her struggle to comply, she shows her mastery circuitously, through her technical skill, which belies her claims of humility (not a new technique for responding to authority, it is reminiscent of Sor Juana Inés de la Cruz in her powerful *Respuesta a Sor Filotea*). The poem works as a rhetorical device, a subterfuge that at once hides and reveals the speaker's difference. The poet's facility is apparent in her management of the poem's composition.

The structure of the lines quoted above, like their content, is similar to the first two lines of the poem. "Que" is repeated in a symmetrical construct that mirrors the conjunction "como" of lines one and two: "Quizá como las nubes, / tal vez como el reflejo que se desliza siempre por la arena" [Perhaps like the clouds / maybe like the reflection which always slips through sand]. The "cristal nocturno" is imagistically related to the "reflejo que se desliza" as both are deceptive, false reflections. They are "sueños en medio de otro sueño," or levels of unreality. The reflection as a motif is repeated in several words Orozco uses in the poem: *reflejo, imagen, copia, cristal, modelo,* and the motif continues to be formally reiterated in the paired constructions: *a veces/a veces, cuando/cuando, o/ o.* This reflexive activity increases as the poem continues:

> Se desmorona y se alza en fantasmales remolinos a medida que
>   avanzo;
> se filtra hasta el subsuelo persiguiendo una engañosa huella en el tapiz;
> se arroja deslumbrada contra un haz de luz dura donde se pulveriza la
>   cabeza.
> A veces se condensa en ídolos aviesos o en blancas
> estatuarias de otra edad. (9)

> [it crumbles and rises in ghostly whirlwinds as I advance;
> it is filtered to the subsoil pursuing a deceptive track in the tapestry
> it is flung dazed against a beam of hard light where the head is
>   pulverized.
> At times it is condensed in perverse idols or in white
> statuary of another age.]

The intent to capture, to reflect something ephemeral crumbles. All effort results in fragmentation, shards, waste of raw material, or in immobility—the stasis of idols or statues. These figures also represent a return to old images, to antiquated forms of representation, to a previous form of poetry perhaps. Sometimes it is this, the speaker warns, and repeating herself, "A veces es un cuenco"—a humble waiting recipient, hollow, a void. The forms that the sculptor's substance can assume are, once more, opposites; one possibility is for the substance to become denser, more compressed, or it can take the negative form of a cavity, an absence. This image of the *cuenco* recalls the Kristevan concept of the "chora," from the Platonic use of the word to mean "receptacle."[8] Kristeva uses the term to indicate a boundary around which meaning forms; it is another sign of the marginal, the feminine, the semiotic (Coward 149). It is a negative way to construct meaning by absence.

Using this image, Orozco denies the model while following it, and in doing so, she makes her object (*cuenco* and poem) more active. The *cuenco* is the image around which the poem takes its shape, but standing in a dialectical relation between presence and absence, full and empty, it impedes the object's reification. The speaker too is in movement, vacillating among possibilities; achieving something always means losing something else:

> Cuando logro una mano, pierdo un pie:
> cuando alcanzo el contorno el resto se disgrega en vana orografía.
> No consigo jamás la semejanza desde el corazón hasta mis labios,
> menos feliz que Adán. (9)

> [When I obtain a hand, I lose a foot
> when I achieve the contour the rest disperses in vain orography
> I never attain the likeness from the heart to my lips
> less happy than Adam]

Her use of the possessive pronoun (instead of "el," "mis") makes this creation explicitly hers and begins to erase the division between sculptor and sculpture. The reference to Adam expands this idea and adds precision to her goal; the sculptor/speaker not only wants to create a replica of the model but a self-reflection (just as Adam obtained his likeness). She seems to long for the "Adamic" word, a supposed unity of meaning before the fall, because here her striving is limited to representation, rather than hope of creating the thing-in-itself. As she is, without her semblance, the speaker cannot obtain the happiness of certain pebbles (*guijarros*), inanimate objects that always have a cumulative function in Orozco's work and so are always among their "fellows." She is not as happy as the protagonists she mentions, the artistic product of another author in another time, who already know their destiny. In each of these cases the poetic subject compares her position with that of an object or product or another's likeness, never with the creator. In this she draws attention to her own constructed nature, for she is the "speaker," voice of the poetic subject. The poet demonstrates a lack of identification between her created "self" and her position as creator. At the same time, in a dialectical movement, she increasingly dissolves the line between the artist and his or her work, for the subject creates the object and the object here is the subject. The creative metaphor in "Esbozos . . ." gains yet another meaning, that of self-construction.

Frustrated, the artist-speaker comes to doubt, to question the pattern. When she tries to touch it, it changes. But she continues to obey its "inhumano" order because she knows her place. "Inhumano" creates an interesting play of meanings for it works in the sense of impossible, cruel, other-worldly, but also as *material*. Her master is an object that controls her as if it were the subject-artist rather than a representation. The "yo" of this poem is the "espejo escaso" [scant mirror], another reflection. She is the "bruma acumulada en el umbral" [mist accumulated on the threshold], the heap of insubstantial material (words?) like the sculptor's clay awaiting a form. She is the question that is never revealed—out of our reach—and she is the answer. "La respuesta" looks like an afterthought, added to the poem by the conjunction "y," and at first glance it seems to offer closure, an end to ambiguity. But it is the answer to the question that we never hear; a kind of anti-answer that results in another question, it denies stasis or repose. Although the answer is never revealed, through reference to the legend of the Sphinx we are reminded of her question to Oedipus and its answer. The answer implied but never pronounced is "Man"; a term that pretends to be universal is unspoken in this poem.[9] Orozco provides us with an indication of the gender of the speaker who identifies herself with that which is unsaid; she does not speak from a position of false "neutrality." She is the other side of Man; like the Sphinx, feminine, an animated statue, the speaker figures herself as another "negativity," another model sprung from the patriarchal cultural code since its genesis (Adán).

"Acaso" [maybe] brings us back to the beginning once more; it is another qualifier, this time of the speaker's destiny. Her fate is to be the "sello irreversible." Not the copy of the law but the seal, in another inverse figure she identifies herself with the object used to make the stamp. Or her destiny is to be the "huella no colmada," an imprint, another negativity, or to exist "por algo que no soy": to be the opposite, the other, a relative and negative definition once more.

The speaker of "Esbozos . . ." defines herself against the model, arriving at meaning in terms of what she is not. She begins by looking for an exact correspondence and ends with the realization that she cannot convert herself into the model, but she can become its negative reflection. The speaker, in effect, takes on language's role as both arrive at meaning only in relation to other words or forms. In "Esbozos . . ." Orozco textualizes her experience as author, which is the activity of writing. She creates a metapoem (similar to "Densos velos . . ."), in which one of the primary themes is the creation of the poetic subject. Orozco maintains a lack of unity, affirming the act of negation, and creates a poetic subject that constantly changes form, that transgresses limits.

The poet both is and is not her lyric voice in "Esbozos . . ." This contradictory identification is reminiscent of Girondo's self-extinguishing language in *En la masmédula* and of his "super" and "anti-yo" constructions. The problem in each case is the same, searching for a different speaking position, not as conventionally centered, uniform, hegemonic. Girondo's "resolution" to this problem is the tension of paradox; language has meaning, yet its meaning is less conspicuous in his poetry than the word's material presence. Meaning is in the words themselves, rather than something outside to be deciphered. Similarly, the speaker he employs is either entirely absent or entirely present but in either situation he dominates the poems. Orozco's subject is in flux; she alternately follows the model, rejects the model, and is the model. This switching between subject and object positions is a fundamental characteristic of *La noche a la deriva*.[10] This speaker subverts the concentration of power in one voice by making herself many. She breaks up a duality that Girondo enforces, and rather than losing a sense of self, she appears to gain strength by occupying a variety of perspectives.

These poets both create a different position for their readers, manipulating the difficulties of identification already present in lyric poetry. Girondo's confrontational style asks for a flexible, perhaps a more courageous reader, but in this he is selecting for a more elite, specialized reader than in some of his earlier poetry. Through his subject-object confrontation often posed in terms of gender differences, he is also inscribing a more unitary "masculine" subject position for his reader. We're forced to identify with a gendered, male "I." Orozco's poetry with its traditional aspects links her more obviously to poets like Verlaine, Rimbaud, and Rilke. She uses a more conventionally acceptable style, making it possible for her to assimilate to the literary canon that precedes her. Orozco's poetry is not overtly radical. When we read it closely, however, we find ourselves identifying with a variety of subject positions, unable to rest in a single perspective. Often at least one of the speaker's positions is gendered as female. When the dominant society is patriarchal, speaking from the position of "other" is perhaps radical in itself. Orozco's poetic voice does not presume to be universal. As such, it does not dominate but remains particular and is contestatory in a very understated fashion.

Both of these poets speak in some way in opposition to convention. As subjects in late capitalist industrial society, they are marginalized as poets in an economy in which poetry has very little exchange value. Perhaps poetry represents cultural capital, but even this is undercut by Orozco's and Girondo's positions as Argentines in relation to world literature. The distribution of their work suffers from problems of uneven social, economic, and cultural development. Both struggle with problems of identity and recognition; both seek a voice through their texts, which mediate between their positions as individual subjects and as members of society. Neither intends to reproduce domination but to appropriate the dominant culture's methodology to his or her own ends. Oliverio Girondo does this with poetry that is radical in appearance but actually produces mixed results, as we have seen. He creates a "revolution in language" that was avant-garde in the moment it appeared because of its nonconformist, challenging qualities. Now his work is being reclaimed more for its linguistic features; it is a revolution in *language* which perhaps represents to many one of the few places where revolution is possible. Orozco's poems, appearing more conventional, provoke underhanded, subtle subversion. The negativity or refusal that Girondo employed in his linguistic structures is present in Orozco's nonunified subjectivity. She carves out a variety of places from which to speak and does not reduce her subject position to only self and other. Her poetry is not avant-garde and, in fact, almost seems to be reacting against this movement in order to represent more classically lyric poetry. But hers is not a neoromantic exploration of metaphysical dilemmas. In Orozco's poetry we see a double movement, both accepting and defying, challenging and conforming. Through a close reading of Orozco's work in relation to Girondo's, rather than seeing her *obra* as an inexplicable break from the prescience of her more experimental predecessors, we see how she shares some of their characteristics and rejects others while adding her own innovations. Reading these poets diachronically, we find that they do not participate in distinct movements but are part of a whole cultural production in which each one affects the others.

CHAPTER 4

The Struggle of Imagination
Alejandra Pizarnik and Olga Orozco

Up to this point in my analysis, I have elected to read comparatively by basically examining one poem of another author in detail and contrasting it to a poem by Orozco. This methodology allows me to use concrete examples of each poet's techniques as representative of the body of their work. With Eliot, we observed similarities through juxtaposition; gaps in time, language, and nationality make the differences between the two poets more striking and allow us to read "Little Gidding" as a prior discourse, a generic forerunner that is implied in the later poet's work. By the time Orozco writes *Mutaciones de la realidad,* Eliot is a part of modern poetry's institutionalization. In Argentina, he exemplifies the values of a literary and cultural elite.

Reading Orozco's work in relation to Oliverio Girondo's, the primary emphasis fell upon his poem "Nochetótem." With Girondo, however, we did not remain as enclosed within a single example, but considered the entire collection *En la masmédula,* while beginning to examine Orozco's *La noche a la deriva.* In comparison to Eliot's poetry, the poems in Girondo's book work more as fragments of a whole; they are shorter than "Little Gidding," not as contained within a formal musical structure. While many characteristics of Girondo's style are very distinct from Orozco's—the construction of metaphors, reliance upon images (or lack thereof), rhythm, tone, length of line, structure of the poetic voice—we still observed some perhaps surprising similarities. Both Orozco and Girondo use their poetry to increase access to the semiotic, and each attempts to force his or her language beyond its significative function.

Orozco and Girondo are closer in both historical and geographic terms than is Eliot, similarities which lead to a more integrated reading of the two. These authors have a specific relation to each other as both participate in the construction of the more qualified genre of twentieth-century Argentine poetry. Their relation is more apparent when they are read as "constituents of a genre," within their larger structuring framework (Culler, 1976: 1394).

Through her open acknowledgments of other authors and texts Orozco frames her work, drawing attention to the continuity of a tradition while signaling her vision of her place in it. Orozco openly acknowledges a "harmony" with T. S. Eliot in the 1988 interview and shows her familiarity with his work through direct quotation. While Orozco has written about Oliverio Girondo and enjoyed a long friendship with him, she does not include him in her list of influences. In my third chapter I have argued that because of Girondo's prominence, his is an inevitable influence; if Orozco's poetry is not immediately comparable to Girondo's, in many respects she is writing against the implied presence of his work. Viewing Orozco in terms of these poets we see her relation to tradition; she is both part of it and diverges from previous patterns. Outside as well as within her poetry, Orozco struggles in a kind of stasis, for she transforms while she remains in her place.

We can see the conflict with tradition in yet another form in Orozco's poetry when we consider all these poets in terms of a more customary rendition of the heroic trajectory. Joseph Campbell outlines the monomyth of the hero as follows: "A hero ventures forth from the world of common day into a region of supernatural wonder: fabulous forces are there encountered and a decisive victory is won: the hero comes back from this mysterious adventure with the power to bestow a boon upon his fellow man" (30). Orozco's speaker often embarks on a heroic quest, enters other realms in her search, and strives to overcome immoderate obstacles (death, barriers to communication, physicality). The poet also associates her quest with traditional pursuits by employing terminology of ancient civilizations, of Greek myths (the Sphinx, the Oracle at Delphi, for example), but she alters her version of the hero's trajectory by eluding victory. We can observe her difference when we consider Eliot's clearer model of Campbell's theory in "Four Quartets." Eliot's speaker wades through the mire, the disintegration of modern life, to find his place in the spiritual order at the end of his journey and communicates a message to his compatriots: "All manner of things shall be one." The hero's journey

in Eliot's work concludes in a very modernist affirmation of art's ability
to provide order (and spiritual renewal) in a disordered world.

This route is more difficult to chart in Girondo's work unless we think
of his speaker as an antihero and the progress of his poems as disintegration rather than reintegration. This inversion of a traditional mythic-
heroic pattern fits with the carnivalesque elements of his poetry and is in
keeping with his avant-garde aims. It is negative, in that his poetry aims
to destroy conventional patterns, replacing them with remnants of the
predominant linguistic structures. Girondo may tangentially recall the
monomyth, in order to use it as a counterdiscourse in his poetry. But in
Orozco's poetry something happens that is quite within the definition of
neither modernism nor the avant-garde; the speaker in this case is not the
traditional mythic hero or does not remain in a heroic role. More often,
her *yo poético* loses her agency and is transformed into a marker on the
hero's road. She *becomes* the Sphinx, the statue, the idol, the continent,
as we have seen, or she is a caryatid as in this example from "El revés de
la trama" [The other side of the plot]:

> Casi todo mi ser es invisible;
> plegado en una brizna,
> sumergido hasta el limo en la inconmensurable pequeñez.
> La mole de San Pedro brillando en el agujero de la cerradura;
> Bizancio en una lágrima.
> Hija del desconcierto y la penumbra,
> avanzo a duras penas con mi carga de construcciones y naufragios:
> cariátide insensata transportando su Olimpo en la nube interior,
> perdiendo a cada tumbo su minúsculo yo como una piedrecita del gran
>   friso,
> un ínfimo fragmento de eternidad que rueda hasta los límites del
>   mundo
> y se recoge a tientas, sin acertar su sitio y su destino.
>   (*Mutaciones* 81–82)

> [Almost all of my being is invisible
> folded in a leaf of grass
> submerged up to the slime in immeasurable smallness.
> Saint Peter's mass shining in the lock's opening
> Byzantium in a tear.
> Disorder and penumbra's daughter
> I advance with great difficulty with my load of constructions and
>   shipwrecks

fatuous caryatid transporting her Olympus on an interior cloud
losing her miniscule I at each tumble like a little stone in the big frieze
an abject fragment of eternity that rolls to the limits of the world
and is recovered in the dark, without finding its destiny and its place.]

Orozco departs from the mythic pattern; she does not find a secure place in tradition or her power in the existing order. Her poetic speaker leads a dual existence; she is a heroine in motion but is also a mute and anchored object, unable to search for alternatives.

Proposing a heroine who is at once speaking and mute, Orozco takes a place in tradition while she refuses it. Uncovering this pattern provides a link to our next textual interaction: that of Olga Orozco and Alejandra Pizarnik. Alejandra Pizarnik is an Argentine contemporary of Orozco's whose poetry takes on the same challenge—How can one speak and yet remain silent? The comparison between these two poets is more common; Pizarnik was born in 1936 and Orozco in 1920, so these poets come from overlapping generations and shared lives. Each one has poems dedicated to the other (Orozco's "Pavana para una infanta difunta" [Pavane for a deceased royal child] and Pizarnik's "Cantora nocturna" and "Tiempo" [Night singer and Time]). They are thrown together by categorists as female Argentine poets, but in fact they shared an actual relation to one another, a real friendship-mentor relationship. It is more difficult in this case to sort out textual from biographical relations, so I will begin with the texts, considering shared themes of silence and death and in the process discuss their different poetic techniques. This will eventually lead to an examination of their lives. In contrasting Orozco and Pizarnik we can explore mutual "influences" more than imprints of prior texts, and because of all the contiguities between the two authors, this will lead to a more integrated examination of their differences.

Silence is a key factor in Alejandra Pizarnik's poetry. In an interview with Martha Moia, silence is one term among others (*jardín, bosque, palabra, errancia, viento* and *noche* [garden, forest, word, wandering, wind, and night]) that the poet qualifies as "signs and emblems" in her poetry (*El deseo de la palabra* [Desire for the word] 246). Silence does not always have the same meaning in Pizarnik's poetry but, rather, shifts over time, as her work and style change, and its meaning changes even within an individual work. *Arbol de Diana* [Tree of Diana, 1962] is Pizarnik's fourth collection, and she emphasizes silence throughout these brief, largely untitled poems. The poems mark a progression in their evocation of silence.[1] In the beginning of the third poem, for example, silence implies the absence of another but it soon shifts (line 5) and becomes at once personalized and distanced:

> sólo la sed
> el silencio
> ningún encuentro
> cuídate de mí amor mío
> cuídate de la silenciosa en el desierto
> de la viajera en el vaso vacío
> y de la sombra de su sombra. (*Extracción* 9)

> [only thirst
> silence
> no encounter
> be careful of me my love
> be careful of the silent one in the desert
> of the traveller in the empty glass
> and of the shadow of her shadow.]

The "mi" of the preceding line becomes the "silent one"; silence is no longer only outside of the speaker, instead she embodies it. Yet this is also a distancing move, for with the transformation the speaker now refers to herself in the third person. This process of separation continues in the series, as in poem six, where the subject shifts from "I" to "she" and it is "ella" who "tiene miedo de no saber nombrar" [is afraid of not knowing how to name] (*Extracción* 9). Pizarnik's "yo" is being silenced in the progress of these poems—fragments of a larger poem—in which the subject is increasingly split into "yo" and "ella." Poem fourteen articulates the paradox:

> El poema que no digo,
> el que no merezco.
> Miedo de ser dos
> camino del espejo:
> alguien en mí dormido
> me come y me bebe. (*Extracción* 9)

> [The poem I do not articulate
> the one I don't deserve
> fear of being two
> the mirror's road

someone in me sleeping
eats and drinks me.]

The *yo*, identified as poet now, is explicitly divided. She has two selves: one feeds off the other, one seems to speak at the cost of the other's silence. She refers to an unspoken poem, another, silent poem. Or is it this poem unraveled, under erasure? The poet speaks yet tells us what she does not say, making us focus our attention on the element of silence.

In poem sixteen the "yo" continues its retreat and "tú" is the actor here:

has construido tu casa
has emplumado tus pájaros
has golpeado al viento
con tus propios huesos.
has terminado sola
lo que nadie comenzó. (*Extracción* 9)

[you have constructed your house
you have feathered your birds
you have beaten the wind
with your own bones
you have finished alone
that which no one started.]

It is a feminine "you" that takes over for "no one" in a double movement that affirms while it negates the speaking self.[2] Pizarnik is both constrained by and takes advantage of paradox, and as *Arbol de Diana* advances, silence is mentioned less as a theme; instead it is implemented. The poetic speaker gives herself to silence, lets it speak through her:

Silencio
yo me uno al silencio
yo me he unido al silencio
y me dejo hacer
me dejo beber
me dejo decir. (*Extracción* 10)

[Silence
I join myself to silence
I have joined myself to silence
I let myself do

I let myself drink
I let myself say.]

Silence is connected to the self; it is not an exterior force in this poetry.
By embodying silence, Pizarnik makes what is not voiced, and therefore
usually unheard, speak. She *becomes* silent, counterpoising her silent self
to the force of language.

Silence dominates these poems spatially as a handful of lines occupy
the pages amid the remaining blankness. Pizarnik uses short lines and a
minimum of punctuation in order to stress the function of space balancing her words. In *Arbol de Diana* there is an irregular pattern of rhymes
(usually assonant), and the poetry depends more upon repetition and
alliteration. It does not have the sonorous quality of Orozco's extended
verses. Pizarnik's language appears to be simpler, more straightforward,
and plain, but her poetry's lack of connective phrases, of mediating ideas
between lines, makes it conceptually more complex than it may first
seem. She and some of her readers note her debt to surrealism,[3] most
apparent in her images, which frequently juxtapose concrete things and
abstract ideas: "Mi infancia y su perfume a pájaro acariciado" [my youth
and its perfume of a caressed bird] ("Tiempo" *Poemas* 16). The lack of
verb in this line is typical of Pizarnik who associates the two images by
joining them with "and." Unlike Orozco's chains of metaphors, Pizarnik's
poetry leaves much unsaid. This understated quality continually reminds
us of the force of silence, never far away.

Orozco's technique of folding one metaphor into another, of extending a meaning through a tripartite grouping of images, fills the page with
words:

> —no importa que las hojas prometieran con cada centelleo
> una gruta encantada,
> que los susurros del atardecer fueran las risas de los desaparecidos,
> que los pájaros cambiaran de color justo a la hora de no ser ya los
>   mismos—("Parte de viaje" *La noche* 18)

> [—It is not important that the leaves promised an enchanted cave with
>   each sparkle
> that the twilight whispers might be the laughter of the disappeared,
> that the birds changed color exactly at the time when they are no
>   longer the same—]

Silence is not as directly a theme in Orozco's work but is one of a
number of threats which the poet fends off through the activity of

writing. Orozco does not dedicate poems to silence, as Pizarnik does, and silence occurs more indirectly in her poetry. It is an action, a reaction, or a characteristic that changes possession. We see inanimate objects speak as speaking subjects become mute or lose the "power" of speech. This last phrase signals an important difference between the two authors, for while Pizarnik calls upon the force of silence, Orozco continues to acknowledge language's strength against silence. In Orozco's poetry silence often is the result of a struggle about who or what is to have the word.

In chapters 2 and 3 we saw this encounter with language in poems where the poetic speaker attempts to follow models and fails ("Esbozos frente un modelo," "Densos velos te cubren, poesía"). In each of these cases she is momentarily defeated or silenced, only to take up the fight and her pen once more on the following page. When Orozco's theme is writing, as it is in these poems, the impasse between the particular subject and larger forces results in silence; however, the impediment in Orozco's poems is more often characterized in different terms. It is frequently spatialized, and instead of silence, Orozco speaks of absence or distance. This is quite clear in her first book, *Desde lejos*—the title itself fixing its remote origin. In this early book there is a more distanced poetic speaker so that silence most often exists outside of the first person voice, in the surroundings: in the "día silencioso" [silent day] (*Obra* 34), the "muda confusión de los días" [mute confusion of the days] (38), or in the "dominios del silencio" [domains of silence] (37). Later, in the collection *Los juegos peligrosos*, the poetic speaker is more prominent and the poem "Espejos a distancia" [Distant mirrors] closes with the same kind of paradox Alejandra Pizarnik will employ: "Voy a empezar a hablar entre los muertos. / Voy a quedarme muda" [I am going to begin to speak among the dead / I am going to remain mute] (*Obra* 89). In this poem Orozco confronts her other half, her mirror or accomplice, significantly distanced, and we find that while one speaks, the other must remain silent. In the poetry of both authors, silence can indicate the unheard, repressed voice of the split subject.[4]

In *Museo salvaje*, Orozco's next book of poetry, silence is seldom mentioned. It is the antithesis of these prose poems to physicality that mimic the body's materiality through a corpus of language. Through the words' physical presence silence is kept outside of these poems or is indicated in passing, as when Orozco describes the mouth as an "oráculo mudo" [mute oracle] (*Obra* 160). In *Cantos a Berenice* [Songs to Berenice], silence reappears with its associated spatial term—absence—and is another form of speech, indicative of memory: "la vida es ausencia amor-dazada / y el silencio, / una boca cosida que simula el olvido" [life is gagged absence / and silence / a sewn mouth simulating forgetfulness] ("VII" *Obra* 171). Silence is constrained; it does not lose its signifying function but, rather, indicates a space where something is not said.

In Orozco's work silence sometimes has power analogous to that of language, but she is not as consistent in this view as is Pizarnik. Orozco's silences, even when full of substance, always imply a struggle with language for there is a decided value in controlling the sign in her poetry. In *Mutaciones* we see that the encounter with language is linked to the construction of subjectivity. The poem "Objetos al acecho" [Objects in wait] provides a provocative example, for in this confrontation, the objects win. Things awaken from their "manso ensimismamiento" [docile self-contemplation] with no explanation and are suddenly menacing, rebellious: "Los objetos adquieren una intención secreta en esta hora / que presagia el abismo" [At this hour objects acquire a secret intention / that foreshadows the abyss]. They become mystical, semi-animate creatures—gargoyles, idols—who change the law and judge the speaker. The poem ends by reinforcing her limitations:

> Y ningún catecismo que haga retroceder esta extraña asemblea que me acecha.
> este cruel tribunal que me expulsa otra vez de un irreconocible paraíso,
> recuperado a medias cada día. (*Mutaciones* 69)

> [And no catechism which might make this strange assembly retreat awaits me.
> This cruel tribunal which expulses me once more from an unrecognizable paradise
> half recovered every day.]

The speaker, whose language has lost its force, is barred from "paradise" or the prerogative of subjectivity, it seems. She loses her uncertain power over her "tribu doméstica" [domestic tribe] as they gain a silent but active authority over her. In this poem there is no possibility of a shared subjectivity; the first person voice does not merge with other voices or things. The objects proffer a silent indictment and through this communication become subjects, able to challenge the primary speaker's power. In other examples from *Mutaciones*, the speaker herself has a tenuous subjectivity and tries to hide her lack of presence through imitation. In "Los reflejos infieles" [Unfaithful reflections] she tries on masks, successive faces, but is unable to disguise her absence. In this instance she has a voice but no presence: "Ningún signo especial en estas caras que tapizan la ausencia" [No special sign in these faces which cover absence] (57). "El resto era silencio" [The rest was silence], the first poem from Orozco's recent collection, *En el revés del cielo,* narrates the speaker's attempt to avoid some distant authority's dictate of silence: "Yo esperaba el dictado del silencio; / acechaba en las sombras el vuelo sorprendente del azar, una chispa del sol, / así como quien consulta las arenas en el desierto blanco" [I was waiting for the dictate of silence / in the shadows I was watching chance's surprising flight, a spark of sun, / just like the person who consults sand in the white desert] (9). The poem ends with the inevitable silencing command: "Había una sentencia en su página blanca, / un áspero dictado caído de lo alto hasta su mano: / 'Y haz que sólo el silencio sea su palabra'" [There was a sentence on his white page / a harsh dictate fallen from on high to your hand / "Make only silence your word"] (10).

There is a progression in Orozco's work, as this last poem demonstrates, toward a more direct confrontation with the threat of silence. This development occurs concurrently with the increasing prominence of the *yo poético.* It is significant that in this most recent example the confrontation is so explicit, as is the speaker's resistance. The initial poem of *En el revés* is a mandate for silence; yet it is the *first* poem, opening a book in which the speaker is obviously not quiescent but speaking in defiance of authority.[5] As we have seen, in Orozco's work silence is seldom a positive attribute but is linked to a lack of power, to rigidity, petrification, objectification, and division. Speaking is identified as a determined and determinant act. Both Orozco and Pizarnik often employ silence to characterize one half of a divided self, and while Orozco increasingly acknowledges and struggles to give voice to this silent side, Pizarnik submerges herself in silence, exploiting its more positive aspects.

For Pizarnik, silence can hide weakness. In "Figuras y silencios," her speaker asks to be silenced:

Manos crispadas me confinan al exilio.
Ayúdame a no pedir ayuda.
Me quieren anochecer, me van a morir.
Ayúdame a no pedir ayuda. (*Extracción* 14)

[Convulsed hands confine me to exile.
Help me not to ask for help
They want to deprive me of light, they are going to extinguish me.
Help me not to ask for help.]

There is strength in suppression for to speak would be to reveal need. To speak also means to use a language that is not one's own as in "Fragmentos para dominar el silencio" [Fragments to dominate silence] (*Extracción* 16), in which "las damas solitarias" [the solitary women], who represent the force of language, sing through the poetic voice while the speaker-subject listens at a distance. The speaker is alienated from language both because of its general lack of referential capability and because it does not work as a means to express *herself*: "Algo caía en el silencio. Mi última palabra fue / yo pero me refería al alba luminosa" [Something was falling in the silence. My last word was / I but I was referring to the luminous dawn] ("Caminos del espejo" *Extracción* 16). Silence has a dual nature; at times it is an arm against language's inaccuracy and at other moments it is an indomitable force that language barely controls.

In a similar sort of inversion, Pizarnik attempts to achieve silence through speech. Her often-quoted lines from "Caminos del espejo" [The mirror's roads], "Deseaba un silencio perfecto. / Por eso hablo" [I wanted a perfect silence. / This is why I speak] (16), hold a variety of possible interpretations. The poet may want to use language to refer to its own limitations, to what is left unsaid, or to the blank spaces so prominent in the pages of her work. Like Orozco, Pizarnik self-consciously calls attention to the "failure" of language. Still another use for poetry is as a kind of purge, the idea being that through using language and exhausting it, one can come to hear silence. Silence is not a passive absence of words in this case but an active relocation of meaning.

In Pizarnik's work, silence is increasingly connected to death. Her poems mark a process of self-annihilation in which the paradoxical interdependence of poetry and silence is mirrored by that of death and life. Correspondingly, death is not an inexpressive void but acquires a more potent voice than life's.

No es muda la muerte. Escucho el canto de los enlutados sellar las hendiduras del silencio. Escucho su dulcísimo llanto florecer mi silencio gris.

III

La muerte ha restituído al silencio su prestigio hechizante. Y yo no diré
mi poema y yo he de decirlo. Aun si el poema (aquí, ahora) no tiene
sentido, no tiene destino. (*Poemas* 75)

[Death is not mute. I listen to the singing of the mourners seal the
fissures of silence. I listen to their very sweet sob make my grey
silence bloom.

III

Death has restored to silence its bewitching prestige. And I will not say
my poem and I have to say it. Even if the poem (here, now) doesn't
make sense, doesn't have a destiny.]

Pizarnik celebrates death's soundless, liberating song. Providing another means of communication, death represents freedom from language's
restrictions; a liberation like that of the plastic arts whose images Pizarnik
finds more expressive because of their proximity to silence.[6] Pizarnik has
been criticized for just this trait, for inverting the usual function of
poetry, its role as lyric or *canto*. Ricardo Herrera argues that instead of
forming bonds with others and affirming human experience, Pizarnik's
poetry leads to isolation and a privatization of the subject. Herrera says,
for example, that Pizarnik, "No es alguien, como Garcilaso, que siente,
ya privado de todo, que al menos su dolor lo une al mundo, sino, por el
contrario, alguien que ha hecho de su dolor el despeñadero del mundo"
[Isn't someone like Garcilaso [de la Vega], who feels, already lacking
everything, that at least his pain links him to the world, but, on the
contrary, someone who has made of her pain the precipice of the world]
(101). The poetic experience is made up of a symbolic transgression—"lo
prometeíco, lo adámico, ¿No es acaso esencial a lo poético?" [the
Promethean, the Adamic, isn't it essential to the poetic?] (100)—and then
a return and reintegration, according to Herrera. Pizarnik does not participate in this classically romantic notion of poetry, so dependent,
as Herrera himself demonstrates, on masculine heroic models. A more
generous reading of her poetry would note its difference as peculiarly
modern, in its reflexive quality, its self-consciousness, and its almost
nihilistic awareness of the limited possibilities of "return." In one sense
this may be true, in that Pizarnik's poetry does record her increasing
distance from society. However, while she constructs a self that is alone,
she is not autonomous. Often pleading for help, she is represented as
unable to survive independently, and the speaker both asserts her isola-

tion and undermines it. But if isolation and exile are this poet's experience, they can also be generalized. The poet describes her duty in terms of a communal function which is "exorcisar, conjurar y, además, reparar. Escribir un poema es reparar la herida fundamental, la desgarradura. Porque todos estamos heridos" [to exorcise, to conjure, and, moreover, to restore. To write a poem is to repair the fundamental wound, the laceration. Because we are all wounded] (*Deseo* 247). "Reparar": by acknowledging separation Pizarnik attempts to overcome it, a desire which culminates in another paradox, as she affirms and refuses her difference.

Separation, distance, silence are all joined in the idea of death which holds an advancing fascination for Pizarnik's poetic speaker. Death implies self-destruction in this poetry, and like the allure of silence for the poet, achieving her desire requires her demise. Pizarnik is not unique in the poetic tradition for her celebration of death—Lautréamont and Nerval, the French "dark poets," are two she cites for their celebration of death's possibilities. Cristina Piña accurately describes Mallarmé as her forebear in the realm of silence and his influence can also be seen in relation to suicide (Prologue *Extracción* 5). Maurice Blanchot describes Mallarmé's positive attitude toward death and the "power of the negative," which offers the French poet the "supreme possibility," the power not to be (7). Suicide is positive in the sense that it means taking control over one's destiny, gaining ascendancy over an otherwise unpredictable fate. This is a romantic idealization of suicide, and romanticization of the theme is augmented in Pizarnik's work by the frequent confusion of her texts with the facts of her life.

Alejandra Pizarnik died in 1972 from an overdose of barbiturates, a death which has been widely interpreted as suicide. The tendency to read her poems as autobiographical fragments is apparent in titles of articles about Pizarnik that frequently read her work as her life (Two examples: "Alejandra Pizarnik: La poesía como destino," or "A Death in Which to Live") and in the tendency to assiduously date her last poems, a practice which encourages the reader to consider them suicide notes. Critics who indulge too completely their autobiographical readings participate in the continual mythologizing of the romantic artist, individualistic and estranged from society. Yet Pizarnik's work does encourage this association, and her biography must be taken into account as a factor in her production, an element in the intersection of text and context. Alfredo Roggiano characterizes this trait of her poetry more precisely when he says, "Es ésta una poesía ontológica, en el sentido de que el hacer poético es más que un acto de crear: es una posibilidad de ser" [This is an ontological poetry, in the sense that poetic activity is more than an act of creation; it is a possibility of being] (55). Pizarnik's awareness of death throughout her poetic production, not only in her last years, allows her to use her art to fashion her survival. In doing so, she consistently expands her particular history into larger, more impersonal existential considerations.

Pizarnik persists by transforming herself in poetry and makes poetry through the sacrifice of self. In the last stanza of "El deseo de la palabra" [Desiring the word] she declares:

Ojalá pudiera vivir solamente en éxtasis, haciendo el cuerpo del poema con mi cuerpo, rescatando cada frase con mis días y con mis semanas, infundiéndole al poema mi soplo a medida que cada letra de cada palabra haya sido sacrificada en las ceremonias de vivir. (*Poemas* 95)

[I wish I could only live in ecstasy, making the body of the poem with my body, rescuing each sentence with my days and with my weeks, infusing the poem with my breath in proportion that each letter of each word might have been sacrificed in ceremonies of living.]

This suggests a mutual sacrifice in the union of self and language. The poem is followed by its reflection, "La palabra del deseo" [Desire's word], in which the poet now laments language's failure to unify:

La soledad es no poder decirla por no poder circundarla por no poder darle un rostro por no poder hacerla sínonimo de un paisaje. La soledad sería esta melodía rota de mis frases. (*Poemas* 96)

[Loneliness is not being able to say it because of not being able to encompass it because of not being able to give it a face because of not being able to make it synonomous with a landscape. Loneliness would be this broken melody of my sentences.]

Desire, originating in the subject, creates language, and in a reciprocal movement, language creates desire. This construction recalls the Lacanian notion that links the individual to the social through the symbolic. The mutuality of the relation between language and desire is exemplary of many of Pizarnik's apparent "oppositions" that in fact form a kind of commutative relation to each other, in which one term can be substituted for its other. The poet "lives" in poetry; her artistic creation allows her to endure. But one of the costs of her survival is objectification, through the self-alienation we have observed, amplified when the poet seeks to become one with her object, poetry.

In "Piedra fundamental" [Fundamental stone], Pizarnik writes:

> No puedo hablar con mi voz sino con mis voces.
> . . . algo en mí no se abandona a la cascada de cenizas que me arrasa
> dentro de mí con ella que es yo, conmigo que soy ella y que soy yo,
> indeciblemente distinta de ella.
> . . . Yo quería que mis dedos de muñeca penetraran en las teclas. Yo
> no quería rozar, como una araña, el teclado. Yo quería hundirme,
> clavarme, fijarme, petrificarme. Yo quería entrar en el teclado para
> entrar adentro de la música para tener una patria. (*Extracción* 21)

> [I cannot speak with my voice but with my voices. . . . something in
> me does not abandon itself to the cascade of ashes that obliterates
> me within myself, with she who is I, with me that am her and that
> am I, unspeakably different than her. . . . I wanted my doll's fingers
> to penetrate the keys. I didn't want to graze the keyboard like a
> spider. I wanted to immerse myself, nail myself, fix myself, petrify
> myself. I wanted to enter into the keyboard in order to enter into
> the music to have a country.]

Finding a homeland in her poetic production entails self-sacrifice and stasis. Reminiscent of Orozco's frozen images, her speaker's union with the objects around her, Pizarnik also loses the power of mobility, agency, in her search for perfection. But she does not achieve perfection or entrance to the world of things: "Las palabras hubieran podido salvarme, pero estoy demasiado viviente" [words would have been able to save me but I am too much alive] ("Los poseídos entre lilas" *Extracción* 26). Death is completion: feared, desired, guarded against. Living is the continuous effort required to remain in tension between the two poles of the beginning (innocence, childhood) and the end (death). This poetry that speaks continually of death is in fact meant to be a life-sustaining process, a means of survival but not transcendence of the situation.

Olga Orozco observes this existential quality and describes Pizarnik's poetry spatially, using a road-of-life metaphor:

> La poesía de Alejandra Pizarnik es un país cuyos materiales parecen
> extraídos de miniaturas de esmalte o de stampas iluminadas: hay fulgores
> de herbarios con plumajes orientales, brillos de epopeyas en poblaciones

infantiles, reflejos de las heroínas que atraviesan los milagros. En estos territorios la inocencia desgarrada recubre paisajes inquietantes y las aventuras con un juego con resortes que conducen a la muerte o la soledad. Para perderse o para no perderse, Alejandra Pizarnik ha ido marcando el camino hacia sus refugios con resplandientes piedrecitas de silencio, que son condensaciones de insomnios, de angustias, de sed devoradora. (Beneyto 25)

[Alejandra Pizarnik's poetry is a country whose materials seem to be extracted from enameled miniatures or illuminated engravings; there are herbalists' resplendencies with oriental plumage, glittering epics peopled with children, reflections of heroines who go through miracles. In these territories torn innocence recovers disturbing landscapes and adventures with a game with mechanisms which lead to death or solitude. To lose herself or not to lose herself, Alejandra Pizarnik has marked the path to her retreats with shining pieces of silence, which are condensations of insomnia, anguish, and devouring thirst.]

A more precise reference is the children's story of Hansel and Gretel ("marcando el camino . . . con resplandientes piedrecitas"), a figure that extends Orozco's characterization of Pizarnik's innocence. At the opposite end of Pizarnik's idealization of death is her idealization of and nostalgia for childhood.[7] Both spaces represent a separation from adult life and Pizarnik's role as poet. Images of childhood involve the desire to retreat, to turn back, and like suicide, they offer a survival strategy stemming from the poet's sense of powerlessness. Pizarnik frequently infantilizes her speaker in a retreat from her adult role as poet-survivor (as evidenced by the recurrent toys, dolls, niñas de papel in her poems). Childhood represents another impossible, utopic freedom, but in figuratively regressing to her youth, Pizarnik denies what power she might possess. In this activity she seems to present a textbook example of Gilbert and Gubar's theory about the woman writer's anxiety of authorship, her consciousness of breaking the limits dictated by society.[8] Yet, at the same time, Pizarnik painstakingly records again and again in her poetry the deeply rooted power of those limits.

While both Pizarnik and Orozco stress process as they grapple with fundamental questions in their writing, each author's poems mark a different lyric route. Pizarnik's poems are often spare, calling attention to space, as we have observed, and to their own fragmentary nature. They are like shards (or, Orozco's term, "piedrecitas") grouped into neat little piles, remnants of an explosive event we never see or hear but that echoes, perhaps, in the surrounding silence. Orozco structures her poem's long lines with complex syntax and internal rhyme, filling the pages of her books with language that works back and forth upon itself and never quite rests in closure. There is no end, only more process. Death is a major theme in Orozco's work and, making it a part of this process, she incorporates it as an essential element of life. Orozco ritualizes death in her poetry, countering the actual loss death represents by directing her poetry to the living. She offers a symbolic resistance to death in her poems, assuring her readers that loss of life does not necessitate loss of identity, but that through poetry, one can affirm a particular person's continuing importance.

Death is a strong force in each of Orozco's books, but in *Las muertes* and *Cantos a Berenice* it is the organizing metaphor. Orozco's challenge to death's strength is evident in the irony of the title of *Las muertes* for these are "dead ones" come back to life. The collection speaks of these characters' lives rather than their deaths, adding yet another level of irony because these are fictional characters who never actually "lived." The poet culminates the ambiguous life-death relation, concluding her book with another contradictory twist as the still-living poet memorializes herself in "Olga Orozco." Orozco immortalizes herself by killing off one of her textual selves; she is at once victim and conqueror of her own mortality. *Cantos a Berenice* plays on this same interdependence of life and death. These poems memorialize the author's cat, Berenice, an activity that lets Berenice reappear (like Lewis Carroll's Cheshire Cat) in her various transformations. Berenice survives through history, through her reign in Egypt, in her role as protective spirit, "el tótem palpitante en la cadena rota de mi clan" [the vibrating totem in the broken chain of my clan] ("X" *Obra* 174), the "otro yo" [other self] of the poetic speaker. The *yo poético* gains strength in confronting death through the death of Berenice. She does not find it empty, an encounter with nothingness, but portrays it instead as a merging with everything. The speaker transcends her self, the limits of her individuality, and in the power of her imaginative unity with death, is able to enter a more collective subject. Confrontation with mortality is an equalizing factor which affects every living being so that the speaker identifies her fate with that of Berenice: "Aunque se borren todos nuestros rastros igual que las bujías en el amanecer" [Even though all of our traces may be erased like the candles at dawn] ("XVII" *Obra* 184), and their fate with the death of all her loved ones:

"Tal vez seas ahora tan inmensa como todos mis muertos" [Perhaps you are now as immense as all of my dead ones] (184).

Instead of finality, death represents another transformation in Orozco's poetry. In her conception of the mutability of life, we can see the influence of gnostic thought and themes, a source which Orozco acknowledges.[9] Gnosticism is characterized by constant transformation, by challenging limits in the desire to overcome all dualisms resulting from a post-edenic separation from God. There is a sense of being caught in this world, which is governed by laws that the individual must either avoid (by living outside of them, denying the world) or must openly transgress. In her article on Antonin Artaud, Susan Sontag provides a cogent explanation of the gnostic sensibility, noting that "It is a mark of all gnostic thinking to polarize inner space, the psyche, and a vague outer space, 'the world' or 'society,' which is identified with repression — making little or no acknowledgement of the importance of the mediating levels of the various social spheres and institutions" (52). Orozco's portrayal of death and her poetry's "retreat from the world" can be explained in terms of gnostic doctrine, but this in itself is not sufficient. It would be reductionist to read her poetry only on this level, to use gnostic principles as keys to unlock a set of clearly defined meanings. A gnostic metatext provides one reading but the influence of gnosticism begs historicization, contextualization. Why is gnosticism one of the influencing ideological discourses at this moment, on this author? How is it inflected in this particular instance? These are questions to which we will return in our examination of Orozco's work. Her use of gnosticism differs from Artaud's; Sontag characterizes the French writer's beliefs as an example of radical individualism, a rejection of the world which inevitably leads to silence (or for Artaud, madness).

Orozco does not embrace silence or death but struggle and transformation. We have seen that her poetic subject is constituted in a dialectical process in which the self is both subject, in control, articulating its desires, and object, at the mercy of laws and forces beyond her control. She may be consistently frustrated, her chance of success negated, but not with self-destruction or annihilation as a result. Death is not personified as an intriguing lover who invites the speaker to join her, as we often see in Pizarnik's poetry; instead, it is an external force that the speaker must integrate into her life.

Death is regularly present in the different elegies that recur throughout Orozco's production. These elegies often have an even more intimate tone than much of Orozco's work; perhaps the most personal example is "Si me puedes mirar" (102) [If you can see me], from *Los juegos peligrosos*, a poem commemorating the death of the poet's mother. Yet the loss of a parent is also a supremely general experience. Orozco increases the application of this poem about her mother by referring to what society designates as typical "maternal," caretaking activities, while avoiding the mention of proper names and excluding any specific dedication. Later, in *La noche,* Orozco memorializes a friend in "Por mucho que nos duela" [However much it may hurt us], and although this loss is another common experience, the dedication "a Josefina Susana Fragueiro" indicates the specific loss of a particular friend. The poem is composed, in fact, of memories and an imagined present and future characterized by the unique essence of this friend:

> ¿Y estarás ajustando más las cuentas,
> borroneando tu torturada biografía con tachaduras que son un signo
>   menos?
> ¿O te retienen por un ala rebelde desde arriba,
> mientras pugnas por desasirte con esos tormentosos aleteos,
> con esta fuerza de bestezuela exasperada con que te
> resistías a las jaulas de cualquier ordenanza,
> acumulando sólo lastimaduras y castigos, con extraña
> paciencia? (35–36)

> [And will you be settling accounts again
> effacing your tortured biography with erasures which are one sign
>   less?
> Or are they retaining you from above by a rebellious wing
> while you struggle to free yourself with those tormented flappings
> with that power of an exasperated little beast with which you
> resisted the cages of any order
> accumulating only wounds and punishments with strange
> patience?]

The speaker creates a future tense for her friend by wandering through her recollections, overcoming temporal and spatial gaps by weaving different places and moments together in the texture of her poem. She joins the customarily separate planes of life and death by enlarging the meaning of commonplace occurrences: "¿Puede ser que no vengas, tú, que siempre acudías antes de ser llamada . . . / Quizás te hayas confundido otra vez el lugar y las horas / y andes como viajera perdida nuevamente entre dunas errantes y encrucijadas circulares" [Can it be that you aren't coming, you, who always came before being called? / Maybe you have once more confused the time and place / and you wander like a newly-lost traveller among errant dunes and circular crossroads] (35). The concept of waiting for a dead friend has an ironic veracity that returns the reader to the speaker's perspective as this elegy is primarily focused on the one-who-has-lost, the survivor. It is the *yo* of the poem who is disoriented (*perdida*) now. Orozco concludes her elegy by figuratively letting her friend go and urging a mutual forgetting:

Asciende, asciende hasta perdernos de vista como a las migraciones de
    este último otoño,
como a los huesos que se disgregan en la playa.
Y olvídanos junto a la loza rota, los calendarios muertos, los zapatos;
olvídanos tiernamente, con esa fervorosa obstinación que tú sabes,
pero olvídanos, por mucho que te cueste,
por mucho que nos duela todavía. (36–37)

[Ascend, ascend until we lose sight of one another like the migrations
    of this last Fall
like the bones which are dispersed on the beach.
And forget us together with the broken porcelain, the dead calendars,
    the shoes;
forget us tenderly, with that fervent stubbornness that you know
but forget us, however much it may cost you
however much it may hurt us still.]

What she proposes is a reciprocal, impossible action for obliteration is the antithesis of the poem's activity.

Orozco takes advantage of a convention of lyric poetry when she employs the elegy, prolonging life by evoking the dead. But she also amends the form by inverting the emphasis in "Por mucho. . . ." The tragic figure here is the speaker who must live with the irrevocable absence of her friend. Death, present indirectly, is not kind or cruel but a fact to contend with. In "Pavana para una infanta difunta" (*Mutaciones* 73), Orozco eulogizes Alejandra Pizarnik, once more modifying the elegiac form. She uses military terms to describe Pizarnik but only to emphasize her nonheroic status. She is a "pequeña centinela" [little sentinel], "sin más armas que los ojos abiertos y el terror," fighting a legion of invaders [armed only with her open eyes and terror] (75). Orozco portrays Pizarnik as a child-warrior who sought salvation in language. Not an original depiction, she is adapting Pizarnik's self-portrait. Orozco describes Pizarnik's attempts to defend herself in the world as ineffectual by putting them in diminutive terms: "Ergías pequeños castillos," "te vestías de plumas," "amaestrabas animalitos peligrosos para roer los puentes de la salvación" [You erected little castles, you dressed yourself in feathers, you tamed dangerous animals in order to gnaw at salvation's bridges] (76). The speaker portrays Alejandra Pizarnik as if she were a child playing with fire, in this case, death. Even the title expresses the infantilization and "otherness" of Pizarnik; "infanta" implies both youth and outdated royalty, placing Pizarnik in another time, another world, neither adult nor modern. The title also has several intertextual resonances: to Maurice Ravel's musical composition, "Pavane pour une infante défunte" and to Cabrera Infante's novel, *La Habana para una infanta difunta* [Havana for a deceased royal child] which, curiously, was published the same year as *Mutaciones*, 1979. Although Orozco's poem shares a dance-like construction with the Cuban novel, it does not resemble Cabrera Infante's parody in content; there is a stronger allusion to the impressionist music of Ravel. Pizarnik is fascinated with its danger and so invites death while attempting to fend it off. Orozco's poem highlights the death-poetry link in Pizarnik's work; we are made to see that the younger poet is unable to create and sustain a self solely in her writing:

> !Ah los estragos de la poesía cortándote las venas con el filo del alba,
> y los labios exangües sorbiendo los venenos en la inanidad de la
>   palabra!
> Y de pronto no hay más.
> Se rompieron los frascos.
> Se astillaron las luces y los lápices.
> Se desgarró el papel con la desgarradura que te desliza en otro
>   laberinto. (76)

> [Ah poetry's ravages, cutting your veins with the edge of dawn
> and your lifeless lips sucking poisons in the word's emptiness.
> And suddenly there is no more.
> The vials broke.
> Lights and pencils splintered.
> The paper was torn with the laceration which slides you in another
>   labyrinth.]

These concise lines, uncharacteristic of Orozco's usual style, indicate a break in the torrent of words with which she recalls Pizarnik's attempts to preserve life. At the same time, the style shift reminds the reader of Pizarnik's phrasing. Orozco is momentarily recreating the poet by adapting her traits, emphasizing her images (the garden, the other side of the mirror, the child-like woman) to chart what appears to be her fatalistic march toward death.

Unlike "Por mucho. . . ," the tone here is not one of mutuality and the focus is not on the speaker's loss. The *yo poético* is indirectly present through most of the poem until the first person voice speaks directly, entering very close to the end with "Pero otra vez te digo" [But I tell you again] (76). She reminds her listener of what seems to be often proffered advice, that "en el fondo de todo hay un jardín. / Ahí está tu jardín, / Talita cumi" [at the bottom of everything there is a garden. / There is your garden, / Talita cumi] (77). Even without the biographical information from which we can infer a mentor relation between Orozco and Pizarnik, this poem records a difference in status and perspective. Orozco adopts the words of an authority to offer hope to the despairing poet even after her death, a stance which delineates their different attitudes toward life and death. Cristina Piña explains the source of "talita cumi," a biblical phrase that Christ directed to the daughter of Jairo, urging her to rise ("Estudio preliminar" 48). Orozco uses the ancient Syrian language (Aramaic) and switches linguistic codes, producing a curious effect. "Talita cumi" obscures meaning and the reader is struck first with the sound of unknown words that have an incantational quality. We expect some unseen door to swing open. The shift in languages also implies intimacy—it functions as a secret code that only the initiated might comprehend and, as the poem is directed to the *tú* of Pizarnik, it suggests a shared, private language between the poets. Once we discover the origin of the words, the language remits us to the past; it is an ancient language, its use far removed from the present circumstances. Orozco's closing line connotes the possibility of a kind of spiritual transcendence through faith then, but it is a breaking of boundaries that might only occur upon escaping from the speaker and addressee's actual place, time, and circumstances (life-death, twentieth-century Argentina, the Western world).

Orozco defies death by proposing faith in the power of the imagination in "Pavana para una infanta difunta," whereas in "Por mucho que nos duela," it is faith in the strength of memory that challenges absence. It is not that the poet overcomes death, but rather that she uses her poetry as a tool to survive. This affirmation of imagination reinforces her belief in her created self and, conversely, in the power of creation. Pizarnik, lacking this faith, is swallowed up by the world. She may admirably push poetry to its limits, but to do so requires a sacrifice of self; Pizarnik yields to a literal, silencing death. Orozco is strengthened by the repeated confrontations with death in her poetry and counters death's transformative, finalizing powers with her own authority to transform. While her imaginative solution may have limited practical applications, it is a significant sign of what contestatory methods are available to the poet. Orozco's engagement with otherworldly solutions points to her perception of a lack of possibilities in this one.

For Alejandra Pizarnik, the ontological attempt to create/save/live in poetry led to existential paralysis. Olga Orozco's creation evidences more separation between self and work. Poetry might enhance life but Orozco seems quite conscious of its limitations. She has, perhaps, not as utopic a vision for poetry as does Pizarnik, who strives for an unalienated connection between art and life, but Orozco's goal is to explore and endure. Pizarnik's utopic vision leads to a dystopic end—silence or suicide (reading both life and work in this instance); only liberating options if we are reading about them and not living them. Making poetry with one's self requires stasis or petrification of a living, mutable identity in order to achieve artistic perfection—in Pizarnik's poetry this moment of perfection is linked to the notion of death. Orozco rejects the possibility of perfection or stasis, embracing its opposite in terms of perpetual failure or transformation.

These poets are similar in that the work of both shows signs of alienation. We see this in their differing constructions of a dissociated self: Pizarnik's distancing of her speaker who shifts from first person through various pronouns to *nadie* [no one]; we see it in her speaker's desire for an object position. In Orozco's work, the speaking persona also objectifies herself by blending her voice with that of her surroundings or becoming mute while the objectile world is given voice. Often linked because of their shared gender, both poets frequently use images drawn from the social construction of their feminine roles: elements of domestic life, girl's playthings, the interior spaces of houses, an identification with Lewis Carroll's Alice, attention to masks, appearances, costumes are all common in their poetry. These shared traits indicate that part of the self-alienation we have observed may stem from Orozco and Pizarnik's shared positions as female poets in a male-dominated tradition. Consciously or not, neither poet employs a speaker as self-assured as Oliverio

Girondo's, nor do we find the undivided speaking subject we noted in the poetry of Eliot. Instead, these two speak with an authority which they also strategically undermine.

Reading Pizarnik as a descendent of Orozco, we can see how the later poet takes Orozco's structuring ideas a step further. The concept of poetry's almost magic power to conjure that we saw in Orozco becomes its ability to exorcise in Pizarnik's production as she makes bigger claims and stakes more on what poetry can do. But rather than being more engaged with the world or reality, Alejandra Pizarnik's poetry is even less engaged. While Olga Orozco is cited for her "indagaciones metafísicas" [metaphysical examinations] (Luzzani 112), Alejandra Pizarnik moves the struggle more completely into language. This increased rejection of reality can be read in terms of the historical process, for in mid-twentieth-century Argentina it is more difficult to evade the reality of sociopolitical events. Describing a possible relation between poetry and politics in terms of a struggle between real events and the imagination, Terrence Des Pres explains that "the question of distance becomes the heart of the matter. With enough space between self and world, the press of the real is diffuse and can be evaded. When this space cramps and shuts down, the real is unavoidable and must be resisted" (23). Olga Orozco, as a member of *el 40*, in many respects participates in this generation's apparent retreat from reality. Pizarnik, who publishes her first book in 1956—one year after the fall of Perón, is a member of the subsequent generation and her work can be seen as not just evading but as *resisting* reality. She actively constructs another space in which to live, pitting her imagination against reality.

Orozco prepares to enter the literary scene in the gap between *yrigoyenismo* and the advent of Perón. Pizarnik's prepublishing moment is during the first Peronist period. As we noted in the introduction, Peronism is a complex movement, difficult to dissect, but it certainly represents a major cultural crisis in Argentina. Through the populism of *peronismo* the working class gains a voice for the first time in Argentine politics. Peronism also coincides with the increasing commodification of culture, the reign of mass communication; this is a global phenomenon, but one which is closely linked to Peronism in Argentina. The movement used the mass media (radio, periodicals, newspapers) to its benefit, creating a cultural alternative to the intellectual realm previously dominated by European models and participated in by an elite. Pizarnik, like Orozco, is at once part of and reacting against this literary elite. Her generation (born in 1936, she is called a member of both the fifties and sixties generations) is different from Orozco's, though, in that it is more clearly self-divided. Some members of these two decades begin to work toward a more politically engaged literature, attempting an active response to social problems.

William Katra, in his dissertation that studies the "Generation of '55," defines this group as sharing a birth date around 1930, as possessing a leftist political orientation, and as being composed of the members who produced the magazine, *Contorno*.[10] The members of this group, writing narrative, essay, and literary criticism, and influenced by Sartre's theory of *engagement*, work to create a progressive, alternative literary tradition. Although none of the authors Katra cites is a poet, a similar desire is also apparent in poetry of this generation, as evidenced by the work of Juan Gelman (1930). Gelman is well known for his choice to write a more openly provocative or "dangerous" poetry, a position that led to his exile during the recent dictatorship.[11] Others of this generation, like Pizarnik (for example, Roberto Juarroz, Francisco Madariaga), continue the surrealist-influenced search for inner transformation, seeking change through a use of language that disrupts conventional modes of thinking. In her historical context Pizarnik's fascination with silence and her self-exile into poetry seem to indicate her belief in the impossibility of achieving unity anywhere else. She has an almost utopian desire for some transformation that might end her alienation, and recognizing the possibility only in art, she removes herself from reality. She "defeats" her sense of estrangement only through death or through making her subject one with its object, poetry (even this is a dubious victory given the fragmentary nature of her poems). In the process, Pizarnik's production emphasizes the distance between literary activity and lived experience.

Olga Orozco writes throughout these social and cultural changes in Argentina, also remaining in the surrealist tradition and evading objective reality. Here we might observe a connection between surrealism, with its "revolución del espíritu" (Poblete-Araya 114), its appeal to the irrational, and its emphasis on exploring other realities, and the mystical, oracular traits that are augmented in Orozco's poetry by gnosticism. In a chaotic world with changing social conditions, it is not unusual to seek a religious metatext to explain human conditions. Gnosticism is an unconventional religion and its "otherness" may appeal to a surrealist-influenced desire for different modes of access to the truth. It is a marginal religion but also one linked to European artistic society and the avant-garde. Gnosticism offers an alternative narrative of the world, one in keeping with Orozco's vision of reality in transformation. Like surrealism, gnostic principles require separation while ultimately seeking restoration (in the case of the former, it is of the severed connection between language and meaning or the conscious and unconscious, in the latter it is the restoration of lost order or meaning).

Gnosticism, like surrealism, stresses the importance of the human soul and provides a pattern for the inner self's relation to the world. Orozco combines these two elements and unites them in another, for this writer primarily reconciles herself with the world through poetry; she exteriorizes her self in her lyric production. This exteriorization is a process of transformation that is marked by a shifting in Orozco's work, a change we have observed through the increasing presence of a first person poetic subject after *Los juegos peligrosos* (1962). This subject, as we have seen, refuses its assigned place in poetry, is transgressive, forges new paths. Through a nonunified subject, the poet undermines her speaking voice by portraying the self as both subject and object while she expands it to release semiotic elements.

We have seen evidence of the poet's sociohistoric position in her figural composition of self. Proposing this self within a system of relations to other texts, Orozco indirectly reveals her feminine social position, for although she aligns herself with male poets, she reveals herself to be alienated from their tradition.[12] She shows her "otherness" through an identification with objects, statues, or animals, or by figuring her speaker as a "península raída" [worn-out peninsula]. Orozco's language and images, while not directly referential, regularly coincide with historical events. Her poetry reveals its role in the social formation; its apparent retreat from social reality can be read as part of an avant-garde inspired proposal of alternative values when faced with modern, increasingly alienated society. Orozco does not acknowledge a political dimension to her poetry, but we can read it there through careful observation of the construction of her texts and subjects that, though not overtly, in content, but rather *formally*, demonstrate an impulse to subvert, challenge, change. In Orozco's poetry we see the locus for changes to come. It forms the roots for the later split we observed that is exemplified in the differences between Pizarnik, who follows the neoromantic, surrealist line and demonstrates an advanced state of alienation in her attempt to objectify herself in poetry, and Gelman, who will explicitly fight against the process of objectification in society.

CHAPTER 5

Succeeding Silence
Recent Women Poets in Argentina

[

Pizarnik and Orozco, as major figures in Argentine poetry after *posmodernismo,* employ techniques that are both sustained and replaced by succeeding generations. Although both authors share traits related to gender, their differences remind us that there is not a single "female" subjectivity but multiple discursive positions constructed in poetry. In this chapter we will see how elements of these poets' gendered positions are shifting and/or being shifted by women poets writing from the 1960s to the present day in Argentina. To do so we will look at a representative selection of poets, namely, Cristina Piña, Inés Aráoz, Liliana Lukin, and Diana Bellessi, in order to observe their links to Orozco and the neoromantic, postsurrealist legacy. The selection of these particular poets is based on when they are publishing (1970s–1980s), their gender, and on their stylistic links (implicit or explicit) to Orozco and Pizarnik's neoromantic, postsurrealist work. As will become clear in the course of this chapter, their work also represents a spectrum of possible outgrowths and innovations, resulting in a set of very different texts that share a similar origin or point of departure.[1] As in every case we have seen, these poets both absorb and counter their predecessors' work; Nélida Salvador has commented about postfifties poets, "Les importa ante todo el contenido dialógico y referencial para lograr que el hecho poético se transforme en intransferible testimonio de un espacio y un momento condicionante" [above all the dialogic and referential content is important to them so that the poetic act might be changed into the nontransferable testimony of a conditioning time and place] (11). This particular selection of poetry forms a gradation and in Piña, Lukin, Aráoz and Bellessi's production we will observe an increasing disruption of cultural codes: image, language, and themes considered to be appropriate for poetry. Our examination of these writers' work will also lead us to broader questions about the changing roles for poetry in late twentieth-century Argentine society. The impact of the violent and authoritarian dictatorship of the seventies radically shifted ideas of Argentine identity and led to a concomitant questioning of the role of culture both during the dictatorship and in its aftermath. I find Nelly Richard's observations about the possibility of cultural dissidence in Chile under authoritarian regime equally applicable to Argentina in similar circumstances: "el arte y la literatura en especial, adquieren valor de sublevación contra el habla disciplinaria y regimentado de la sociedad" [art, and literature in particular, acquire a rebellious quality against the society's disciplinary and regimented speech] (76). Poetry's figurative capacity augments ambiguity, even anarchy, in societies seeking clarity and imposing unity. In this situation the feminine, in its difference, is one of several possible contestatory discourses that disrupt the apparent univocality of the "institutionalized word" (Richard 77).

One of the recurrent themes in the preceding chapters has been the importance of reading in gendered terms. I would argue, along with Nancy Gray, that the necessity of understanding how gender is constructed by culture is a *survival* need, for gender constructs can produce real oppression (2). We have seen that, although most of the authors studied do not specifically identify their poetic speakers in terms of gender, gender is an issue in every case. The universal, "human" subject has been revealed to be, in fact, a male subject, and when the subject is female this difference must be specified. It follows then that difference is often revealed in women's writing through a continual assertion of self. This personal focus is evident in early twentieth-century female poets, the *posmodernistas,* such as Delmira Agustini or the notable Argentine, Alfonsina Storni, whose defiant assertion of a female perspective pervades the oft-cited "Tú me quieres blanca" [You want me white] or the rebellious speaker of the first poem from her last collection, "A Eros" [To Eros]: "He aquí que te cacé por el pescuezo / a la orilla del mar, mientras movías / las flechas de tu aljaba para herirme" [And so here it is that I caught you by the neck / at the sea's edge while you moved / the arrows of your quiver to wound me] (185). No slave of love, Storni's speaker dispenses with Eros by catching him and dissecting him before tossing him into the sea.

Pizarnik's work both supports and undoes this female tradition, for in her poetry the central movement is an alternation between the denial and the assertion of self. All the other elements in her work are read, often reductively, in terms of this primary opposition (variously characterized as death/life, being/not-being, writing/living, etc.).[2] In *Death in Quotation Marks: Cultural Myths of the Modern Poet,* Svetlana Boym proposes that this kind of self-effacement has become necessary to the process of artistic production in the postromantic Western tradition (it is indicative of the Mallarméan "elocutionary disappearance of the poet") (12). Many feminist critics have observed that this authorial "disappearance" is different for female poets who have been traditionally constrained to silence (Ostricker, Homans, Chávez Silverman). Boym also specifies an alternate process in the case of a woman writer, suggesting that the figurative "death in writing" that appears to be self-erasure of the author can have another, lifesaving function. For the woman who writes, killing "the traditional feminine heroine in herself" can be "an act of self-defense so that this heroine will not in turn be able to kill the poet in her" (206). Boym's analysis helps us to situate Pizarnik's struggle as part of a more generalized battle against mythologized, discursively produced images of women, one of which is the silent, self-sacrificing heroine.

The feminine figure as an object, inanimate, is an image which also occurs in the poetry of Cristina Piña (born: 1949). A literary critic who is widely known for her work on Pizarnik, Piña is also an accomplished poet who has been awarded poetry prizes and published several collections: *Oficio de máscaras* [Office of masks, 1979], *Para que el ojo cante* [So that the eye sings, 1983] and, most recently, *Puesta en escena* [Performed, 1993]. The title of her first book calls attention to the concept of multiple identities, to the play among the various speakers, masks, and faces featured in these poems. The introductory poem in this collection, entitled "Cariatide," evokes the classical Greek column in the form of a woman. The image is both perfect and horrifying in its static beauty:

pulida
atroz
radiante en la ilusión del mediodía
clavada entre las huellas
de un naufragio final
clara en el vasto horizonte
enceguecido. (11)

[polished
atroz
radiant in midday illusion
nailed between the vestiges
of a final shipwreck
clear on the vast blinded
horizon.]

Piña's poem does not seek to impress us with the formal grace of the caryatid but, rather, undercuts the figure's quiescence through her speaker's analytical reaction to it. The fact that it is clearly situated in the past ("recuerdo de armonías / que abultaron el grito / de un tiempo entre barrotes" [remembrance of harmonies / which increased the cry / of a time amidst heavy bars]) contrasts with the speaker's present and implies a distance from this female figure; a distance which is increasingly closed as the speaker's reaction to the statue becomes more emotional, more personal:

espectáculo obsceno
su equilibrio
desde tu espejo
se descalza otra máscara
el horror. (12)

[obscene spectacle
her balance
from your mirror
takes off another mask
the horror.]

This is an ambiguous mirroring for the referent is unclear; we don't know if the horror comes from gazing at the column and encountering a reflection, at the speaker's regarding her own true image (in contrast to the caryatid's mask), or at the mask-like quality of her (*tu*) image in the mirror (although there is no explicit gender identification of the speaker in this poem, because of the association with the caryatid and the use of a clearly female perspective in many other poems in this book, I have chosen to use a female pronoun here). Piña confuses subject and object as she emphasizes her speaker's identification with and dissimilarity to her classical counterpart. She reveals the limitations of the caryatid's static beauty through another female vision of it.

The exchange between the terms *yo/máscara/rostro* echoes other themes in this book: language (*palabra*), exile (*exilio*), and death (*muerte*). We find a typical example of the interplay between these concepts in the title poem "Oficio de máscaras." This poem appears in the section, "Los oficios nocturnos," prefaced with an epigraph from Alejandra Pizarnik that announces the poet's shadowy preoccupations with language and representation: "Toda la noche espero que mi lenguaje logre configurarme" [All night I hope that my language might succeed in configuring me].[3] The poem itself begins with a conjunction and a lowercase letter, technically connecting this poem to the previous one while drawing attention to the episodic quality of this search for language.

y yo busco un lenguaje
toda la noche buscaba un lenguaje
de silencio aherrojado buscaba un lenguaje
en el tajo del grito
y la voz exiliada
¿pero no ves sus rostros
tatuados en tus manos
las manos asesinas
que sitian tu estricto silencio
entre palabras
las palabras que te aluden te eluden
te soplan pájaros de sombra
en la zona iluminada?
ella busca un lenguaje
viajera y obstinada persigue la palabra
desde el borde
hacia los bordes
la ciega la baldada
el vejamen del sonido
trae. (54)

[and I look for a language
all night I was looking for a language
of chained silence I was looking for a language
in the cut of a cry
and the exiled voice
but don't you see its faces
tattooed on your hands

the murderous hands
that set siege to your strict silence
between words
the words that allude to you elude you
shadow birds blow you
in the illuminated zone?
She looks for a language
obstinate traveler she pursues the word
from the border
toward the borders
the blind one the paralyzed one
the humiliation of sound
brings.]

Piña is following the path of Orozco and Pizarnik, looking for a language in "la voz exiliada" (a line which recalls "yo inauguro / la patria del exilio" from "Máscara en el atardecer" [I inaugurate / exile's homeland] (17), the second poem in the collection, and signals a kind of "desde lejos" positioning). Distance increases as the subject in each verse recedes, changing from *yo* to *tú* to *ella*. By means of these multiple perspectives (or masks), the speaker, clearly female here, withdraws herself from the search, from the poem and the act of writing. The process is left incomplete, for the poem ends with "el vejamen del sonido / trae." Without an object "trae" is mysteriously cut off; sound seems to have sucked up the speaker in midsentence. The poem, in effect, enacts her exile or death in language.

Piña's search seems to reach some resolution, perhaps, in the next section, "Los gestos," in which language achieves a kind of physicality through sensual experience. Her poem entitled "La escritura del cuerpo" [The body's writing] (67) clearly associates writing and the body in a manner that recalls French feminism and associated ideas that came to the forefront in the 1970s.[4] Not evoking the "fluid femininity" of Luce Irigaray, this poem is more reminiscent of Hélène Cixous, for whom writing is an erotic act and "writing the body" produces *jouissance*. Piña sings with the body here: "el cuerpo / es el canto de la tierra prometida" [the body / is the song of the promised land] (68), and lovemaking is rendered in grammatical terms:

fuga
adherida a las vocales

fuga
eludiendo consonantes fuga
fuga a consonantes vocales
los cuerpos se trenzan
la cópula esperada
   incipiente
   palabra. (70)

[escape
stuck to vowels
escape
eluding consonants escape
escape to consonant vowels
the bodies intertwine
the awaited copula
   incipient
   word.]

Play in language is analogous to physical play and both offer liberating possibilities, but these possibilities are transitory for silence is restored at the end of this poem. This silence suggests the limits of language's
expression, referring to the nonverbal "cópula" which cannot be commu-
nicated in language. While this part of *Oficio de máscaras* is like Orozco's
Museo salvaje (published four years earlier) in its focus on the body, "Los
gestos" [gestures] is very different in technique. Piña is less narrative, less
metaphorical, than Orozco in this section of her book. Using a very
personal perspective, these poems attempt to forge an erotic linguistics in
which silence is taken into account, accepted as an element—often a
defining boundary—of language's (or desire's) structure.

This particular combination continues in the section, "El cuerpo y el
poema" from Piña's next volume, *Para que el ojo cante*. There is a
combination of sensuality and materiality in the poems, "Cuerpo como
poema" [Body like a poem] (79), "Poesía pura" [pure poetry] (87), and
"Desafío" [Defiance] (71), the latter echoing the style of "Oficio de
máscaras" in its opening lines: "Y hago el silencio / como un amor a
solas" [And I make silence / like a love alone]. In many of these poems an
assertive subject confronts the conventional alliance woman/body (an
accord which customarily excludes the intellect) and restructures it. Piña
intellectualizes the body by mixing mind/body and language/referent
oppositions. Writing, like passion, arises from a desire for an impossible

union, and although its goal is untenable, it produces pleasure in the process.

While the body-word nexus continues, perspective becomes a central figure in this collection. Again, language is the theme that links all topics, for language structures vision (as evidenced by the synesthesia of the title) and Piña's focus makes us see differently, often restructuring cultural codes. In the four poems which comprise the "Sobre Casandra" [On Cassandra] segment, for example, the poet takes on the mask of Casandra and rewrites a mythic persona in a manner similar to Orozco's later "Penélope" poem. In "Casandra llega a su madurez" [Cassandra arrives at maturity], an unnamed speaker decrees that Casandra must reject her vision of the world; the next poem repudiates the first, and in "Casandra dice no" [Cassandra says no], the prophet refuses to surrender her vision. In the last two poems, "Casandra traicionada" [Cassandra betrayed] and "La muerte de Casandra" [Cassandra's death], escaping the imposed image of this world, Cassandra rejoins the cosmos. She is an active subject in these poems, her prophetic powers emblematic of the force of women's speech, which may be thwarted but is ultimately recovered by Piña's evocation of her powers. In this series in particular, Piña can be seen participating in the broader project of a feminist rewriting or re-visioning of historical, mythologized portrayals of women.[5]

The connection between vision and re-vision is not only apparent in terms of gender, it also has historical features in these poems. The writing-sensuality link as a tool to gain access to reality is explored in "Alquimia nocturna" [Nocturnal magic] (59). Piña establishes a superficial tranquility in this poem through the repetition of "bebes tu vino" [you drink your wine] while a variety of other sounds are introduced: "Alguien aúlla detrás de los espejos / alguien raspa" [someone howls behind the mirrors / someone scratches], increasing the tension between appearance and noise. The strain is broken at the end of the poem with the cup and the production of writing: "Rompes tu copa / tocas el liso vientre / del poema" [You break your cup / you touch the smooth belly / of the poem]. The image of the poem is sensual, almost maternal (*vientre* recalls the womb-like potential offered by the poem). Poetry springs from the pressure of the unarticulated (sounds in the dark), from the necessity of self-examination (scratching on the mirror), and also from a consciousness of the outside world (groans and death "on the other side"). The poem is a call to listen again, then to rewrite, breaking the wine-induced silence. In this case writing includes drawing in the referent, for the references to moans, death, terror, fear, and bodies suggest the press of history unacknowledged during the dictatorship.

Calling this poetry neoromantic would be stretching the term too far. Although there are some obvious correspondences to Orozco's work in Piña's rewriting of myths, her dialogic relation to other artists, her metapoems in the later book, and the recurrent figures of masks, faces, and ceremonial, often nocturnal settings for her explorations in the first collection, Piña concentrates her attention more consistently on language and adds an erotic element seldom present in the earlier poet's *obra*. Piña shares more formal elements with Pizarnik (the use of lowercase letters, often abbreviated lines), and both poets include themes of death, exile, and a preoccupation with language. Language, however, is not a refuge from reality for Piña, as it is in Pizarnik's late work. Instead Piña questions language and what it can do, while exploring what poetry can be in changing cultural conditions. Like both of her female predecessors, Cristina Piña employs an expressly female speaker at times and often connects writing to a specifically female erotic experience. But the relation between the body and writing in Piña's work is still primarily structured through conventional rhetorical figures: the simile of a "Cuerpo *como* poema" [The body as poem] or a conjunction, "El cuerpo y el poema" [The body and the poem]. Liliana Lukin's more recent poetry will more radically rework the writing/body relation. Gender is still an important element in Lukin's production but writing's relation to recent events takes precedence. The question here becomes how does the lyric maintain an alliance to its aesthetic tradition and yet "meet the challenge of history?" (Milosz 92).

Liliana Lukin's (born: 1951) first book of poetry, *Abracadabra*, was published in 1978. The title makes explicit reference to the performative properties of the word, a reference which is elaborated through the following epigraph: "La palabra cabalística 'abracadabra' nos viene de los gnósticos. Para ellos se trataba de un término mágico al cual se atribuía la propiedad de curar la fiebre y ciertas enfermedades, se recomendaba escribir sobre un papel dicha palabra en once renglones, con una letra menos en cada uno de ellos, y sujetar al cuello del enfermo este talismán" [The cabalistic word "abracadabra" comes to us from the gnostics. For them it was a magic term to which they attributed the ability to cure fever and certain illnesses, recommending that the word be written on a paper on eleven lines, with one letter less per line, and that this talisman be tied around the neck of the sick person].

Lukin begins invoking the ritual, magic elements of language, very much in the style of Orozco and Pizarnik; she reinforces the power of the word. Pizarnik is one author of three (García Lorca, César Vallejo) among the opening epigraphs, and her name will appear again in this book. Lukin's style is reminiscent of Pizarnik's. In one of the first poems, "Denuncia" [Accusation], the speaker begins characterizing herself in diminutive terms: "Es preciso que yo, pequeña / especie de mujer, / escribiente nocturna / de la poca vida" [It is necessary that I, small / type of woman / night writer / of little life]. Once more, this poet uses a nocturnal setting, aligning herself with the *poetas malditos,* those who work or see by night in a neoromantic conception of the poet (who never writes in/of or explores the pedestrian daytime). What follows is her confession as she tells us what she does not have, of her lack of strength; after a chain of increasingly self-deprecatory adjectival phrases, we find out what is *preciso*—that she is driven by the need to return "todo el daño / que me han hecho" [all of the injury / they have done me]. The speaker sets up an impossible task for herself, and in an indirect strategy, in the course of describing what she *cannot* do, she accomplishes some part of it. Writing is described in terms of what it is not throughout *Abracadabra.* In "Arte poética," creation is a process of selection, laden with sadness or with pain, a process whose final product is described as follows: "Un poema es un desastre de amor / Una palabra desnuda con los brazos en alto" [A poem is a disaster of love / a naked word with its arms raised]. The word here is a metaphorical captive, failure, or victim (like the *yo poético* of "Denuncia"), a criminal caught in the act. Lukin questions the function of language, and poetry in particular, as a means of expression while she reinforces its expressive capacity in her poems.

In an interview, Lukin acknowledges that Alejandra Pizarnik was important to her early artistic creation:

> Para toda mi generación Alejandra Pizarnik fue un mito: ejercía una fascinación esa escritura, semejante a la que provoca un abismo. Es una escritura que yo llamaría "limítrofe," al borde siempre de la *idea* de la locura de la *idea* de la muerte, (no de la locura y la muerte), que buceó desesperada en las formas de la desesperación y en la subjetividad entrevista en el desgarramiento de estar solo, con nada más que las palabras. He dejado de creer en ella, aunque me sigue conmoviendo. (*Inti* 238)

> [For all of my generation Alejandra Pizarnik was a myth; that writing exercised a fascination, similar to the one provoked by an abyss. It is a

kind of writing I would call "liminal," always at the limit of the *idea* of madness, the *idea* of death [not of craziness and death], which desperately dove in the forms of desperation and subjectivity glimpsed in the pain of being alone, with nothing else but words. I have stopped believing in her, even though she continues to move me.]

The last phrase is significant: "creer en ella" reinforces the substantial sway Pizarnik has held over ensuing generations. In *Abracadabra* Lukin's poetry evidences many of the characteristics she observes in Pizarnik's, but this poet finds that they lead her in a series of concentric circles. *La desesperación* and limits of language may be interesting to explore, but the only way to escape the spiraling effect of these questions is to reformulate them in terms of specific circumstances or to abandon them. Lukin does not relinquish many of the themes of this first book; language will continue to be a central preoccupation, but these concerns are articulated differently in her 1986 collection, *Descomposición*.[6]

The opening quote from Roland Barthes' *The Pleasure of the Text* calls our attention to certain texts that make their readers "listen indirectly" in order to hear beyond what is being said. This is the first indication of how we are to read this poetry. Lukin then introduces the first section, ironically entitled "Epílogos," with another quote, this time from Kafka's "In the Penal Colony": "Usted ve—dijo el oficial—dos tipos de agujas en variada disposición; cada aguja larga tiene una corta junto a sí; es que la larga escribe y la corta expele agua para lavar la sangre y mantener la escritura siempre clara" [You see—said the official—two types of needles in different arrangements; each long needle has a short one next to it; the long one writes and the short one squirts water to wash away the blood and to keep the writing always clear]. This passage describes the "harrow," an instrument used to write the prisoner's sentence on his body, a tattooing which makes that crime indelible. The body is a surface to be read by others (or, analogously, the book is a kind of body), inscribed in a painful process that contradicts the "pleasure of the text." In a kind of inverse mirroring, *Descomposición* closes with "Prólogos" and another Kafka quote from the same work. This time it is about reading and explains how, because he cannot decipher [the text written upon his body] with his eyes, "nuestro hombre" reads with his wounds. Frank Graziano, in his recent study *Divine Violence: Spectacle, Psychosexuality, and Radical Christianity in the Argentine "Dirty War,"* also refers to Kafka's story and to the harrow. Graziano argues that the harrow "articulated quite explicitly what 'dirty war' torture and discourse only imply: The symbolic relation between the punishment and its crime is 'written' on the victim's body, in the Argentine case with the *picana*-phallus" (165). With these epigraphs Lukin reinforces the idea that we are to read otherwise, and that reading, like writing, is both a disturbing and corporeal process. The inverse ordering and the echo of Kafka at the end create a circular structure in this book, and the postponed prologue invites us to read again. But this arrangement also makes reference to other, extratextual events; the text is the epilogue to a prior event and prologue to another, opening itself to the future. This reading is strengthened by the fact that, although the collection was published in 1986, it unites texts written between 1980 and 1982 (*Inti* 237); it is positioned at the end of the dictatorship and "dirty war," and the Kafka quotes evoke that time period. Lukin's almost allegorical imagery encourages this reading for it frequently makes indirect reference to incidents connected to the "dirty war" while making more direct reference to the general postrepression intent at recuperation characteristic of Argentina in the 1980s.

The author continues to add to her introductory information; after the Kafka epigraph the opening poems appear before the first numbered division in the book (I—"Del silencio" [On silence]), making them stand as another kind of epigraph to the collection. Lukin layers her materials, calling attention to the intertextuality of her work and making the book into a kind of onion, which the reader enters by peeling back layers only to discover new ones underneath. By means of this orchestrated indirection, Lukin makes the connotative aspects of poetry work to the maximum, continually reminding us of the multi-referential capacity of the word. "Esa manera de estar . . ." [This way of being . . .], the first poem, exemplifies this through its images which suggest torture, impotence, dissociation from the body, and distance from the self. It is a transient state, signaled by the use of *estar* rather than *ser,* and abstract, for the speaker examines his or her situation from both interior and exterior perspectives. In a shift from *Abracadabra,* Lukin uses lowercase letters and slashes reminiscent of Juan Gelman to punctuate her poem. This style continues in the next poem, an extension of the first, which is more about a place than a situation. Through the use of vague deictics (them, around there, someone, this place), however, we cannot quite establish the action or the actors. There are disconnected sounds, vomit, and bodies. The last two lines are characteristically evocative yet imprecise:

"cuando en el mover sacuden las ideas violentan / mientras rajan / por los huecos / sube un olor" [when upon moving the ideas shake do violence / while they cleave / through the holes / an odor arises]. Both "they" and "ideas" could be the subject of "violentan" and "rajan," verbs that imply force and suggest that we might read the fragmentation of the last line—the slashes—as wounds. What is left at the end of the poem is a smell, evidence, the sense that something critical has occurred.

The sense of smell recurs throughout *Descomposición* in continual reference to the decay suggested by the title: "apesta," "pudre," "oler," "el olor de nuestras llagas" [turns putrid, rots, smell, the smell of our wounds]. The author translates background noise to background smell—there is invariably something rotting. Of course, the title also evokes writing/composition and its antithesis, decomposing or taking apart in this instance to expose latent content. Lukin's poetry never remains solely on an intellectual level, for she relies upon physical elements to increase meaning, to direct our focus outside of language. As the author herself explains it, a connection between writing and the body is integral to her work:

> Creo que una clave en mi escritura es el "tema" del cuerpo: un cuerpo en descomposición, quebrado en la tortura, en el dolor, cuerpo que se reconstruye en la memoria y la mirada. En mis dos últimos libros: *Descomposición* y *Cortar por lo sano* el cuerpo de la escritura y el cuerpo muerto son el mismo, lo mismo: un cuerpo que cae, su visión y su reconocimiento. Un cuerpo que es también el cuerpo del deseo o el de una Historia con demasiados cadáveres, nunca contemplados pero que la escritura inscribe, pone en escena. (238)

> [I think that one of the keys to my writing is the theme of the body: a decomposing body, broken in torture, in pain, a body which is reconstructed in memory and in the gaze. In my two latest books, *Decomposición* (Decomposition) and *Cortar por lo sano* (Cut to the quick), the body of writing and the dead body are the same: a body which falls, its apparition and its acknowledgment. A body is also the body of desire or of a history with too many corpses, never seen but which writing inscribes, dramatizes.]

Lukin practices a style of writing that, in some ways, reveals the body(ies) through consideration of its own materiality or textuality, indirectly inscribing what has not been acknowledged—the atextual.

Language, a symbolic system, cannot make its referent present, so in a sense it always embodies absence; Lukin uses this quality to make absence present. In this way she deals with language's limitations while managing to break out of them.

She continues this project in *Cortar por lo sano* (published in 1987, written in 1983). The title extends the metaphor of writing as a kind of wounding, in this case, cutting to the quick, and Lukin perseveres in her disruptive activity. In a kind of negative or inverse communication she draws attention to perforations:

No poder
   recordar un rostro
   sus ángulos ajenos
hace huecos en el discurso del dolor
muele penumbras trazos líneas
mancha el papel. (7)

[Not to be able
   to remember a face
   its alien angles
makes holes in pain's discourse
grinds shadows traces lines
stains the paper.]

Not being able to remember disrupts discourse, grinds lines, and stains paper; destroying order and lineality, absence calls attention to itself. Like the "huecos" here, there is something missing in most of these poems, some kind of disappearance. They are largely untitled (two are numbered) and are grouped under three headings: "la caída de un cuerpo" [a body falling], "un cuerpo que se piensa donde ya no está" [thinking about a body where it isn't], "libro de viajes para un cuerpo en fuga" [a book of trips for a body in flight]. This series of *cuerpos* forms a corpus, not only poetic but historical: "la historia es / un cuerpo sin explicación sobre la escena / su carne expuesta / al amor y a la duda" [history is / a body without explanation on the scene / its flesh exposed / to love and doubt] (11). Bodies signify, taking on a variety of connotations in a discourse which resists disappearance by making phantom bodies reappear. Lukin's work participates in the historical recovery process, not concealing or refilling absences but making these absences meaningful. Frank Graziano observes that the "dirty war" produced a double disappearance, for its victims disappeared both from life and from death; there were most often no bodies to recover, no ritual, no closure: "No grave sealed the *desaparecido*'s fate; these dead were never covered over. Their unresolved absence was imbued with a haunting vitality" (187). The lack of body (a symbolic, significant form) takes on its own meaning in this historical situation and alters the customary relation between form and meaning. The absence of a form takes on new significance.

When bodies are directly mentioned in Lukin's poetry, their meaning shifts. In this poem from *Cortar por lo sano,* the body is not a surface but an instrument that might engrave its image on the eye:

si yo hubiera visto
la retina dejaría de ser
un instrumento
ahora habría en ella una marca
el hueco que su cuerpo imprime
en la pulida lente
despojar de palabras—es la idea—
estos despojos que no se ven
que aquí no quede nada
nada nada
salvo esa costra alrededor
de la figura—en la córnea—
la materia torturada
que un deseo
pueda conservar. (10)

[if I had seen
my retina would stop being
an instrument
now there would be a mark on it
the space that your body imprints
on the polished lens
to strip away words—is the idea—
these unseen mortal remains
that nothing remains here
nothing nothing
except this crust around
the figure—in the cornea—
the tortured matter

that a desire
might preserve.]

To strip words away from the remains makes the parameters of the
tortured material, a figure, visible—yet it remains undescribed. Once
more we are called upon to see, to read otherwise, in order to reevaluate
or undo the recent history of language used to obfuscate, to deny. Liliana
Lukin's work displays a profound distrust of language carried over from
earlier poetic generations, but in her last two books especially, this doubt
is articulated in relation to specific circumstances. Her poetry takes part
in a struggle with language, but this struggle becomes intimately allied
with the effort to come to terms with the shocking facts of recent
Argentine history. Lukin does not approach her subject directly; this is
not open denunciation, but through continued signaling, she demonstrates how terror can infiltrate life. In *The Witness of Poetry*, Czeslaw
Milosz examines the posttraumatic possibilities for poetry, observing
that reality can surpass "any means of naming it." When this occurs, "it
can be attacked only in a roundabout way" (93). When the unspeakable
happens, Milosz continues, it also compels those involved in aesthetic
production to focus on the fragility of civilization or culture and how
these can be used against us (97). Milosz's remarks about changes in
Polish poetry written after World War II are remarkably applicable to
Argentina after the dictatorship of the seventies; recovery from both
experiences depends upon putting a culture, formerly perceived as or-
derly and highly civilized, on trial (82). Taking part in this project,
Lukin's work does not display a horrific reality nor does it attempt an
oneiric distancing from it—instead, by reshaping our vision through her
use of language, she makes her readers aware of hidden meanings and
profound changes in both history and art.

In Lukin's latest works, gender questions become secondary to her
broader interests in coming to terms with recent events that affect both
women and men. The reader does not encounter gendered bodies or
speakers in *Descomposición* or *Cortar por lo sano*. Inés Aráoz (born:
1945), the next poet we will consider, follows the opposite trajectory,
employing a "neutral" or ungendered speaker in her first book and
revealing more gendered elements in her later work. Still, from the first,
she positions her speakers outside of convention; in *La ecuación y la
gracia* (1971) [The equation and grace], her poetic voices frequently take
on an antiheroic or pseudoheroic stance. There is a *yo poético* at the

center of many of these poems who appears to recount a series of amazing feats, but most of them are unrecognizable. Aráoz creates a tension between various discursive modes; poetic components contend with narrative or realistic elements, analytical with ritual (as evidenced by the title, which unites mathematics to faith with that delicate conjunction "y"). In this way Aráoz departs from vanguard projects with their focus on disruption and renovation and moves toward the "postmodern."

Inés Aráoz plays between clarifying and muddling information in her poetry. This example, one of the untitled poems from *La ecuación y la gracia,* seems to be recounting a series of events. The poem hinges on a succession of verbs in the preterit, but all of the "events" here are poetic and recount a metaphorical, personal "history":

> Me he montado en el vientre vasto de la
>   tierra y cabalgo los vientos más
>   adiestrados.
> Quise horadarlo todo, todo; hasta el tem-
>   ple duro y frío que me asomaba, a
>   veces.
> Hundí las manos en la arena y extraje
>   deliciosas tallas, formas rebeldes,
>   transparencias nocturnas y cálidas,
>   sólida roca, antiguas narraciones. (57)

> [I have mounted the vast womb of the
>   earth and I ride the most dexterous winds.
>   I wanted to perforate everything, everything; even the
>   cold hard courage that at times peeped out
>   at me.
> I dug my hands in the sand and extracted
>   delightful sculptures, rebellious forms,
>   warm nocturnal transparencies
>   solid rock, ancient narratives.]

The poet creates little blocks of text and her line breaks reinforce the arbitrary form rather than rhyme or meaning. Extending the first line into the left margin in a kind of inverse indentation makes these blocks function as antiparagraphs, suggesting prose (as they suggest narrative), but at the same time going against it. The unexpected images or combinations of adjectives and nouns give this poem a surrealistic aura, but again, these are purposely juxtaposed to other techniques that imply a more logical order. When we reach the end of the poem Aráoz brings us to a present moment, but rather than offer us closure, she increases our perplexity:

Y esto que viene ahora, esto que me inun-
    da, es el tiempo ya sólo. Es cosa de
    antaño, que busca; ensayo simple,
    casta, celebración.

[and this that comes now, this which inundates me
    is now only time. It is a matter of
    old times that searches; a simple attempt,
    chaste, celebration.]

The vague references to time (*esto, cosa de antaño*) only increase indeterminacy. The reader has the sense that something has changed, that time has passed, but we are not sure what or when.

Aráoz's poetry here is not primarily designed to convey a message (as Lukin's later work may be) or to exist as an object for our contemplation or sonorous enjoyment (a modernist trait more apparent in Eliot and Orozco), instead, with Aráoz we begin to see the intrusions of "noise," interruptions in the channel of communication. William R. Paulson uses Michel Serres's term to describe literature's function in the information age as a "source of differences," creating perturbations in "the circulation and production of discourses and ideas" (iix). Aráoz's continual mixing of diverse conceptual and linguistic spheres manifests a "productive ambiguity" (Paulson 79). She includes realms frequently excluded from poetry in order to call attention to poetry's difference. We find another example of this in the poem that follows the one just cited and that includes several references to concrete systems: *lenguajes, estructuras, datos* [languages, structures, facts], which one might *transitar, ortorgar, amplificar* [move, award, expand], but these terms that pretend exactitude, scientism, actually produce more confusion:

Si sucumbo, tampoco los niños quieran
    saber lenguajes y estructuras. Esto
    es como transitar halos de papel,
    entrada gratis y acontecimientos
    circenses de verdadera carne, timba-
    les esclarecedores que has ortogado

(no importa quien seas) aún sin
saberlo. Yo y tu magia concertados
en la nave central del universo, muy
cercana. Lo que pudiera añadir sería pertubador porque no existen
más datos. (60)

[If I succumb the children might not want
to know languages and structures either. This
is like travelling paper halos
free entry and circensian happenings
of true flesh, illuminating drums that you have awarded
(it doesn't matter who you are) even without
knowing it. I and your magic assembled
in the central ship of the universe, very
close. What I could add would be
disturbing because there is not any
more data.]

Aráoz joins magic and technical idioms in her accumulation of images/objects that come together at the poem's end: "siluetas, escudos, paraguas, los objetos / del mundo han caído frente a mí y / me adoran" [silhouettes, shields, umbrellas, the objects / of the world have fallen in front of me and / adore me] (61). This odd combination of suddenly animate objects completes the assemblage of incongruous elements and draws attention to the subject here. The objects adore the speaker, positioning him or her as a deity and, at the same time, losing their object status to become subjects (subject to the power of the speaker and able to respond to him or her). In this way Aráoz not only questions the subject-object separation, she parodies it, exposing its underlying power relations.

Aráoz's style reworks vanguard principles that depend upon the disruption of convention to create new meanings in relation to fresh concerns, and in this she comes closer to the "postmodern" than any of the other poets we have considered thus far. Charles Russell, in his book *Poets, Prophets and Revolutionaries,* provides a condensed and useful definition of the characteristics of postmodern art, which he opposes to the vanguard and describes as being both an expression of and an oppositional practice in society: "This paradoxical situation defines the postmodern arts. It is evident in the four related premises of postmodern criticism and literature: the confusing multiplicity of meaning systems and the apparent devaluation of specific meaning; the focus on the structure of discourse as opposed to its operative function; the loss of subjective definition in culture and discourse; the denial of historicity in social and linguistic change. Each of these premises serves to radically qualify, if not deny, the resurgence of the avant-garde spirit" (268). The paradoxical impasse often reached in Olga Orozco's work is extended, multiplied in the poetry of Inés Aráoz. Aráoz uses techniques that expand her work beyond modernist and vanguard characteristics; we see this in her attention to the artificiality of form, tension between unity/disunity, which will move toward emphasizing the gaps, cracks, moments, fragmentation, and the integration of "nonpoetic" elements of late twentieth-century culture. All of these practices apparent in *La ecuación y la gracia* are resumed in her next book, *Ciudades* (1981).

The city as a theme is worked and reworked in the first eleven poems of this collection. The poet draws out multiple meanings of the city, not attempting to fix a single figure. In "Ciudad Tomada," for example, the speaker is allied with the city, both are feminine, the "extranjera" to a group of "hombrecitos-ciudadanos" who attack her and abandon her, leaving her as fertilizer/field for corn: "me desgarra / ron y destruyeron y como última / celebración me dejaron, extranje / ra, abandonada entre maíces que / de mí germinarían" [they clawed / and destroyed me and as a final / celebration they left me, foreigner / abandoned among corn grains that / would germinate from me] (19). But this is not a simple poem about (masculine) destruction and (feminine) cyclical regeneration although it includes both of these ideas. Once more Aráoz dismantles elementary oppositions; the "hombrecitos" destroy the city but also, in a sense, reseed her with their "cerbatanas" [peashooters]. "Ciudad," like the associated terms "cultura" and "civilización" (all feminine in Spanish), is returned to its "natural" productive but also passive state as "tierra" in the end. The contemporary almost science fictional atmosphere of the first part of the poem, in which the speaker (at once metropolis and inhabitant) uncovers pods in a deserted city, contrasts with the pre-Columbian earth mother image at the end; however, this is not a call for a return to an idealized past but the intersection of various temporal states. Inés Aráoz makes conventional categories more dynamic by establishing new relationships between them.

In her next poem, "Gran Ciudad," the tension between man/men, the community, and the individual is more explicit. Here the first person speaker observes the city in value-laden terms; it is "voraz," "tormentosa," an "amante terrible" [voracious, stormy, a terrible lover]. This city contains a variety of men: criminals, those who are naked, catastrophic, questioning, the first and last, united in their disorder and in their individual yet collective existential dilemma:

> Oh! Qué puede un hombre so-
> lo, realmente solo, sino abrirse las
> entrañas y contemplar en ellas,
> aturdido, las magnificencias, las
> matanzas, el eterno abismo y so-
> bre todo, esa apenas hebra que
> cohesiona a la gran ciudad. (22)

> [Oh! what can a man alone,
> really alone do except open up his
> guts and contemplate in them,
> bewildered, the magnificent things, the
> massacres, the eternal abyss and
> above all, that scant thread which unites the big city.]

The city is not a figure as in the previous poem but a tenuous relation between its inhabitants. Aráoz uses the antiparagraph form again in this book; like the city, it is a structure which barely holds together disparate parts. Creating pressure with every element in her compositions, Aráoz omits the customary inverted exclamation points or interrogation marks that let the reader know how the sentence will be inflected. Instead she makes certain sentences both statements and questions/exclamations—or perhaps they begin as statements and change in emotional tone—in either reading, their heterogeneity questions and restructures tradition. The poet uses both formal and conceptual elements against themselves, to disturb habitual associations and make her readers aware of her constructions.

This poet's focus on rupture, her attempts to disjoint the joints, is enacted most completely in her 1986 collection, aptly titled *Los intersticiales* [The interstices]. Like "ciudades," "intersticiales" is a term whose meaning proliferates within each poem and from poem to poem in numbered succession. The first poem (I) presents a stream of associations stimulated by the word "intersticiales":

> Estampar los intersticiales con voces recogidas donde-
> quiera (en una sala de espera, por ejemplo). Entién-

dase por intersticiales la hendedura entre un mundo y
otro, los huecos del sentido, los espacios que median
entre una y otra letra en la palabra, entre dos palabras, entre textos; los silencios de Beethoven, lo que
cabe en la sinapsis pero mucho más simplemente, el
exceso de luz que filtran los desgarrones y tisaduras
del toldo precisamente frente a mi mirada ya cansa-
da de curiosear los disparates de las nubes que a veces pasan por esta sala, mientras se espera.

[To stamp the interstices with voices gathered anywhere
(in a waiting room, for example). Understand
for interstices the fissure between one world and
another, the gaps of meaning, the spaces that mediate
between one letter and another in the word, between two
words, between texts; Beethoven's silences, what
fits in the synapse but even more simply, the
excess of light which the holes and tears of the tent filters
exactly in front of my gaze, already tired
of inquiring into the absurdities of the clouds that sometimes pass by this room while one waits.]

The long list of meanings in this poem pretends to offer us an explanation of the title but, instead of clarifying, it complicates the message. This
is true of every poem in the collection, and it lends the book an episodic
quality. The poems are like little vignettes that continually return to the
spaces, the silences, the pieces with their disruptive and illuminating
potential: "la brecha sugestiva" (II), "El punto ignoto" (XI), "Oh tú,
fragmento!" (XVI), and the "Palabra caza-bobos" [the suggestive break,
the unknown point, oh you, fragment, and the fool-hunting word].

Amid this fragmentation unity is created, not only through repeated
themes, but also by means of a travel metaphor. In the first poem quoted
above, a waiting room is the setting for the speakers' interstitial meditation; the place itself has an in-between quality and a role, both temporal
and spatial, in the larger evocation of a trip. Elements of travel recur
throughout these poems, although no specific locations or destinations
are ever mentioned. We begin to realize that this is a multifarious trip:
through memory, an ontological trip, a trip through the said and the
unsaid, through writing, through nowhere in particular, a dream trip.
The waiting room is "intersticial," a moment of stasis in the layers of

movement Aráoz constructs, analogous to the fragments, words, gaps, all interspersed through the text like flashing lights that illuminate. Momentary illumination is this author's *modus operandi*, and she creates an unconventional narration in *Intersticiales* by communicating through (in the sense of both across and by means of) the cracks. Aráoz tells her readers as much in the last poem in this series, "Interlocutor distante." In this poem her listener is both hypothetical yet necessary to her production, existing in that "exact crossing of possibility and impossibility":

> En ese preciso umbral—punto de nostalgia
> para mí, instante semimágico, eternidad, digamos—
> empieza a funcionar el interlocutor y se levanta así-
> mismo la suspensión, pero ya todo es lenguaje es inaudi-
> ble; usted se ha ido.

> [On that exact threshold—a nostalgic point for me
> a semi-magic instant, eternity, let's say—
> the interlocutor begins to work and suspension rises like-
> wise, but everything is already language, is inaudible;
> you have gone.]

There is movement—indicated by the process of crossing, the threshold, and the disappearance of the interlocutor—and this journey is marked by a series of connections (*instantes*). These moments emphasize the nexus (rather than the lexis) in the larger narrative, signaling a new location for meaning and opening up other possibilities in language. It is not silence or distance but this momentary relation between terms that Inés Aráoz makes speak in her poetry.

Like Lukin, Aráoz creates meaning indirectly, forcing the nonverbal to reveal itself. The last two poems, appearing in the section "A Che Efe" are love/loss poems, in which the author employs a more conventional poetic theme and a speaker who is lost in language. Love is evoked through metaphor, and the female speaker is erased by the process of love: "Y yo nada, mis cabos sueltos, mi fuerte mirada ya só- / lo en el amado, en él disuelta, / yo nada" [and I am nothing, my loose ends, my strong look already / only on the beloved, dissolved in him, / I nothing]. In many ways these features are reminiscent of an earlier, more traditional form of love poetry. The speaker cannot reach her beloved and there is a collapsing of the categories of love, writing, and death; even with what appears to be a conventional theme, the poet sustains her focus on the lost conjunction so apparent in the preceding poems. Read in the context of the other poems, of the *poemario*, these last love poems provide yet another instance of the nonnarrativity of Aráoz's work, for the limits of language remain its most expressive feature.

The body as theme or metaphor is not present in Inés Aráoz's poetry; she focuses instead on the text. In fact, in the three poets examined so far in this chapter, we can observe a kind of progression from the problematic construction of subjectivity, the representational problems presented in Olga Orozco's work toward an increasing emphasis on artifice, on the nature of language itself. We have moved from Cristina Piña's engagement with and response to conventional images of women and her rewriting of the relation body-text to the slippage between the two which occurs in Liliana Lukin's work. In Lukin's poetry, the body itself increasingly functions as a kind of writing, sharing many of the same difficulties presented by language. Aráoz uses language to call attention to the nonverbal in her texts, reminding us of language's (and poetry's) constructed nature. Diana Bellessi, the next poet to be considered, will offer us still another version of the junction between language and the body by exploring the sensual, erotic elements of both.

Bellessi returns us to the literal body in her 1988 book, *Eroica,* in which she reworks the mind/body split through the perspective of an always female poetic voice. Bellessi arrives at this particular position gradually, for although all of her work can be linked through its continuing attention to identity, in her early books this feminine, corporeal theme is not so apparent. In *Destino y propagaciones* [Destiny and propagations, 1972], her first book of poetry, the dominant theme is childhood, the past, which the poet evokes in a personal tone that is not nostalgic but simply acknowledging the end of an era. Her 1985 collection, *Danzante de doble máscara* [Double-masked dancer], continues some of the same themes from her first book (identity, family history—particularly in the final section "Detras de los fragmentos" [Behind the fragments]) while adding new ones: an anticolonial, specifically American consciousness. "Amazona," an early poem in the collection, is a good example of Bellessi's combination of traditional myth and celebration of female strength with a specifically American manifestation, summoning images of both the river and female warriors with its rhythmic intonation. The inclusion of local elements make this collection more Argentine—including references to accordion music, the New World, and Italian immigration. A utopic idea of community is the inspiration behind this *poemario* (made explicit by the epigraphs, e.g., "La utopía no es un lugar a alcanzar, es un motor a utilizar" [Utopia isn't a place to get to, it is a stimulus to use] and the endnotes), and epitomized through the recreation of indigenous myth in the series of poems at the book's center, "Waganagaedzi, el gran andante" [Waganagaedzi, the great wanderer]. Myth has a political function here; it is a means of revealing hidden (or lost) unity.

In *Danzante de doble máscara* the concept of identity is predominately autobiographical, national and regional, rather than gendered. This idea of a political identity takes on broader proportions in 1988, when Bellessi publishes *Paloma de contrabanda* [Contraband dove], a collection of writings produced in workshops in the prisons of Buenos Aires. Bellessi's introduction makes clear the importance of giving voice to marginalized perspectives for both those inside and outside the prison's walls. In her work in the prisons and in the resulting text, we see her continued interest in building a community. In this same year Bellessi published *Eroica,* a book that features specifically "woman identified" female voices whose particular experiences reshape their relationship to language. This book is not as different from *Paloma de contrabanda* as it may first appear to be, for like prison writings, in *Eroica* the very personal brings us back to the political domain.

The title has multiple resonances; uniting hero and Eros, it suggests a heroic love, feminized. The opening poem, "Acceso a la imagen" [Access to the image] presents a reader/writer/lover who attempts to enter, gain access to, penetrate, the text/body/image. At least partially successful in her attempt, the speaker ends with questions remaining: What's behind this wall of language? Can the speaker make it hers? The poem works on the levels of both body and language, for the erotic experience is activated "*in* and *as* language," a process that will be continued throughout this book (Gray 136). Although it employs what appears to be a phallic eroticism, the poem also implies that the lovers are two women: "Soy la primera que / penetra aquí / y aquí entró / la especie entera" [I am the first woman who / penetrates here / and here entered / the entire species] (9). Bellessi reclaims patriarchal language and uses it against itself to express the customarily suppressed, to "attain the unattained body in words" (163).

The poet ceaselessly unites text and body by conceptually linking the two: "El texto / el cuerpo común avanza" [the text / the common body advances] (23), "la palabra liberada / de deseo deja / de ser palabra" [the word liberated / from desire ceases / to be a word] (53), and at times with overtly sexual language referring to female sensual experience such as "dilatado el pezón" [dilating the nipple] (14) or "dedo adentro" [finger inside] (16). Bellessi augments her construction of a sexual textuality through poetic devices such as her frequently fragmented, rhythmic repetition, acceleration, and alliteration, which makes language's surface slippery, as in this example, the beginning of "Murga":

Tierra
Palpitar del parche en la planta
del pie
Destello
Resuello rozando el estandarte. (25)

[Earth
palpitation from the patch on the sole
of the foot
sparkle
I breathe noisily grazing the banner.]

The individual poems echo one another in tone and language, creating a kind of fluidity in this volume, a dissolution of boundaries between the individual units. The fact that this sexuality is specifically lesbian is sometimes overt (especially in the final section, "Amar a una mujer" [To love a woman]); in other instances it is encoded, as we see it in the reflection theme, the mutuality of "Dual":

devuelve
bordado en plata
la imagen astillada
en otro espejo
pero doble
la boca reflejada
y aquella que refleja
se unen
en opaca contracara
    detrás
    el beso en
    plata
    del espejo

[it returns
embroidered in silver
the splintered image
in another mirror
but double
the reflected mouth
and that which reflects
unite
in an opaque about-face
    behind
    the kiss in
    silver
    of the mirror]

Oddly enough, with all this libidinal energy set loose, we find that the speakers assume a curiously distanced tone. The *yo poético* seldom speaks directly of her desire but rather of Desire in general, often sliding from first to second to third person. With this technique she overcomes the subject/object opposition common to love poetry and replaces it with a more reciprocal relation. Bellessi not only rewrites tradition, then, but writes "what has not been written before" by writing as lesbian, a position, according to Monique Wittig, that exists outside of social relations (she is neither man nor woman, the latter always formed in relation to man). In fact, Nancy Gray's eloquent description of Wittig's project in *Le corps lesbien* could easily be applied to *Eroica*:

> The speaker of this text uses words to travel throughout the whole body of a beloved, a body like but other than her own. She does not gaze upon that body or recite its characteristics, but uses all her (and our) senses to move through it, inside and out—through every cell, muscle, secretion, excretion, taste, touch, smell. As she moves, the words make melodious, sometimes rapturous, arrangements on the page even as they probe what we have learned to fear and recoil from as well as what we have learned to regard as pleasurable. Consequently, on many levels at once we must give up notions of what is appropriate or not (for language and for the body) and accept instead the impact of the whole. This leaves us with a sense of having seen what has not been (seen). (164)

Like any good poet Bellessi uses language and sound in new ways. Beyond this, she also challenges phallogocentricity by redefining terms, making her private language public, as she does in "Matinal," which is not only "daybreak" in the poem of that title but "una manera de besar." The word recurs like the tolling of a bell, signaling a forbidden kissing of "aquella boca" [that mouth]. These final poems are openly transgressive in their celebration of the proscribed, for Bellessi blatantly challenges her reader's gender assumptions by giving us another vision of female sexual experience.

Diana Bellessi continues Wittig's enterprise in *Eroica,* but Bellessi's work has a different impact in a context so distant from France. *Le corps lesbien* was published in 1975, and although quite militant, it was one of a number of radical texts analyzing the position of women that was produced in Paris in the 1970s. This, of course, is the same decade which ushered in the recent dictatorship in Argentina, a regime whose conservativism was accompanied by a fierce repression of homosexual activity. Although by 1988 there was an incipient lesbian feminist community in Buenos Aires and a certain audience for *Eroica* (as is made evident by its very publication in Tierra Firme's series "Todos bailan," which is dedicated to publishing new, often controversial poetry), Bellessi's book materialized in a potentially more reactionary environment than Wittig's.[7] Writing and publishing openly lesbian poetry in this atmosphere is to confront prejudice and heterosexist assumptions head-on, an outspoken political move. As Bellessi herself explained in a 1991 report on Gay Pride Month:

> En momentos en que a la CHA (Comunidad Homosexual Argentina) le es negada la personería jurídica, con argumentos difamatorios y homofóbicos que han quedado reflejados en medios masivos de comunicación, donde resulta increíble seguir oyéndolos en personajes que detentan el poder público o monitorean la opinión de la gente, es necesario recordar que nadie es libre sobre la opresión ajena. . . . Que lo personal es político y que sólo si, desde cada espacio de exclusión específica nos soldarizamos activamente con las otras personas, sobre puntos programáticos en común, podremos llevar a cabo un movimiento de liberación humanizadora. (*Feminaria* 38)

> [At a time when the Argentine homosexual community is denied its legal recognition with defamatory and homophobic arguments that have been reflected in the mass media, where it is incredible to keep hearing them in people who retain public power or monitor public opinion, we must remember that no one is free from outside oppression. . . . That the personal is political and that only if we, from our

specific marginal positions, actively support each other, recognizing our common points, will we be able to realize a movement of humanizing liberation.]

Bellessi's self-consciously female subjects do not pretend to speak for all women but break the silence of a particularly marginalized group within the larger community of women. In this she is following the transgressive path of Artemis, which she outlines in her article "La diferencia viva: El poema eres tú" [The lively difference: You are the poem]: "El caso de Artemisa es comparable al de la poeta que necesita representar algo de lo imprepresentable desde su particular sitio de exclusión, sin renunciar por eso a todos los recursos existentes dentro y fuera del discurso dominante. Su deseo es valerse tanto de la caótica y amorosa ley de la espesura como de la rígida impecabilidad que infunde al texto el discurso del padre." [The case of Artemis is comparable to that of the female poet who needs to represent some part of the unrepresentable from her particular site of exclusion, without—by so doing—renouncing all of the resources existing inside and outside of the dominant discourse. Her desire is to make use of both the chaotic and loving law of abundance as well as the rigid impeccability which the discourse of the father infuses in the text] (9). Bellessi proposes another rewriting of Woman (the given image or definition) using the inherited, patriarchal tool of language that has effectively excluded Her in the past. She accomplishes this, not by avoiding the sexual or the essential physicality that differentiates male and female, but by maximizing gender differences through heightened attention to female sexuality. Her *yo poético* is never neutral or universal and this very specificity makes her readers reflect on her speaker's distinct positions. We can see this quite clearly in the final poem of *Eroica*, a poem whose last lines act as both a coda and a commentary on the preceding texts:

Aria final
La Diva lanza el aro
y me abraza
   Su voz resuena
   en la fosa de los músicos
   y golpea
   contra la cúpula del techo
   Silencio

Estruendo del aplauso
Altera el orden: la creación empieza. (123)

[Final aria
the Diva hurls the ring
and embraces me
    Her voice resonates
    in the orchestra pit
    and pounds
    against the ceiling's dome
    Silence
    Thunder of applause
Alters the order: creation begins.]

The diva is breaking loose in order to create (it has only begun here at the end), and when the poet says that the diva's voice "resuena" we can read it in a double sense—to turn up the volume and to sound again, remake the sounds. Rather than conceiving of poetry as ritual, a solemn perhaps solitary occasion, Bellessi offers her readers poetry as celebration: of women, the female body, and language through *Eroica*'s lesbian textuality.

Through these representative readings we have come to see how many contemporary Argentine women poets have moved toward the idea of a gendered language. In her introduction to *Feminism, Bakhtin and the Dialogic*, Dale Bauer has proposed that feminine language has inherently dialogic characteristics for it is "marked by process and change, by absence and shifting, by multivoicedness. Meaning in feminine language is always 'elsewhere,' between voices or between discourses, marked by a mistrust of the 'signified'" (11). This strategic shifting, the use of silence and paradox, are primary characteristics in each of these poets' work, and they can be used to illuminate other poets' works as well. Liliana Ponce, for example, is another poet whose work descends directly from Orozco's. The poems in *Composición: poesía 1976–1979*, are abstract, situated in an alternative realm, "un tiempo sin ninguna circunstancia" [a time without any circumstance] (43), with a speaker who often confronts emptiness, an abyss—her poetry is marked by characteristics of dislocation and search we have seen in her predecessors. Ponce's style also recalls Orozco's with its long lines and rhythms, and she takes up similar themes: thresholds (one section of this collection is entitled "Las puertas

del agua"), cats ("Un gato," named, coincidentally, Oliverio), reflections—"sin límites, meros reflejos que entrelazan / los contornos referidos
al objeto" [without limits, pure reflections that entwine / the contours
relating to the object] (49). In lines like these we see Ponce's continued
attention to the metaphoric quality of language.

The concept of language as trope is also central to the work of Tamara
Kamenszain. In her 1977 book, *Los no*, the ritualized Japanese theatre
"No" is the primary comparative term, linked to life and poetry here.
Several of these poems begin with similes, "como el bailarín," "como el
actor," "como el público," "como los músicos," "como el teatro" [like
the dancer/actor/public/musicians/theatre], creating a series of associations that culminates in a denial:

> Los términos de la comparación
> que buscan uno en otro
> no se parecen al teatro no
> igual a sí mismo. (19)

> [the terms of comparison
> that look for one in another
> do not resemble the No theatre
> the same as itself.]

These figures cannot communicate the reality of the theatre, itself a
representation. The idea is expressed in language that doubles back on
itself, for negation is part of the No theatre's definition; according to
Kamenszain, it exemplifies the renunciation of representation.

This problem of understanding and expression is continued in Kamenszain's *La casa grande* [The big house, 1986]. The collection opens
by highlighting the eye in its capacity to provide interior access and as a
way of comprehending the exterior world. The eye is a bridge between
the past/memory/subjective experience and the present, objective reality,
a mediating function analogous to that of language. The composition of
the book extends this analogy, for the first two sections are a succession
of verbal snapshots that make the reader focus on the surface, on the act
of representation through dense word play, tongue twisters, alliteration,
and structural repetition. The third section comes closer to narrative,
joining images into a kind of filmed return to childhood, but writing itself
is always part of the subject matter. *Vida de living* (1991) continues *La
casa grande*'s semisurreal evocation of daily life. The space here is a

"cuarto ambulatorio" [walking room], peopled with fragments of family life, marriage, and "el peso de los amigos / muertos viviendo aquí / en el living de esta charla" [the weight of dead friends / living here / in the living room of this speech] (48). Language is spatialized and we are reminded that the past only "exists" in language.

Delia Pasini, like Kamenszain, presents her readers with a neosurrealist disarticulation of a family house in *Un decir que se repite entre mujeres* [A saying that is repeated among women, 1979]. There is no apparent speaking subject in most of these poems and the objects in the house exist by themselves, as if through ghostly observations of the past. Pasini uses simple sentences, creating images rather than action, and it is their juxtaposition that produces the surrealistic effect. She draws attention to the poetic subject through its self-conscious absence, a technique Pasini adeptly uses to evoke the "feminine" position. We see this especially in the last poem of this collection, "Una mujer todavía joven" [A woman still young], which animates the figures in a David Hockney painting. Entitled "Mr. and Mrs. Clark and Percy," our vision of the painting focuses on the woman, but it is a view from outside, a third person perspective that sees "una mujer" and "Mrs. Clark." The perspective seems to shift to Mrs. Clark's own view through the use of first person, then it slips back to a third person "Mrs. Clark" again:

Tomo el libro y comienzo a leer.
Abro la ventana, para disipar el aroma.
No puedo perturbar un orden.
La lluvia se arremolina sobre la acera.
Un gato blanco salta sobre la alfombra
y mira con sus ojos transparentes.
Mrs. Clark, de pie ante el balcón,
se ausenta en su sonrisa. (79)

[I take up the book and begin to read.
I open the window to weaken the aroma.
I cannot disturb an order.
The rain whirls on the sidewalk.
A white cat jumps on the rug
and looks with its transparent eyes.
Mrs. Clark, standing in front of the balcony
drifts away in her smile.]

Mrs. Clark moves in and out of the same plane as the objects in the room (including Mr. Clark and Percy the cat), and this vacillating perspective brings us to the mysterious last line of the poem: "Sus ojos me recorren" [Your/his/her/their eyes run over me] (80). Is this Mrs Clark's perception again, the direct object of her husband's gaze? of our gaze? Is it the viewer's "I" (perhaps "una mujer")? Or is it a personification of the last object seen, a book, speaking to us, making reference to our reading? The indeterminacy of the shift in perception of this last line means that all of these possibilities must coexist. The subject is made slippery in this case not to do away with it but to reveal how it is constructed, to illustrate how easily it moves from object to subject and back. Pasini subtly reconstructs a female subject by looking at her, looking away from her, directing our gaze through her. Extending Oliverio Girondo's self-cancellation and Orozco's dislocation, Pasini demonstrates how one can be in the poem and outside of it at the same time.

The work of each of these poets evidences continued attention to the subject's position in language while it displays the range of writing by female poets in Argentina today. Rather than forming a uniform group or generation, however, these writers are united by the variety that their work embodies, exemplifying the diversity that exists within "feminine" language. For the term "women's writing" does not refer to a style or a school but a biographical coincidence, like nationality, that may or may not unify a body of works. The writing studied in this chapter is marked by multiple traits; it is at times contestatory, antiauthoritarian, metacritical, proclaiming gendered specificity yet universal; it is at once transformative of and transformed by history. These contemporary poets use their precursors as jumping-off points and assume their own differences in order to engage in new struggles, to innovate and revitalize Argentine poetry.

CHAPTER 6

The Author as Subject

[]

We have examined the construction of subjectivity in the lyric through-out this study. In this chapter we will take another slant on the subject and examine its fabrication in a different form, the literary interview. The interview itself is rarely examined as a text, in terms of its discursive construction of a subject. It is more commonly read as a portrait of the author, lacking a specific perspective and almost always serving the same ends: to illuminate the author's process of production while reinforcing the link between the person and his or her work. In a Latin American context, the literary interview can be situated between the related genres of autobiography (a subject's self-construction, which, however, elimi-nates the dialogic exchange of the interview) and testimonial writing (with which the interview shares an oral component, "historical" expec-tations, and at times, a dialogic presentation, but as we will see later in this chapter, the *testimonio* supports different social objectives). The interview is considered to be less "literary" and more "veridical" than fiction, which is by definition an imaginative text, or poetry, which emphasizes the extrareferential function of the word. It is a text con-structed to feed our interest in the person-as-producer, and in the process, it frequently augments a romantic idea of the individual artist. By focus-ing on the literary aspects of the interview, the discursive and figurative strategies used by interviewer and interviewee to create the subject(s) of the interview, this chapter will work against unitary notions of subjectiv-ity. This constructivist perspective may make some progress toward undoing the fetishization of the artist and uncover the ideological under-pinnings of the genre while providing us with another angle on the poet as subject.

The literary interview can be a means of reinforcing authority, in that it both "creates" the author and "authorizes" his or her sense of the meaning of the work in question. My approach to the creation of literary authority in the interview has been influenced by increased attention to the construction of the author in the last 20 years. In his well-known essay, "The Death of the Author," Roland Barthes calls attention to the authorial role as a particular position and a way of reading. Barthes suggests that the author does not control the meaning of his work but has a subordinate relationship to his product: writing. In his essay published a year later, "What Is an Author?" Michel Foucault responds to Barthes's ideas. Departing from Barthes's premises, Foucault historicizes the notion of the literary work and suggests that the author has a "classifying function"; a particular discourse or set of writings is united and validated through the concept of the author. According to Foucault, authority is an operation that can be dissected, revealing indications of social relations that govern textual production in a specific historical moment. Foucault also poses the important question: Who has access to this authoritative discourse? We will see that this is a fundamental consideration in the literary interview that affects an exposition of the author but in reality is a dialogical construction of, or contention for, authority.

In this reading I am also following in a tradition fictionalized in Argentina by Jorge Luis Borges in his "Borges y yo"—not reading the author as self but rather as an author-persona, a not-always-complacent combination of variously constructed selves and others. Olga Orozco offers us a particularly provocative example of the creation of subjectivity in the interview examined here (one which I carried out in Buenos Aires in 1988) because she, in some ways, struggles against the form. Writing in a neoromantic lyric tradition still strong in Argentina, Orozco tries to poeticize the process of the interview. As will become clear through our examination of the text, the author's resistance to the interview form is part of a larger struggle to control meaning. We see this in Orozco's combining written and oral responses to my questions, in her hesitation to single out literary antecedents, and in our discussions about the meaning of certain poems—discussions which become circuitous competitions for authority, conflicts about who will control this jointly authored text. While we refer to poetry in the interview, we arrive at Orozco's lyric production indirectly, exploring instead how the author-as-subject is constructed in a variety of discourses and how the author constructs herself within the limits of the interview. Reading this interview as another textual representation of self gives my argument an additional dimension; it will add biographical data and make reference to a different interpretation of Orozco's poetry (not just *any* other interpretation but the author's commentary), providing still another means to see her in a relative, historical position instead of in terms of a self-enclosed, single-voiced discourse. In the process the comparisons with other Orozquian subjects—her poetic subjects—disclose the different ideological demands imposed by the limits of distinct genres.

The interview has strong dialogical aspects that are contained in the etymological origins of the word; from the Old French "entrevue," or to see each other, the interview is an eminently reciprocal activity. In this interview we will see how I, the interviewer, construct Orozco, my subject, through the questions that I choose and in my revisions of and decisions about how to present the resulting text. I formulated my questions in preparation for this interview with Orozco in response to her poems, to other interviews I had read, and to historical, contextual information. In a way then, my role in the interview situation becomes a vocalization of my reading process. Olga Orozco, in turn, reacts to me and to what I represent in her responses to my questions: I am a younger, middle-class, North American white female, on my first visit to Argentina, representing an academic institution, and coming to my work with the perspective of a literary critic. Orozco's position is that of author; she is an experienced interview subject, as there are numerous examples available, and we see her in a moment of public presentation, for she is conscious of the exposure, the nonprivate nature of our exchange. As Philippe Lejeune, a theorist of the literary interview remarks, "C'est une forme de contrat autobiographique vis-à-vis du public" [It is a type of autobiographical contract with the public] (Royer 119). Like autobiography, the literary interview is another means of producing a subject in language (a social context) and as such, is determined by a variety of ideological practices.

In the introduction, we examined several different theories about the process of production of subjectivity and touched on Althusser's definition of ideology as the "imaginary relationship of individuals to their real conditions of existence." According to Althusser, ideology constitutes individuals, making us subjects who see ourselves as originators of our actions (Easthope 40).[1] In his book, *The Ideology of Power and the Power of Ideology*, Goran Therborn expands Althusser's explanation of the formation of subjectivity by including the problem of "how classes are constituted as struggling forces, resisting exploitation or actively engaged in it" (9). Arguing that Althusser's work allows us to see subjectivity as a process, Therborn adds that we must situate this process in a particular social context and include the possibility of contradiction. He gives us a variety of ideological categories among which there is interplay, contention. Therborn makes four broad distinctions among the various ideological discourses that interpellate a subject; these are categories that we have seen more indirectly and in less social terms in the poetry but that are nonetheless present there, though they are more clearly delineated in the interview form. Because the oral interview is a type of conversation, meaning is not as controlled as it is in poetic production, for the text is not written and rewritten, honed to create a desired effect. These less "composed" qualities of the interview make it easier to identify some of the different discursive strands in the ideological process of subjection, the creation of the author-figure.

Therborn's first distinction among his four categories is that of inclusive-existential ideological discourses, which are those that provide cosmic, existential meanings and define "life-purpose." An example of this would be the gnostic influence in Orozco's poetry or many of the mythic, ritualistic traits that combine to form the poet's own existential ethos. Significantly, we see less evidence of this category in the interview, which proves to be more strongly rooted in experience, less a philosophical exchange. Inclusive-historical ideologies, Therborn's second division, define us as members of the historical or social world, that is, in terms of our citizenship, religion, nationality, and so forth. This category is indirectly present in Orozco's poetry, evidenced by allusions to exterior events ("rhymes" with history). We see an example of this category in the interview when Orozco refers to the dictatorship and the exile of many Argentines. The third grouping, positional-existential ideologies, shares some traits with the first category, but differs by qualifying one for a particular place in the world in relational terms: self-other, male-female, old-young. We find this continually in the construction of the poetic speakers and see it in the interview in the author's response to questions about "women's writing." Positional-historical ideologies are also relational but are social rather than individual and include the subject's family status, education, occupation, and class (Therborn 23–27). When asked about work in the interview, Orozco answers, "No tengo ningún empleo" [I don't have a job], telling us that in her society writing poetry is not "work" because it is not a means of material sustenance or, perhaps, that poetic production is somehow "different" from a remunerative occupation; Orozco later speaks of it as a "calling." All of these discursive characteristics exist in a matrix, some ideological discourses dominating at one moment, in one context, and changing in another. These divisions are useful in separating the strands of Orozco's text to illuminate the conflicts and coincidences among discourses we find in this interview. There are contradictions between the author's portrayal of the artist-subject and the poetic subject, and by contrasting aspects of the two, we find that what is potentially subversive in one subject can work quite differently in the other.

My request for an interview is an action that positions Orozco in her role as writer; it is a positional-historic interpellation from the outset as I make her my subject. Often an interview is a verbal exchange, audiotaped; however, in this case a completely impromptu format was undermined as I gave her my questions to preview and she presented me with a written set of answers. When we met, we talked about her written responses (a conversation I recorded) and in the interview included in the appendix, I have integrated prewritten and recorded answers (the latter appear in italics to differentiate between the two texts). This changes the text in that some answers are well thought out and elaborate and others are obviously conversational. I have included my questions in the interview to specify my role in eliciting answers. This practice is not integral to the interview format, for answers can be extracted and the interview presented as a monologue, hiding the role of writer, interrogator, or structurer and yielding different results.

This pseudomonologic style is the one Alejandra Pizarnik chose in her 1964 interview with Orozco that appeared in *Zona Franca*. Pizarnik describes the general lines her questions followed: "Se referían, en particular, al acto de escribir poemas: ¿Qué pasa en usted cuando escribe un poema? ¿Cómo y por qué sucede? En suma, deseaba averiguar algo sobre los instantes en que escribió los hermosísimos poemas de *Los juegos peligrosos*" [They referred, in particular, to the act of writing poems: What happens when you write a poem? How and why does it happen? In all, I wanted to find out something about the moments when she wrote the beautiful poems of *The Dangerous Games*]. This interviewer's situation is quite different from mine—she is in the position of another poet, younger, admiring, a compatriot and friend, interviewing Orozco after the publication of her most well-received book at the time. Pizarnik's questions elicit responses that describe the writing process, while I approach the conversation from the perspective of a literary critic and pose questions that have more to do with how the author's writing functions and how she situates herself in the world.

In talking about her work in the Pizarnik interview, however, Olga Orozco characterizes herself in several ways that coincide with my analysis of her poetic speakers. She speaks of a kind of transmutation of identity that takes place in the process of poetic production: "Pero mi singularidad, como la de todos, sólo consiste en vanos esfuerzos por dejar de ser yo sin desaparecer del todo, y la revelación sólo se manifiesta en el hecho de seguir siendo yo cada mañana" [But my singularity, like that of everyone, only consists of vain efforts to stop being me without totally disappearing, and the revelation is only seen in the fact that I continue to be myself every morning]. She oscillates between identifying herself as singular and recognizing herself in others. In a similar vein, she speaks of her alienation, "Lo cierto es que actualmente nos sentimos impotentes, separados y ajenos, en un mundo donde las fuerzas ya no son una sino que se oponen" [What is certain is that today we feel impotent, separate, alienated, in a world where the forces are not united but in opposition to one another]. This seems to place the poet in the social realm, but she qualifies her statement later by calling attention to her position: she speaks from the territory "del destierro, de la nostalgia y la esperanza" [of exile, nostalgia, and hope]; she is on "los umbrales del exilio" [the threshold of exile]. As we have frequently observed in her poetry, she puts her author-self outside of historical time, in an affective, almost mythological realm. This move fits with her desire to use the magic power of poetry, and in Pizarnik's interview, Orozco employs a heroic discourse that repeats many images in her poetry—the word is her weapon. But it is a heroic intent that fails, for she declares herself "vencida" [defeated]. The interview ends on this note of "failure," with a consciousness of the poet's limitations, like many of Orozco's poems, and provides us with an example of a coincidence between poetic speaker and author speaker. The lyrical prose style in this interview goes against generic expectations, for instead of giving the reader a closer view of the author, the lyricism undermines the appearance of "truth" or authenticity. Pizarnik's inquiry is not so much a narrative as a poetization of the interview situation. Presenting the author in this format in effect distances the historical subject while preserving the poetic one.

In my interview, which took place 25 years later, with a different slant to my questions and a less lyrical presentation, we can find much of the same language in Orozco's depiction of herself as author. Examining details of her self-dramatization will demonstrate how the rhetorical strategies and the figures of speech this author uses define her as poet and determine her characterization of the poetic process (her reaction to categorizations, control of meaning, publishing guidelines). Even while discussing more prosaic issues and using more concrete language, we will find that Orozco uses similar patterns to distance herself from her author persona. This movement—which could be described as an attempt to hide or separate herself from her texts—is similar to the displacement of the speaking subject that takes place in her poetry. Or we might relate this slippage to another trait of one of her poetic speakers, who often loses its voice while an inanimate object gains the power of speech. The *yo poético,* in effect, loses her individuality in these transmigrations, breaking boundaries to become something other than herself. This is a change that obviously implies loss of self, the humbling of a controlling self in the face of another; but at the same time, it can also be an indirect way to gain ascendancy. When the poet's speaker becomes Miss Havisham (in her book, *Las muertes* 1952), for example, she is rewriting Dickens, superseding his authority by extending his production and making it hers. Orozco follows a similar pattern in my interview. In this text there is an interplay between controlling meaning (who's going to do it, author or critic) and subverting or challenging it. In an analogous movement, Orozco vacillates between making herself singular as an author and acknowledging her profound connection to others.

The interview begins with relational questions about Orozco's production in comparison to three of the other poets I singled out for my intertextual approach to her work. The poet's answers to my questions about her antecedents and successors provide us with insight into an aspect of Orozco's definition of authority—what it means to be an author. Other literary relationships are elaborated in later discussion about influences; this line of questioning springs from my desire to position the poet (to explore her positional-historical ideological formation). Orozco does not see stylistic relations between her poetry and that of Oliverio Girondo but tells us that Girondo was more influential in forming her mode of public interactions as Poet. Girondo modeled the attributes of an author for the younger poet, such as a "comportamiento retraído frente a las solicitaciones exteriores (nunca tuve ansiedad por publicar, no acepté invitaciones de los medios masivos de comunicación, sino que procedí discriminadamente, inclusive rechazando premios cuando

provenían de entidades que consideré reprobables)" [my restrained behavior when faced with outside requests (I never was anxious about
publishing, I didn't accept invitations from the media but was discriminating, including rejecting prizes when they came from entities I considered objectionable)] (Appendix, 149). What stands out in this list of
characteristics is the distance required to be an author with a particular
status in Argentine society of the 1930s and 1940s. Orozco reinforces
these values of separation from the mass media and exclusivity in choosing where one's work will be received in her answer to my later query
about how she chooses where to publish. Maintaining aesthetic value
seems to require one to proceed discriminately; from this we learn that
differentiation is a necessary element in the construction of a poet-
subject.

While this is what Orozco says about her publishing procedure (in
both the written section of the interview regarding Girondo and later in
the oral follow-up about publishing guidelines), the long list of magazines
and newspapers in which she has published contradicts her position
(158–59). The author notes the nationality of the different publications,
details that give us an idea of her international distribution, and adds that
even this long list is incomplete. The list belies her stated values and
indicates instead a healthy desire to publish and pride in her work. This
contradiction provides evidence of a conflict between the exigencies of
Orozco's figural position as author (constructed under the influence of
Girondo and romantic individualism) and the practical demands of twentieth-century authorship, which requires wide publication.

Speaking of the other poets, Orozco calls attention to several of her
stylistic similarities to T. S. Eliot—in their use of time, their love of cats—
and to the themes she shares with Pizarnik. But in the latter case, she
distinguishes the temporal order of relations, reminding us that Pizarnik
was significantly younger and therefore (by implication) the influenced
one. A little later Orozco acknowledges that Pizarnik has also been
influential in the development of younger poets: "La [influencia] de
Alejandra fue más bien abrumadora, ya que adoptaron su manera como
receta fácil: dos o tres imágenes, un corte brusco u otra imagen desconectada, sorpresiva" [Alejandra's influence was more overwhelming, since
they adopted her style like a simple recipe: two or three images, a sharp
cut or another disconnected, surprising image] (150). "Abrumadora" is a
curious word choice here for its double meaning indicates both the
breadth of Pizarnik's influence and its overwhelming quality (in the

pejorative sense, it is excessive). To influence, while it may appear to aggrandize an author's importance, is not a particularly positive activity in this characterization. Orozco accepts the term "influence" in this question but, interestingly, cannot see how she might have influenced others: "*me lo dicen miles de veces pero yo no lo advierto. Por lo mismo que te digo, [. . .] tú no lo encuentras a alguien en la calle y piensas cómo te pareces a mí, ¿verdad? Puede ser que la cara se parece a la de un amigo tuyo pero no a la tuya, ¿verdad?*" [*They tell me thousands of times but I don't spot it. For the same reason I'm telling you, [. . .] you don't meet someone in the street and think how much she looks like you, right? It could be that her face looks like a friend of yours but not your own*] (150). The figure she employs, which compares poetry to faces, clearly associates her creation with herself and she tells us that she is too aware of her particularity to see herself (her work, influence) in others. This is different from other authors who "*tienen mucha avidéz por verse reflejado, tanto que tienen la fantasía que influyen a todo el mundo*" [*are very interested in seeing themselves reflected, so much so that they have the illusion that they influence everyone*] (151). In one sense, Olga Orozco makes limited claims for her work by stressing its individuality, while she also values its unique qualities.

When I changed the question to naming some of *her* aesthetic influences, the word "influence" became problematic. Orozco prefers "preferencias," "exaltaciones," or "admiraciones." She explains the difficulty: "Las influencias literarias, por dentro se sienten, sin duda, como una prodigiosa concordancia, como una bendita hermandad, como un sabor tribal. Por fuera suenan como una acusación de plagio, de usurpación, o por lo menos de falta de originalidad, cuando en realidad es más legítimo que todos provengamos de alguien" [Literary influences are felt inside as a great agreement, a blessed brotherhood, a tribal flavor. But from the outside they sound like an accusation of plagiarism, of usurpation, or at least a lack of originality when in reality it's very legitimate that we all come from someone] (151). Her acknowledgment that some authors can influence subsequent generations is not unusual but it is significant that Orozco is hesitant to specify her bonds in these terms. She recognizes antecedents in a general way, using communal, kinship language, while her consciousness of the claims of her authorial role with its different ideological demands (primarily the need for originality) limits how precise she can be. In order to preserve her "individuality," the author must deny her social role while she simultaneously acknowledges it. This move is not a personal one but the result of certain ideological constructs (for example, the demands of liberal humanism typical of capitalism which calls for "free," "autonomous" subjects) requiring Orozco to accede to one of her society's definitions of the poet's place.

We can see a similar sort of conflict between individual or self-definition and a more openly social intent to define when Orozco speaks of the "Generación del 40." She tells us that the concept of a generation only works if it is defined in very broad (almost meaningless) terms and that the elements of this definition "no bastan para autorizar el uso de tal rótulo, como no basta el color de la envoltura, ni el lugar y el momento del canto para clasificar las especies zoológicas" [are (not) enough to justify the use of such a label, just as it is not enough to have the same color wrapping, or the place and time of the song in order to classify a zoological species] (152). The author continues, expanding this biological metaphor that equates the intent to categorize to a cage that encloses living beings who must be maimed to fit within its confines: "Basta recorrer sus nombres y sus obras [those of the forties poets] para comprobar que sólo forzadamente, cortando brazos, mezclando plumas y agregando piernas, se los puede encerrar en una sola jaula" [One only has to run through their names and works to prove that only with force, cutting off an arm, mixing feathers, and adding legs can they be enclosed in a single cage] (152). Categories are artificial limitations imposed from the outside. They are social constructs that do not originate from the artist's production and only reinforce "artificial" coincidences of time or theme. In opposition to these cages, the artists and their production are naturalized through Orozco's use of a biological trope. These poets' "natural," individual selves are restrained by civilization's awkward, overly incorporating constructs.

The definition of the poet's role that I am constructing in my reading of this text is expanded when Orozco speaks directly about the function of the poet in the world. The terms shift between question and answer in this instance. My question is: "¿Cuál sería la función de la poesía en nuestra sociedad?" [What is the poet's function in our society?] (153). This "nuestra" is suspicious on my part as I inadvertently collapse differences between North American and Argentine societies. Orozco's interpretation of the question personalizes it, changing its focus from the product, poetry, to its producer, the poet (or from object to subject). The underlying assumption in this shift is a common postromantic one: that poetry is "above all a matter of subjectivity" (Easthope 30). Orozco explains her concept of the function of poetry by focusing on the poet's role, which is that of intermediary between self and others. The poet has a social function no matter how isolated the author might appear to be:

> Por antisocial que parezca, el poeta ayuda a las grandes catarsis, a mirar juntos el fondo de la noche, a vislumbrar la unidad en un mundo fragmentado por la separación y el aislamiento, a denunciar apariencias y artificios, a saber que no estamos solos en nuestros extrañamientos e intemperies, a descubrir el tú a través del yo y el nosotros a través del ellos, a entrever otras realidades subyacentes en el aquí y el ahora, a azuzarnos para que no nos durmamos del costado más cómodo, a celebrar las dádivas del mundo y a extremar significaciones, ¿por qué no?, cuando la exageración abarca la verdad. (153)

> [No matter how antisocial he may seem, the poet facilitates great catharsis, helps us to look into the depth of the night, to illuminate unity in a world fragmented by separation and isolation, to denounce appearances and artifice, to know that we are not alone in our longings and in bad weather, to discover the "you" through the "I" and the "we" through the "they," to catch a glimpse of other underlying realities in the here and now and to incite us so that we don't comfortably fall asleep, to celebrate the world's gifts and stretch meaning—why not?— when exaggeration contains truth.]

The poet gives us a unifying vision, an activity which Orozco later qualifies as part of the poet's attempt to change life ("*cambiar la vida*"). But poetry's power is limited and, as we have seen both in Orozco's poetic speaker and in the author-persona she projects in the Pizarnik interview, the poet's attempt to provoke change is destined to failure. This vision of the constricted power of the word is linked to the isolated realm in which it is permitted to function. Ineffectuality seems to be a characteristic of this definition of poetry (an "innate" quality—circumscribed in inclusive-existential ideological terms). This presents the problem of which limitations came first, those of language or genre—a dilemma that becomes a moot point when we read against the grain and recognize that both aspects are socially and historically determined. Read historically, poetry and language are seen as problematic and have differing degrees of social impact at different moments in history.

In this interchange about what poetry does, we can see some of my assumptions and perceptions as interviewer-reader in contact with the author-respondent's ideas. For example, in the "our society" phrase of my initial question, I meant to evoke a temporally specific response. Orozco gave me an atemporal definition, in keeping with her views, and strengthened the timelessness of her perspective by quoting herself in an earlier discourse on poetry (from her own 1980 speech). Reinvoking her words implies that the poet's definition is equally valid in 1988. At the same time, in citing a previous textual self, she further distances or "others" herself. She retrieves her author-self as represented in language from another moment and, with this move, reinforces her "present" creation of an author-persona.

We have observed certain qualities that are necessary to shape an author-subject up to this point in our examination of the interview: distance and exclusivity, originality or singularity, "natural" or unconstrained expression, and a consciousness of language's limitations. These are not discrete categories but are terms that overlap, slide into one another. All are properties that make the poet appear to speak as an individual voice, obscuring the material and social process of its production. As Althusser explains it, these attributes combine to create an "obviousness" about the subject's identity:

> Il s'ensuit que, pour vous comme pour moi, la catégorie de sujet est une "évidence" première (les évidences sont toujours premières): il est clair que vous et moi sommes des sujets (libres, moraux, etc.). Comme toutes les évidences, y compris celles qui font qu'un mot "désigne une chose" ou "possède une signification" (donc y compris les évidences de la "transparence" du langage), cette "évidence" que vous et moi sommes des sujets—et que ça ne fait pas problème—est un effet idéologique, l'effet idéologique élémentaire. (*Positions* 111)

> [It follows that, for you as for me, the category of the subject is a primary "obviousness" (what is obvious is always primary): it is clear that you and I are subjects (free, ethical, etc.). Like all things which are obvious, including those that make a word designate a thing or possess a meaning (therefore including the obviousness of the transparency of language) the "obviousness" that you and I are subjects—that it isn't problematic—is an ideological effect, the elementary ideological effect.]

In terms of poetry, we can read the presentation of the poet-subject as a singular, transcendent ego as an ideological effect (Easthope 39). That the subject could be a not-so-complacent position constructed through discourse is an idea that struggles against this convention. Speaking of herself as a poet, Orozco portrays herself in dialectical terms that expose the contradictions of her position, for she must both speak for the tribe and distinguish herself from it.

Orozco does not speak as directly about meaning as a topic, yet her responses tell us something about her ideas concerning the creation, control, and limitation of meaning—another element in her construction as author. The problem here is the "author-ization" of meaning, which is one way to "shield" discourse or protect one discourse from the invasion of others (Therborn 84). Contention arises about "who can make valid assertions" (84) or which meanings are "correct" and who has the power to affirm these meanings. The author-critic difference of which we see evidence in the interview can be constructed in broader terms as the divergence between public and private property. Textual production may be conceptualized as a "private" experience, an arguable point, but publication certainly makes it just that—public. Copyrights may control duplication but they do not limit meaning. There is an underlying polemic in this exchange about what the role of the reader (as opposed to the author) is in producing a poem and/or how the moment of reception is different from the moment of production.

Various examples of the confrontation between different interpretations occur when I observe some feature or figure in Orozco's poetry. For example, on page 155 of the interview, I comment on a series of objects that undergo what I call a process of immobilization in Orozco's poetry. She responds, noting her reaction to these objects, but supersedes my observation by adding other traits that are more significant to her.

Pero creo que la lista que das no es correcta. La esfinge no me desasosiega por su inmovilidad sino por su sabiduría secreta y por la sanción que corresponde a mi ignorancia. La mujer de Lot, o sea la estatua de sal, está presente más que por estatua por mirar hacia atrás. La "estatua de azul" es otra cosa; es como el calco que el alma dejó en la eternidad y al que debe volver a animar; lo dejó al nacer y regresará al morir. (156)

[But I think your list isn't correct. The Sphinx does not disturb me because of her immobility but because of her secret knowledge and the sanction with which my ignorance is answered. Lot's wife, or the salt statue, is present more because of her looking backward than as a statue. The "blue statue" is another thing; it is like a tracing that a soul

leaves in eternity and which it must reanimate; the soul left it at birth
and will return upon its death.]

The subtext here: the author's meaning is the determining one, one
that prevails not simply because she provides additional detail but because she fixes it; her meaning does not seem to change. Another example
of this occurs later when we are talking about the sculpting metaphor and
the author adjusts meaning: "La cantera no alude a la escultura sino a un
depósito de piedras" [The quarry does not refer to sculpture but to a
stone depository] (157). A quarry, as a source of stones, does bear some
relation to sculpture but this is not the "author-ized" connection between
images. Orozco first denies the relation but obliquely affirms it in her
explanation, in which she describes stones as representing the potential
for sculpture: "Para mí las piedras tienen vida interiormente. Y así como
quitando piedra, 'esculpiendo' está la estatua, que ya estaba antes en
materia informe, así quitando vocablos al lenguaje está el poema" [For
me stones have an interior life. Therefore, as chipping away stone,
"sculpting," produces a statue which was already present in the unformed material, so it is that chipping away words from language reveals
a poem] (157). Control over meaning in this interview must stay with the
poet.

The exchanges differ slightly when we are discussing the theme of the
body. In this case, I pose a question: Why this theme in that moment?,
wanting to know if the author observes any relation between her theme
and historical events. In her response Orozco indirectly tells us that she
does not see an external relation, and in fact, she further interiorizes the
theme by explaining that it originates from a very personal experience of
sickness and death.

Aunque toda esta extrañeza de la que hablé está de manifiesto en uno y
otro momento de mis diferentes libros, en la época en que escribí *Museo
salvaje* pasaba por una etapa de cierta objetividad que me hizo posible
sumergirme hasta el fondo de mis tejidos, mis vísceras, de mis ojos, etc.,
y extraer ese puñado de poemas. Claro que esa observación casi de
entomólogo se interrumpía a cada instante, alterada por una tensión
progresiva hasta un punto insoportable. [. . .] *Además y curiosamente
me fuí deteriorando mi organismo. Escribí el poema sobre el ojo, por
ejemplo, se me producía algo extraño, iba al oculista y tuve presión en
un ojo. Escribí el poema "La sangre," tenía diabetes.* (157–58)

[Although all of this strangeness that I've spoken about is present in various moments in my different books, at the time when I wrote *Museo salvaje* I was going through a more objective stage which enabled me to submerge myself to the depth of my tissues, my viscera, my eyes, etc., and extract this handful of poems. Of course this almost entomological observation was interrupted every so often, altered by a progressive tension [which rose] to an almost intolerable point. [. . .] *Moreover and curiously, my body began to deteriorate. I wrote the poem about the eye, for example, and it produced something strange in me, I went to the oculist and I had pressure in an eye. I wrote the poem "Sangre" [Blood], and I had diabetes.*]

The change in terms from a social-historic emphasis to an eminently personal one indicates that we approach meaning from very different positions. I try to control meaning according to the presuppositions and linguistic tools I possess while I structure *her,* author-as-text, in her context. Orozco attempts to control meaning according to her different goals: constituting herself as author, composing her poetry.

Author-critic is one kind of opposition, defining the subject in terms of its position. There are various other counterpositions that we can identify in this author's construction as poet. These alter-ideological positions indicate possible alternative positions (Therborn 61) and define the subject in a negative relation; we find out how she characterizes herself through a process of elimination, by learning what she is not. We have already seen this movement when Orozco distinguishes herself as not of the 1940s generation; in the process she explains her disagreement with many categorizations. Another category she rejects is that of gender. Her first argument against it is that she does not understand the division, then she describes it as a discrimination that she does not believe in, and finally she acknowledges it, but only in a derogatory sense. "La acepto apenas en un sentido peyorativo, cuando la usan para designar la forma descuidada, la expresión carente de rigor, de estructura y medida, propia de las mujeres que no vieron en la escritura una misión o un destino sino una descarga o entretenimiento" [I accept it only in a pejorative sense, when it is used to indicate a careless form, expression that lacks rigor, structure, measure, the style of women who didn't view writing as a mission or a destiny but as a release or entertainment] (155). Good writing is qualified by the terms "misión" and "destino." Orozco describes her writing process as guided by a universalist impulse; she is a heroic Odysseus called by the siren song of the poem on a voyage:

> Escribo *con* toda la humanidad y *para* nadie en particular. Podría hablarte horas acerca de todo lo que experimento desde la primera llamada de alerta que me arrebata hacia el poema hasta el último oleaje que me devuelve otra vez a la costa conocida, pero puedo asegurarte que en ningún momento de este viaje he tocado la "isla de las mujeres" ni mi lenguaje ha padecido ninguna catalogación genética. (155)

> [I write *with* all of humanity and *for* no one in particular. I could talk to you for hours about all I experience from the first call to arms which stirs me to the poem to the final wave which returns me once more to the well-known coast, but I can assure you that in no moment of the trip have I ever touched the "isle of women" nor has my language undergone any genetic [*sic*] categorization.]

The author employs classical allusions to assert her stake in legitimate "Poesía" in contrast to what she terms the "falacia de la 'poesía femenina'" [the fallacy of 'female poetry.']

The heroic stance of the author recalls Orozco's portrayal of the writing process in her interview with Pizarnik. It also coincides to some extent with her poetic subject, who frequently embarks upon a heroic quest, but who cannot maintain a heroic identity or unity. The courageous poetic speaker does not succeed in its mission. Its identity is always unstable, marked by signs of conflict, slippage, the influence of other identities. Orozco's author persona is more centralized and identifies with a traditional masculine (though supposedly ungendered) universalist model, disidentifying with the feminine. A feminine speaking position is seen only in terms of its differences, which are perceived as weaknesses. It does not offer Orozco an alter-ideological stance, a site of resistance to the dominant one, but instead it is an inferior position that the author strongly rejects. The poetic subject and the author subject are in contradiction in this identification. The poetic speaker gives us a greater sense of its mutability; it offers increased possibilities, while the author subject presents itself within the terms of a more rigid definition. Orozco's poetry's distance from social reality appears to allow the speaker more freedom than her authorial role. Qualifying for authorship is a social process that puts the poet in direct contact with her sociopolitical reality (for example, the real discrimination under patriarchy against "women's

writing" that identifies itself as such), and this proximity ironically seems
to require the poet's acquiescence to a dominant subject position.

Universality is a reigning value that is invoked throughout the interview, and in order to stay within its demands, the poet must reject traits
that indicate a particularity of voice or vision. By implication this means
that there are only certain themes appropriate for poetry, personal experiences with which we all can identify and as such are generalized,
transcending the individual. Historically specific references are too defi-
nite, limiting. Orozco acknowledges that she is not a social poet: *"Te
digo en la gente que tiene una tónica de poesía social. Yo no sé, yo nunca
lo he tenido"* [*I mean in the people who write social poetry. I don't
know, I've never written it* (160). She stakes out another territory in
which to ground her poetry. Defining herself in opposition to social poets
creates a conflict between the previously acknowledged communal function of the poet, requiring certain responsibilities and offering other
possibilities ("por antisocial que parezca . . .") and the author's particular position as Argentine or female, too narrow an identification it seems.
She is inevitably subjected as a citizen of Argentina, however indirectly,
in an inclusive-historical ideological interpellation. Even without concrete references, we encounter various moments in her poetry when
language or images rhyme with history, and I propose that posing oneself
in opposition to social poetry is in itself a historically determined strategy. In the interview, Orozco speaks to this problem more directly and
concedes that the dictatorship did affect poetic production (because of
increased exile) and also might have produced more "oppressive" traits
in the poetry of those who remained (160). Although she does not
acknowledge this in her own case, I argue that, like all writers under
repressive dictatorial regimes, she is subjected by the discourses of power
and torture that surround her.[2] We have seen traces of this discourse in
chapter 4, in "Presentimientos en traje de ritual" [Premonitions clothed
in ritual], in which an unknown "they," "llegan como ladrones en la
noche" [arrive like thieves in the night], or in this example from "Parte de
viaje" [Part of the journey]: "no importa que las hojas prometieran con
cada centelleo una gruta encantada, / que los susurros del atardecer
fueran las risas de los desaparecidos" [it isn't important that the leaves
promised an enchanted cave with each sparkle, / that the twilight whispers might be the laughter of the disappeared] (*La noche a la deriva* 18).
Orozco is also affected by the discourses of other poets and critics, as
evidenced by her sensitivity to the problem of exile, to the dilemma of

whether to stay or go under oppressive circumstances, and which response is most difficult or effective. Staying means survival, but one must
pay the price in silence, interiority, or hidden opposition; exile gives an
author increased freedom of speech but also distance and possibly elimi-
nates the chance of return.

Orozco stayed in Argentina during the dictatorship of the seventies
and continued to write a similar style of poetry while the context shifted
around her. But not without affecting her, for the meaning of her work
changes when it is situated in circumstances of institutionalized repression. Michel Foucault, in *Discipline and Punish,* explains that one of the
functions of the repression of dictatorships is to produce more obedient
subjects. In this context torture can function as an official discourse and
even be made to reflect the "justice" of the punishment inflicted (128).
Torture was a characteristic of Argentina's recent dictatorship but without the presence of inscribed bodies; official "speech" took place instead
in a discourse of disappearances. Under these circumstances we can
suppose that if a lack of bodies is a silent, subjecting discourse, then the
appearance of bodies would be a counterdiscourse, a response. Orozco's
books published during the years of official repression are *Museo salvaje,*
with its intense attention to the body, *Cantos a Berenice,* a memorial to a
Cheshire catlike figure that appears and disappears, and *Mutaciones de la
realidad,* a volume that records the constant transformation of reality
and its observing subject. These books can be read as an attempt to delve
deeper inside experience, but their subject matter also records the impossibility of avoiding contextual intrusion. They in some ways propose
alternatives to "official" reality. We see another conflict here in that,
intentionally or not, the author does have a historical position, one that
cannot be avoided or written around. Examining various texts and their
contexts, we get a sense of the contrary assumptions about the require-
ments of author-ity and what an author produces; the author is to be at
once universal and particular, but even if defined as "not social," the
author is restrained or influenced by circumstances.

A similar contradiction exists in the poetic subject itself. Orozco
constructs her subject in a humanist fashion to be "neutral" and does not
recognize a positive possibility for gendered writing. Yet when we read
her work, we find that she includes many images and structures common
to women's poetry: muteness, invisibility, objectification, a reworking of
female figures common to Occidental culture, a divided self, and a
transgressive self that overcomes the traditional self-other division.[3] In

the interview, Orozco presents an author-self that represses "female" elements, allowing us to see in this case how she is subjected by her society. In order to gain authority, a stronger speaking position, the poet's possible recognition of her particularity must accede to the demand for universality. On the other hand, the self-imposed discipline of poetry produces a disobedient subject—one that is both subject and object, that at once is and is not the author.

The author can be more courageous in her poetic production, oddly "truer," and more direct. Orozco's poetry creates another world against the social one. This world is populated by voices—*tú, yo,* other characters, objects, animals, witnesses. The poetic space is an alternative space that is maintained through a continual distancing: "otro es el acceso a los lugares del verdadero encuentro" [Other is the access to the true meeting places] (*En el revés del cielo* 94). Yet it is a tenuous position for there is a constant sense of being invaded, displaced, for Orozco's speaker continually figures herself as an exile, from *Desde lejos* to this example in her 1987 collection: "Toda una confabulación de lo invisible para indicar apenas que no soy de este mundo, / sino tan sólo un testimonio adverso contra la proclamada realidad, / una marca de exilio adherida a las grandes cerrazones donde comienza el alma" [All a collusion of the invisible elements to barely indicate that I am not of this world / but rather an adverse attestation against so-called reality / a gauge of exile stuck to the large thunderheads where the soul begins] (102). In her poetry, the subject is always already outside of this world and therefore affected differently by the world's demands.

While the author-subject portrays herself as a heroic Odysseus, the poetic speaker in *En el revés del cielo* is the "Sibila de Cumas" [Sibyl of Cumas] (71), or she focuses on Penelope instead of the conventional hero from the traditional story. This last example is significant because Penelope is the one who stayed home; she is the refuge, the prize, a place or thing who does not take part in the voyage but who actively embroiders a story in Orozco's poem and is identified with the poetic speaker:

Penélope bordaba el periplo de Ulises.
Bordaba con realce el riesgo y las hazañas, la penuria y la gloria.
Recibía el dictado de los dioses copiando su diseño del bastidor de las
    estrellas.
Anudaba los hilos con los años.
Pasaban por el ojo de su aguja el caballo de Troya,

los horizontes indominables—esos que no someterán jamás al
    obstinado—
los cíclopes, los vientos, los frutos que procuran el desarraigo y el
    olvido,
y punzaba de paso el corazón de otras mujeres, horadaba otras dichas.
Deshacer cada noche su labor equivalía a conjurar la suerte,
era deshilvanar cada aventura, volver atrás las puntadas del tiempo.
También tú, repudiada, bordas ahora el viaje de otro ausente,
Infiel como las nubes, fabulador como el artero mar. (45)

[Penelope embroidered Ulysses's voyage.
She prominently embroidered the risk, the feats, the poverty, and the
    glory.
She received the gods' decree copying their design of the stars' canvas.
She knotted strings with the years.
Through the eye of her needle passed the Trojan Horse,
the indominable horizons—those which will never submit to obsti-
    nacy—
the cyclops, the winds, the fruits procured by expulsion and forgetful-
    ness,
and along the way she pricked the hearts of other women, she pierced
    other fortunes.
Undoing her labor every night was a way to conjure luck,
it was unthreading each adventure, reversing time's stitches.
You too, rejected one, now embroider the voyage of another absent
    person,
unfaithful like the clouds, a storyteller like the cunning sea.]

Knotting and unknotting, sewing and weaving, are tropes that figure
prominently in this collection. These activities are attempts to mark time
and to influence its progression. They also evoke a different type of
storytelling, drawing on a "feminine" tradition of home arts in which the
woman's adventure is the reconstruction of myth, changing its perspective. The adaptation of myths fits with Orozco's universal impulse, but it
does not take the form of a nostalgic desire to return to a golden past.
Rather, through myth, the author makes the past into a present, dominates it, and rewrites it. Orozco can undo the power of the conventional
mythos by shifting the focus in her poetry to previously marginalized
characters.

This renarration with another protagonist works in some ways like the release of semiotic elements we observe in her poetry, indicative of presubmission to the Oedipal myth narrative. The activation of the semiotic elements and revised narration of old stories both arise out of the subject's condition of "heterogeneous contradiction," a position that enables Orozco to take advantage of what Kristeva describes as the more subversive possibilities in poetry. She explains the condition of the subject of significance as a "heterogeneous contradiction between two irreconcilable elements—separate but inseparable from the process in which they assume asymmetrical functions." These functions are dialectical in that they maintain "both 'delirium' and 'logic'" while they move literature "beyond madness and realism" (*Revolution* 82). Kristeva asserts that modern twentieth-century poetry "had to disturb the logic that dominated the social order and do so through that logic itself, by assuming and unraveling its position, its synthesis and hence the ideologies it controls" (83). Orozco's poetic subject both assumes the dominant logic and unravels it, allowing her a kind of controlled transgression; she subverts while she remains within the tradition. In the lyric, Orozco produces poetic texts and is reciprocally reformulated in them in the guise of a mutable poetic subject. This subject, while sharing traits with the author, is not her replica because the poetic subject responds to different ideological demands; these differences allow it to take positions that are to some degree unstable, revisionary, or counter to the demands of author-ity. The author-subject that we uncovered in the interview is also at once the author and her creation, a mask of herself. This author-character is produced as a subject by other ideological influences, many of which place conflicting demands on Orozco and highlight her relationship to the extraliterary realm. Contrasting the production of subjectivity in the interview and in the lyric demonstrates that, although by divergent means, each genre produces conflictive subjects whose discourse repudiates their apparent distance from the social world.

The interview in this chapter also makes my role as subject and subjected reader, critic, interviewer, and re-producer of texts more explicit. I come from a different interpretative community than the author and from another moment and so I approach these texts with a perspective that challenges some assumptions that have been, perhaps, naturalized. All of the subject positions we find in this reading—author, poetic, reader—exist in an interdependent relationship constituted by social realities. Not taking subjectivity for granted, we recognize that it is not unified and autonomous but contradictory and interdependent; in this contradiction we see the intersection of various ideological discourses and possibilities for change.

My examination of this interview with Olga Orozco also leads us to some more general conclusions about the literary interview as genre. At the beginning of this chapter, I noted that the interview shared problems of subjectivity, historicity, and authority with autobiography and testimonial literatures and hinted at the fact that these forms have different ideological functions. Autobiography usually supports the unicity and power of the subject, as does the interview, but the literary interview also privileges the institutional power of literature while distancing itself from its own constructed nature (the "graphic" function that is more apparent in autobiography). Differentiating itself from both forms, testimonial literature is a genre that undoes the individual perspective, representing a collective voice. René Jara has defined *testimonio* as a "narrative of urgency," stimulated by a particular event (or events) and seen through the perspective of an observer who represents a larger group (2). John Beverley reiterates this definition, adding that *testimonio* is a transitional form that always challenges the status quo (15,9). Thus, the interview may be the most conservative form of the three, valorizing the individual artist and reinforcing his or her role not only as producer but as the source of meaning, feeding our desire for some privileged truth available only through the artist. At the same time, this form frequently disguises the role of the interviewer as co-creator while inviting the reader to consume this textual product as "history" (the story of the author and her work, but not of the interview as part of that work). One way to plant seeds of dissent in the interview, however, as we have seen, is to change our way of reading it and call attention to its generic specificity. Indicating the generic expectations of the interview has allowed us to reconstruct these expectations, arriving at a different, less monolithic portrait of the artist, and enabled us to contrast the production of this subject with the creation of poetic subjects.

Shifting Subjects

◻

In reviewing early twentieth-century literary schools in Argentina in the Introduction, we noted that, although competing ideologies were able to coexist in the aesthetic worlds of Florida and Boedo, they became increasingly polarized in the course of the 1940s. Argentine poetry of the 1950s made this difference more explicit (as we saw in chapter 4), roughly marking a split between poets who sought a more pragmatic, functional role for their work and those who continued the turn toward self-examination, the metaphysical, away from the world. This separation of poetry's operations into two realms was, in fact, a transnational phenomenon in Latin America, a movement that has its roots in modernism. Both North American and Spanish American modernist forms shared an emphasis on language, a valuation of dense expression that obscured any referent outside of poetry. But the contrasting historical positions of the Americas made for different political situations in South and Central America, for in Latin America modernism coincided with an increase in regional consciousness and the modern shift of global powers. The linguistic facility of Rubén Darío may have proved cultural strength, but it was not enough; it did not keep Roosevelt out. As it became clear that a sense of national identity and enhanced cultural capital were not going to preserve or create independence in a world of multinational capitalism where borders were increasingly meaningless, we have encountered a move toward poetry that is more concrete, accessible to readers, increasing its link to the world through more open forms. At the same time the more formalist strain does not disappear.[1] The work of Pablo Neruda, who is still the most outstanding figure in twentieth-century Latin American poetry, significantly embodies this division, and many contemporary poets and *aficionados* split along the lines of whether they prefer the early work—with its more traditional, universalist, metaphysical concerns—or the politically engaged Neruda of *Canto General*.

The division was already in place, then, when Olga Orozco began to publish, and as she continues to write it becomes more pronounced. While prose became more "poetic" with the boom of the sixties, moving away from earlier naturalism and social realism, and implying, therefore, a synthesis among forms, in poetry there was a rupture. Perhaps this is because the poetic genre, which provokes self-contained readings, is supremely literary and calls attention to its own textuality. But lyric poetry traditionally has an oral element as well, a performance aspect, for the lyric exists on the border between music and language. Depending upon which of its elements is emphasized, it can unite voices in community or it can distance itself from the social world through its structural complexity. Orozco's work is indicative of this division—she builds verbal perfection and stresses the imagination in a way that is representative of the line of poets whose work excludes the historical word, yet she speaks of herself as the voice of her tribe. As we have seen, her poetry has a hybrid function, its other-worldly quality is distancing yet her imagination is also an *arma*. By repeatedly signaling its distance from political activity, Orozco's work reacts against it, shows the degree of threat it poses, and at the same time, indirectly reinforces it. The historical world is in some sense "present" most vociferously in her poetry because of its notable absence.

Just what is kept outside of poetic territory changes, for Orozco continues to write through Peronism's various manifestations, subsequent political upheaval, and the recent dictatorship and its demise. Her poetry, like that of Alejandra Pizarnik, continually works to preserve a place that is separate from the encroachment of a fluctuating world, a space in which to write poetry. We observed how both Orozco and Pizarnik held on to aesthetic values in a rough sea of change, a reaction which still has ideological strength in Argentina—as can be seen in the work of those younger poets who group themselves around the publication *Ultimo Reino*. In the introduction to the recent collection *Antología Ultimo Reino,* editor Victor Redondo reiterates this group's view of poetry: "*Ultimo Reino* busca un lenguaje donde la belleza no esté confrontada con el sentido" [*Ultimo Reino* searches for a language in which beauty is not confronted with sense] (6). Redondo's statement demonstrates the continuing attraction of an aestheticism that avoids the larger contextual framework, a perspective that values language in terms of its formal beauty.

This is not the case in the work of the poets studied in chapter 5. In this strain of recent Argentine poetry, the relationship between history and poetic practice returns to the forefront. Unlike the ultra/surrealist vanguard[2] with its high level of linguistic innovation (not necessarily accompanied by more profound changes) and the distance taken by poets of the forties, this poetry evidences an increasingly dialectical relation between language and historical processes. Recent events and elements indicative of the author's gendered identity infiltrate these texts. Although their primary purpose is not to denounce, these authors figurally evoke the atmosphere of the seventies; the dictatorship is a specter shaping their poetry. There is a link between the political situation and gender, for another aspect of a repressive regime is the "feminization" of society, producing an increased consciousness of the struggle required to obtain subject status in a society dominated by patriarchal models of authority. "Shifting Subjects" refers to my own methodology, to the destabilization of conventional subjects, to new themes, to different speaking subjects, to subjects who transform. Calling attention to the construction of subject positions may also produce new readers—less subjected, potentially more creative and interactive with texts, moving away from reading these poets in isolation, seeing them instead as voices in a historically produced cultural constellation.

Appendix

Note to the reader: The text that follows is actually the compilation of two texts; the comments that appear in regular print are the written questions of the interviewer (J.K.) and the written answers of the respondent (O.O.). The italicized section of the text represents the oral portion of the interview that took place when I received Olga Orozco's responses and then had the opportunity to ask her to elaborate on certain points. While the oral and written responses are unquestionably different products, they are also dependent upon one another, and so I have chosen to present them together while distinguishing between the two modes of expression. The English translation follows the text in Spanish.

Entrevista en Buenos Aires, 13 octubre, 1988

J.K. En mi estudio propongo hacer una lectura intertextual de tu poesía en relación con la poesía de T. S. Eliot, Oliverio Girondo, y Alejandra Pizarnik. Pregunto, ¿qué tipo de relación ves tú entre tu producción y la de estos poetas?

O.O. Creo que no hay ninguna. A Oliverio Girondo me ligó una larga y estrecha amistad, y tal vez haya influído de alguna manera en mi comportamiento retraído frente a las solicitaciones exteriores (nunca tuve ansiedad por publicar, no acepté invitaciones de los medios masivos de comunicación, sino que procedí discriminadamente, inclusive rechazando premios cuando provenían de entidades que consideré reprobables). Con T. S. Eliot, a quien siempre admiré, hay alguna concordancia en el sentido del tiempo, por el hecho de que cada uno incluye a los otros, y en el amor por los gatos. Alejandra Pizarnik, de quien fui muy amiga, era bastante menor que yo, de modo que si hay alguna similtud de temas ("las niñas que yo fui," las aventuras infantiles, las máscaras que hay en cada rostro, etc.) mira el libro que publicó antes de que nos conociéramos y saca tus propias conclusiones.

J.K. *¿Y qué de la negatividad en la poesía de Pizarnik? ¿Comparten ustedes este tema?*

O.O. *Mi poesía no es de la negación, tampoco lo de Oliverio—no, no, para nada.*

J.K. *¿Y la poesía de Pizarnik sería de la "negación"?*

O.O. *Yo no creo que sea de negación. Yo creo que es de desamparo, que es de falta de vitalidad, inclusive. Creo que es la poesía de un ser que estaba perdido, que es una poesía de petición de auxilio. Si tú lo quieres resumir fácilmente dices: "estoy sola, tengo hambre, tengo sed, ayúdenme, tengo frío. . . ." Ella dice, "hablen ustedes, cobardes!," como si fuera muy valiente pero es el ser más débil y más cobarde del mundo.*

J.K. *Tengo dificultades con la palabra "negación" en términos de tu poesía también. Quizás mejor palabra sea "rechazo. . . ."*

O.O. *Sí rechaza algunas cosas pero lo hace para afirmar otras, mientras que yo creo que lo que rechaza Alejandra es la vida misma y se prende de la palabra como si fuera una tabla de salvación y evidentemente la palabra no te puede compensar la vida misma. Inclusive llega un momento en que no hay con que alimentar la palabra porque tu vida se ha quedado árida, se ha quedado sin amor, se ha quedado sin jugos, y la palabra no va a bastar para sustenerla.*

J.K. ¿Cuál sería la influencia de ustedes en otros poetas de las generaciones posteriores? ¿Participas en algún taller de poesía o algo así?

O.O. La influencia de Oliverio sobre los jóvenes fue relativa en el terreno literario; fue más bien una adhesión hacia su espíritu y sus actitudes. La de Alejandra fue más bien abrumadora, ya que adoptaron su manera como receta fácil: dos o tres imágenes, un corte brusco u otra imagen desconectada, sorpresiva. La mía, si existe, no la reconozco en nadie, como es difícil encontrarse en la cara de otros. No participo en talleres de poesía; no tengo condiciones didácticas ni ejerzo profesionalmente la poesía.

J.K. *Entonces, ¿no hay nadie que siga en tus pasos, poéticamente?*

O.O. *Es que, yo no me doy cuenta realmente. No sé . . . hay gente que me dice, "ay, Fulana, qué influencia tuya tiene!" o "Mengano, cómo te sigue"; me lo dicen miles de veces pero yo no lo advierto. Por lo mismo que te digo, [. . .] tú no lo encuentras a alguien en la calle y piensas cómo te pareces a mí, ¿verdad? Puede ser que la cara se parece a la de un amigo tuyo pero no a la tuya, ¿verdad? . . . Inclusive esta mujer que ha sacado ahora el premio en La Nación, los otros días Enrique Molina me decía: "Claro que sí, seguro que lo*

tenías que interesar" (él la votó con mucho entusiasmo); me tenía que interesar
porque "tenía muchas cosas en común contigo." Pero yo le decía, "no tiene
nada que ver con mi tono, con nada mío," y empezó a señalarme asuntos y
cosas . . . a pesar de eso, yo no la veo.

J.K. *¿Te parece común en un autor, no poder ver relaciones entre su obra y*
la de otros?

O.O. *No, no me parece común; me parece más bien todo lo contrario. Me*
parece que en general tienen mucha avidéz por verse reflejado, tanto que
tienen la fantasía que influyen a todo el mundo.

J.K. Se han hablado en varias entrevistas de la influencia en tu obra de
autores como Dostoievski, Poe, Cernuda, Baudelaire . . . me impresiona la
falta de autores latinoamericanos en las listas. ¿Puedes decirme a quién calificas
como influencia estética? (y no quiero decir sólo autores).

O.O. Creo que hay una tendencia generalizada a confundir "preferencias"
o "exaltaciones" con "influencias." Jamás he dicho que tuviera influencia de
los escritores que mencionas; dije que sentía gran admiración por ellos.
También me bastó decir que la sentía por Luis Cernuda para que dos o tres
comentaristas dijeran que era mi modelo. Falsedad absoluta. Naturalmente
que tengo más admiraciones, inclusive en Latinoamérica, pero ya me parece
peligroso mencionarlas. Las influencias literarias, por dentro se sienten, sin
duda, como una prodigiosa concordancia, como una bendita hermandad,
como un sabor tribal. Por fuera suenan como una acusación de plagio, de
usurpación, o por lo menos de falta de originalidad, cuando en realidad es más
legítimo que todos provengamos de alguien.

J.K. También en otros lugares se habla de ti como una "poeta pampeana."
¿Cómo dirías tú que se ve esto en la poesía, y qué la llevó a Buenos Aires?

O.O. Soy "poeta pampeana" simplemente porque nací en La Pampa. No sé
cómo se verá esto en la poesía, ni qué quieres decir con eso; en cuanto a mí, en
cuanto a cómo lo veo yo, puedo decirte que en mi poesía hay muchas alusiones
a ese paisaje, a esa visión infinita, hacia ese vértigo hacia arriba que produce la
llanura árida. Por otra parte, allí transcurrió mi infancia que sigo llevando
conmigo, que es siempre presente, como todos mis tiempos, de modo que esta
región entró íntegra con mi niñez en mi libro de relatos *La oscuridad es otro*
sol y continúa entrando en el que estoy escribiendo y que se titulará *También*
la luz es un abismo. ¿Qué me trajo a Buenos Aires? Mis padres, naturalmente.
Vine a vivir aquí cuando era apenas una adolescente, después de pasar unos
pocos años en Bahía Blanca.

J.K. *Lo que quería decir es que me parece que crea un problema caracterizar*
a alguien solamente por de donde viene uno. Por ejemplo, ¿Crees que hay un

movimiento en tu poesía más hacia la ciudad, que lo más reciente es más urbano?

O.O. *Yo no sé. Yo creo que es una cosa de cualquier parte, lo mío de después; no creo que haya muchas cosas del local, quitando el paisaje infantil.*

J.K. También, generalmente apareces colocada como miembra de la generación del 40. ¿Qué quería decir ser miembro de tal generación? Hay dos versiones que he observado; una, que la describe como un intento de ahondamiento en un lirismo subjetivista u otra, que dice que hubo una preocupación con "la condición humana" en contra de la posición lúdica de los martinfierristas. ¿Cómo era el panorama intelectual de aquel entonces?

O.O. Siempre negué la existencia de tal generación. Si por generación entendemos solamente un conjunto de personas contemporáneas, ligadas por una vocación común, que disponen de los mismos escasos medios de difusión y se reunen para fundar otros, diría que existe una compacta y definida generación del 40. Pero creo que estos elementos no bastan para autorizar el uso de tal rótulo, como no basta el color de la envoltura ni el lugar y el momento del canto para clasificar las especies zoológicas. Los criterios estéticos, las edades, la formación general, las tendencias, los odios, los amores y hasta las actitudes vitales de los poetas que han sido agrupados bajo esa denominación eran tan variados que de algunas clases existía un solo ejemplar en el muestrario. No importa que exégetas afanosos los hayan empadronado en líneas generales en el neorromanticismo y les hayan adjudicado una preocupación común por exaltar los mismos accidentes geográficos con igual lirismo y llorar las mismas penas con idéntica nostalgia. Basta recorrer sus nombres y sus obras para comprobar que sólo forzadamente, cortando brazos, mezclando plumas y agregando piernas, se los puede encerrar en una sola jaula.

El panorama intelectual de esa época era mucho más agitado que el actual, más inquieto, más viviente. Estaban todavía en plena actividad escritores de otra generación como Macedonio Fernández, Oliverio Girondo, Norah Lange, Ricardo Molinari, Jorge Luis Borges, Martínez Estrada, Francisco Luis Bernárdez, Leopoldo Marechal, Raúl González Tuñón, y muchos más. Estaba el contingente de refugiados españoles, los visitantes extranjeros, y la revista *Sur*, que a veces traía a artistas y pensadores extraordinarios y publicaba además los últimos hallazgos culturales simultáneamente con Europa. Estaban también las reuniones polémicas en los cafés y los encuentros de grupos, que duraban hasta el amanecer.

J.K. *En realidad, tu obra trasciende una generación, como todavía produces.*

O.O. *Sí. Mira este asunto acerca de las generaciones—de si existe o no* *existe una generación, o si existe una escritura femenina—puede llevar años y no llegar a ninguna conclusión, ¿no?*

J.K. *Es una manía de categorización.*

O.O. *Sí, es que todo se hace más fácil si se puede ponerlo dentro de un rótulo.*

J.K. Ampliando nuestra visión, entonces, ¿Cuál sería la función de la poesía en nuestra sociedad?

O.O. La función de la poesía en nuestra sociedad sería la de siempre en todas las sociedades. Te transcribo aquí algo que ya he dicho acerca del papel del poeta en el mundo: "Reduciendo al máximo su misión en este mundo, prescindiendo de su fatalidad personal y sus propios fines, y limitando su destino al papel de intermediario que desempeña frente a los demás, aun sin proponérselo y por antisocial que parezca, el poeta ayuda a las grandes catarsis, a mirar juntos el fondo de la noche, a vislumbrar la unidad en un mundo fragmentado por la separación y el aislamiento, a denunciar apariencias y artificios, a saber que no estamos solos en nuestros extrañamientos e intemperies, a descubrir el tú a través del yo y el nosotros a través del ellos, a entrever otras realidades subyacentes en el aquí y el ahora, a azuzarnos para que no nos durmamos del costado más cómodo, a celebrar las dádivas del mundo y a extremar significaciones, ¿por qué no?, cuando la exageración abarca la verdad" [This quote is from the "Discurso pronunciado con ocasión del Gran Premio del Fondo Nacional de las Artes," December 16, 1980].

J.K. *Esta definición me parece atemporal.*

O.O. *Claro, a mí me parece que es atemporal la función de la poesía en el mundo—que intenta cambiar la vida pero es tan difícil que llegue a cambiar la vida. No creo que la vida se puede mejorar a través de la palabra, desdichadamente. A menos si convenciera a todo el mundo que escribiera poesía; si todo el mundo escribiera poesía, todos estarían mejores.*

J.K. Hay una unidad orgánica en tu poesía, una retoma y ampliación de temas, pero ¿hay también etapas que ves en tu producción?

O.O. Naturalmente que los hay. No te circunscribiré aquí los límites de cada una, porque no puedo marcarlos con un tiralíneas, ya que en una se anuncian ya los resplandores de otra, pero justamente cada ampliación de temas, cada inmersión en una zona más profunda de lo desconocido, cada avance dentro del territorio del lenguaje, ¿no constituye una etapa dentro de lo que llamas la unidad orgánica de mi experiencia poética?

J.K. En su libro reciente, Elba Peralta trató *La oscuridad es otro sol* con detalle pero no mencionó los fotomontages de Enrique Molina que me fascinan. ¿Cómo ocurrieron éstos y cuál sería su función dentro del texto?

O.O. A veces me desconciertan tus preguntas porque las respuestas son obvias. La función de los collages de Enrique Molina es la que tiene toda ilustración: completar, ampliar, enriquecer a través de las imágenes visuales el mundo que el lenguaje proyecta sobre los planos de la imaginación. No se trata de sumisiones a la letra, por supuesto, sino de creaciones dentro de un ámbito determinado. Enrique Molina, además de poeta es pintor y ha trabajado mucho en collages hechos con viejos grabados, material que utilizaron siempre los surrealistas. Le sugerí utilizar en este caso fotografías en las que había una niñita real, una abuela real, un paisaje real y algunos otros elementos, con los que se podrían componer representaciones paralelas a los estados de ánimo que sugieren los relatos.

J.K. *Sí, yo también podía haber dicho que complementan el texto pero es interesante lo que dices de la fuente de estas fotos . . . ¿Es significativo que sean collages?*

O.O. *El hacía collage con grabados, con libros de física antiguos, como lo hacían Max Ernst y el grupo surrealista en general, ¿no? Viste que Enrique se manejaba casi siempre con libros del siglo pasado, inclusive se manejaron mucho algunas ilustraciones de los libros de Julio Verne; daba una cosa más generalizada, el colage con estos elementos, más imprescindible acerca de quien era cada cosa.*

J.K. *Y la repetición de la niña es uno de los elementos más impactantes.*

O.O. *Claro, claro, esa criatura cerrada y amedrentada está tan de acuerdo con el desasosiego que tiene el libro, ¿verdad?*

J.K. *Pero no has empleado ilustraciones en tus poemarios así que ¿te parece que son más útiles en una narrativa?*

O.O. *No sé, tal vez. . . . nunca me ocurrió con un libro de poemas. No sé; quizás porque los relatos tienen una unidad de personajes y una unidad de panorama, todo se desarrolla en el mismo sitio, ¿no? Mientras que la poesía tiene una unidad interna pero los asuntos son muy otros cada vez y más irrepresentables inclusive. Hay más abstracción, cosas que son más metafísicas, envueltas en sensaciones.*

J.K. También en *La oscuridad es otro sol* se ve la importancia de muchas figuras femeninas: Laura, la reina Genoveva, la "Virgen María," Nanni Fittipaldi, y se ve repetidas veces la abuela en tu poesía y ese poema tan bello dedicado a Josefina Susana Fragueiro.

O.O. Mi casa fue una casa de mujeres. Un hermano muerto cuando tenía cinco años; otro medio hermano en Europa; papá quince días con nosotras y dos meses en pleno campo, y mamá, mi abuela, mi tía, mis dos hermanas y yo en la casa. Supongo que cuando dices "la Virgen María" te refieres a la Lora, una protegida de mi abuela. Pero Nanni Fittipaldi es un hombre; es el loco cantante refugiado en el granero. ¿Qué puedo explicarte? Tengo lazos profundos con las mujeres de mi familia (también tengo un poema a Emilio, otro a Francesco, mis hermanos; uno a E.V.L., mi sobrino; menciono en varios a mi padre), como tengo lazos profundos con Josefina Susana Fragueiro, que fue una gran amiga. La gravitación de la Reina Genoveva y de la Lora se explica por la extravagancia de sus figuras y el patetismo de sus historias. También la tuvo Nanni.

J.K. Se habla hoy en día de la escritura femenina, si hay tal cosa, de la diferencia entre el hombre y la mujer que escribe. ¿En tu opinión existe esta diferencia? ¿Se la puede ver en el género que escogen las mujeres, el estilo, lo que esperan del lector?

O.O. En primer lugar no entiendo esa división, ya que no veo por ningún lado algo que se llama "escritura masculina," sino simplemente "escritura," así como no hay "pintura femenina," ni "escultura femenina," ni "ciencia femenina," etc. No creo en ella. Pienso que es una discriminación más a la que no me acojo. La acepto apenas en un sentido peyorativo, cuando la usan para designar la forma descuidada, la expresión carente de rigor, de estructura y medida, propia de las mujeres que no vieron en la escritura una misión o un destino sino una descarga o entretenimiento. Si bien en la prosa hay elementos que pueden ser mejor manejados por las mujeres (labores, telas, asuntos domésticos, crianza de niños, etc.) y otros por los hombres (mercado de va- lores, asuntos del ejército y armada, política, etc.) no constituye una regla ni justifica la diferenciación, ya que se trata de los materiales del escritor y no del estilo. Yo siento que la creación poética no tiene sexo. Escribo *con* toda la humanidad y *para* nadie en particular. Podría hablarte horas acerca de todo lo que experimento desde la primera llamada de alerta que me arrebata hacia el poema hasta el último oleaje que me devuelve otra vez a la costa conocida, pero puedo asegurarte que en ningún momento de este viaje he tocado la "isla de las mujeres" ni mi lenguaje ha padecido ninguna catalogación genética.

J.K. ¿Te parece válida la idea de antologías de mujeres?

O.O. No, no me parece. Me niego a participar. No quiero ser excluída de la legítima "Poesía" a secas para ingresar en la falacia de la "poesía femenina."

J.K. ¿Tienen las mujeres en la Argentina las mismas oportunidades para publicar, ganar premios?

O.O. Sí, tienen las mismas; no así en el territorio de los empleos, las profesiones y los cargos públicos.

J.K. Otras figuras o imágenes que parecen ejercer una fascinación en tu obra son las de la esfinge, estatua, cariátide, mujer de Lot—todos objetos semianimados, mudas pero no mudas a la vez. ¿Quieres comentar este proceso de "inmovilización" en tus poemas?

O.O. Sí, me inquietan los objetos, como si estuvieran al acecho, presenciándome, dispuestos a cobrar vida, ¿Cómo no habrían de intranquilizarme las estatuas, figuraciones de personas, de animales, de monstruos o de emisarios del más allá, cuyos propósitos me son desconocidos y que con su inmovilidad sólo parecen esperar una señal ignorada para intercalarse en esta vida, tal vez por un solo momento, tal vez para un solo acto. Pero creo que la lista que das no es correcta. La esfinge no me desasosiega por su inmovilidad sino por su sabiduría secreta y por la sanción que corresponde a mi ignorancia. La mujer de Lot, o sea la estatua de sal, está presente más que por estatua por mirar hacia atrás. La "estatua de azul" es otra cosa; es como el calco que el alma dejó en la eternidad y al que debe volver a animar; lo dejó al nacer y regresará al morir.

J.K. ¿Y la imágen del cuenco? Me parece frecuentemente un punto de balance en los poemas; es un objeto humilde que espera contener algo.

O.O. Como decía, creo que cualquier objeto, aun el más anodino, puede cargarse en determinado momento de significación y de intenciones. Por otra parte, aunque no creo mencionar muchas veces el cuenco, no más que la copa, la vasija, o cualquier otro recipiente que deba contener agua, lágrimas, recuerdos u olvido, o lo que sea, el cuenco es liso, liso, y su misma inexpresivida tiene algo de fatalidad ciega.

J.K. *¿Qué quiere decir "fatalidad ciega"?*

O.O. *Lo que pasa es que yo he soñado a veces con gente que tenía unas caras sin rasgos.*

J.K. *¿Como cóncavas?*

O.O. *Como cóncavas; entonces eran también como cuencos, ¿ves? Entonces, no sé, estas cosas que no tienen de donde tomarse como punto de referencia, te parecen que pueden conducir a cualquier parte. Una cara como un cuenco te puede traer cualquier sorpresa tremenda y fatal, mucho más que las caras más horribles, ¿no ves?*

J.K. *Por su falta de definición sería.*

O.O. *Claro, por la falta de referencia total.*

J.K. ¿Puedes decirme un poquito acerca de la relación que ves entre las artes plásticas y la poesía? Tienes los poemas a Hieronymus Bosch, Van Gogh, varias referencias al proceso de esculpir y terminología que parece asociada con esto—"la cantera de la sabiduría," por ejemplo.

O.O. Todas las artes son complementarias y hasta actúan de manera intercambiable en relación con los diferentes sentidos (la música se hace color, la palabra tacto, etc.), pero sobre todo colman deficiencias: la simultaneidad que me da la pintura no me puede dar la literatura, que en cambio me da una sucesión en el tiempo que en la música se hace quintaesencia privilegiada. La cantera no alude a la escultura sino a un depósito de piedras. Para mí las piedras tienen vida interiormente. Y así como quitando piedra, "esculpiendo" está la estatua, que ya estaba antes en la materia informe, así quitando vocablos al lenguaje está el poema que ya estaba antes en el Verbo, y quitando al mundo está Dios, al que yo cubro.

J.K. Otra imagen o más bien actividad que es recurrente en tu obra es la del testigo ("Esbozos frente un modelo," "Al pie de la letra") que parece señalar una relación específica a la realidad (atestiguar es distinto, por ejemplo, de contemplar). ¿Cómo ves esta relación?

O.O. Siento que nada es indiferente. Personas y cosas están animadas de fuerzas de afirmación y de fuerzas de oposición. Hay aliados y enemigos que acompañan unos y otros actos, unos y otros recuerdos, y que testimonian en tu favor o en tu contra. Los seres y los objetos que están indisolublemente unidos a tu vida serán tus testigos hasta el último día, hasta el juicio final.

J.K. En *Museo salvaje* (74), el tema es el cuerpo. ¿Por qué esta temática en aquel momento?

O.O. A lo largo de mi vida pasé por momentos de angustia extrema, los motivos, los temas, absorbentes hasta el desarreglo, enajenantes hasta el peligro y la inminencia del abismo, variaban. Pero uno de los más recurrentes era el extrañamiento súbito frente a mi propio cuerpo, frente a cada parte de mi anatomía y la imposibilidad de que me contuviera, me representara, me expresara. Sí el cuerpo, tan próximo y tan ajeno a la vez; tan desconocido, y sin embargo nuestro único intermediario frente a lo inasible, frente al alma, frente a Dios. El cuerpo que hace posible la vida y la limita, a la vez; que obstruye con su forma densa la posibilidad de prolongarse más allá de la realidad sensorial. El cuerpo, al que estoy adherida y al que quiero, de tal modo que no puedo renunciar a la resurrección de la carne (A pesar de que en algún lado gesta el arma que me matará).

Aunque toda esta extrañeza de la que hablé está de manifiesto en uno y otro momento de mis diferentes libros, en la época en que escribí *Museo salvaje* pasaba por una etapa de cierta objetividad que me hizo posible sumergirme hasta el fondo de mis tejidos, mis vísceras, de mis ojos, etc., y extraer ese puñado de poemas. Claro que esa observación casi de entomólogo se interrumpía a cada instante, alterada por una tensión progresiva hasta un punto insoportable.

J.K. *Esta técnica me parece aun más interesante después de haber leído tu* *último libro,* En el revés del cielo, *que tiene mucho que ver con las limitaciones del cuerpo también.*

O.O. *También, claro, inclusive el poema que se llama "Catecismo animal," que es mi resistencia al dejar el cuerpo, mi protesta porque el alma deje al cuerpo—una petición por la resurrección de la carne, totalmente este poema. Veo esta relación también con muchos otros momentos de mi obra; aunque no sean como poemas unitarios hay alusiones a este extrañamiento o enajenación que produce una u otra mirada contemplativa del cuerpo en un poema u otro poema de distintos libros míos. Y sobre todo desde el comienzo está en* La oscuridad es otro sol *y muchas veces ¿no?*

J.K. *Sí, yo diría que es un tema constante.*

O.O. *No, no, sí, porque es algo que me ha sucedido siempre.*

J.K. *Pero hay libros que toman este tema con más fuerza, ¿no?*

O.O. *Ah bueno, claro. Allí está explicado que justamente cuando me dio tal vez un cierto respiro, la permanencia de la angustia me animé a trasladarlos en este libro que forma* Museo salvaje *que luego tenía que hacer entrecortadamente porque en cuanto incursara un poco profundamente en el asunto, inmediatemente tenía la alteración y otra vez me sumergía en la angustia. Además y curiosamente me fuí deteriorando mi organismo. Escribí el poema sobre el ojo, por ejemplo, se me producía algo extraño, iba al oculista y tuve presión en un ojo. Escribí el poema "La sangre," tenía diabetes.*

J.K. *Era como presentimiento casi.*

O.O. *Escribí el poema al esqueleto—artrosis, pero sucesivamente distintas cosas. Decidí terminar de una vez porque ya había este llamado a través del organismo que se estaba deteriorando. No sé qué era antes.*

J.K. Tú trabajas en *Vuelta,* he oído que has tenido lazos con la Universidad de Buenos Aires, ¿tienes otros empleos? ¿Hay alguien que pueda ganarse la vida con la poesía?

O.O. No trabajo en *Vuelta;* sólo pertenezco al consejo de redacción. Con la Universidad no tuve otros lazos que mis estudios en la carrera de Letras. No tengo ningún empleo. En otros tiempos trabajé como periodista en la editorial Abril y fui secretaria técnica de Fabril Editora. Nadie puede ganarse la vida como poeta, salvo unos poquísimos privilegiados a los que su talento, prestigio y suerte les proporcionan conferencias y premios internacionales.

J.K. ¿Dónde has publicado? ¿En cuáles revistas y por qué?

O.O. La lista de revistas y periódicos en los que he publicado es larga. Menciono algunos: *Sur, La Nación, La Gaceta, A partir de cero, Xul, La tabla redonda, Ultimo reino, La Opinión, Vuelta* (Argentina), *Novembro* (Angola), *La Razón* (Bolivia), *O Globo, Jornal da Bahía* (Brasil), *The Raddle Moon*

(Canada), *Eco, Gaceta, Revista de la Universidad* (Columbia), *Les Lettres nouvelles, Cuadernos, Libération* (Francia), *Nouvelle Europe* (Luxemburgo), *Cuadernos Americanos, Vuelta, Revista de la Universidad de México, La Gaceta* (México), *Las moradas, Cuadernos trimestrales de poesía* (Perú), *Dunganon* (Suecia), *El Nacional, Revista de la Universidad, Zona Franca* (Venezuela), *El Día* (Uruguay), *Via, Escandalar, Hispamérica, Mid-American Review, American Poetry Review, Alaluz* (EE.UU.), etc., etc.

¿Por qué? Porque me solicitaron colaboración, porque estaba de acuerdo con sus líneas generales.

J.K. *¿Y cómo serían estas líneas generales?*

O.O. *Bueno en un sentido de la estética o que no eran revistas en algún momento . . . qué sé yo, franquistas, suponte si se da en España la cosa o no estaba de acuerdo con el staff de colaboradores que había, digamos. Por eso digo líneas generales, sin especificar.*

J.K. *¿Depende de la revista o. . . ? Porque me parece que estás señalando cosas más políticas en vez de estéticas.*

O.O. *De todo depende . . . de la categoría de la revista, aunque a veces he publicado en revistas de jóvenes exclusivamente como ayuda a los jóvenes— que no te pagan un centavo, naturalmente, y ni siquiera te mandan después la revista. Pero bueno, les he dado la colaboración algunas veces cuando veía que valía la pena ayudarles. Pero al contrario, naturalmente que me he fijado en la categoría estética de la revista misma.*

J.K. Una pregunta un poco fuera del tema, pero desde que he estado en Buenos Aires me he fijado en la influencia de la teoría psicoanalítica acá. ¿Has leído mucho de eso, tiene algo que ver con eso? ¿A qué se debe este interés en lo psicoanalítico, Lacan?

O.O. Sí, he leído bastante. No es extraño que la gente quiera asomarse a sus zonas oscuras para conocerse mejor, pero es inadmisible que convierta su vida interior en una maquinita de resortes y pretenda hacer calzar al prójimo en una cuadrícula somera e improvisada. [. . .]

J.K. *¿Estás en contra de su manera formuláica de operar?*

O.O. *Estoy en contra de todo estereotipo, naturalmente, y de las clasificaciones generales. Creo que cada cosa es particularísimo; que uno puede conocerse un poco mejor a sí mismo pero no tratar de catalogar al prójimo y meterlo así por fuerza en ese rótulo cualquiera. . . . Fulano es compulsivo por tal razón y por tal otra este otro es angustiado.*

J.K. *¿Y te parece un acercamiento válido a la literatura, estas teorías psicoanalíticas?*

O.O. *Yo no sé. Creo que toda cosa que termina en una formulación así tan* *rotunda se hace hasta convencional. Yo creo que están bien los elementos pero sin la clasificación, ¿no?*

J.K. *La última cosa que yo quería saber es que si tú crees que durante los años de la dictadura, o como acá se llama "el proceso". . . ¿Por qué se llama "el proceso"?*

O.O. *Nunca he sabido; da la impresión de que hubieran adivinado que iba a terminar en un proceso la cosa, ¿no?*

J.K. *Sí. Yo, al principio, creía que hablaba la gente del fin de la dictadura como "el proceso" pero ahora entiendo que es todo el periodo.*

O.O. *Sí, sí, sí.*

J.K. *¿Pero crees que hubo un cambio en la producción poética, del tipo de libro publicado, menos lectores, cosas así?*

O.O. *¿Durante el proceso? No lo que se suponía desde ya es que iba a haber montones de libros acerca del exilio, etc., etc., que es lo que se produjo.*

J.K. *¿Y eso pasó?*

O.O. *Sigue sucediendo, ¿no?*

J.K. *Sí, ahora, ¿pero durante el proceso?*

O.O. *Ah, no durante el proceso nadie se atrevía a hablar de nada.*

[. . .]

J.K. *Lo que quiero saber, entonces, es que si por lo que tú sabes de este momento, ¿si hubo menos libros publicados acá en Buenos Aires, quizá por falta de interés o falta de ánimo o falta de otras cosas o algo así?*

O.O. *Yo creo que muchos poetas se fueron. Muchas editoriales cerraron; hay también por medio una cuestión económica que fue también paralela a la cosa e inclusive la cultura empezó a resultar un poquito solitaria.*

J.K. *Sí, porque hay gente que dice, por ejemplo, que se escribió más poesía durante la dictadura, hay otros que dicen que se escribió menos poesía.*

O.O. *Yo creo que se escribió lo mismo. Lo que cambió en algún aspecto fueron los temas por los que estaban lejos y los temas por los que estaban acá.*

J.K. *¿Y cómo sería este cambio por los que estaban acá?*

O.O. *Y bueno, en los que estaban acá tal vez se vea una cosa más opresiva en algunos en los que no se animaban a hablar abiertamente. Te digo en la gente que tiene una tónica de poesía social. Yo no lo sé, yo nunca lo he tenido.*

J.K. *Se dice que en Chile, por ejemplo, el poeta Enrique Lihn, al no poder hablar abiertamente empleaba la forma del soneto (anacrónica, restringida) para mostrar los confines de su situación. ¿Se podía ver algo semejante en la Argentina?*

O.O. *No, yo no he advertido nada de eso. No, no acá la gente no se animó a hablar durante el proceso, ¿Para qué vamos a hablar? No sé, después habla* *todo el mundo, normalmente; además entiendo muy bien que nadie hablara porque naturalmente el que hablaba desaparecía. Te digo que los que se fueron les reprochan a los que se quedaron al no haber hablado. Hablar desde afuera es más fácil que hablar estando. Pero todas las cosas son duras; no solamente es duro irse, también es duro quedarse entonces, ¿no? Pero te hablan como si hubiera que haber patrocinado el vaciamiento del país. No es sencillo. No se tiene veinte años tampoco. Además nos tachan de habernos {¿escamoteado/escamoneado?} y de haber colaborado.*

J.K. *No, me parece difícil, la cosa entera. Por ejemplo, la otra noche pasaron en la televisión la película "La noche de los lápices," que realmente me impresionó mucho.*

O.O. *Sí, sí, claro y por supuesto. Pero te digo que los que se fueron, todos creen haber sido heróicos, tampoco fueron heróicos. Entonces cuando volvieron pensaron que tenían que tener puestos extraordinarios ... bueno, no sé, ni para unos ni para otros; todos hemos padecido de las mismas cosas. Además claro que uno no se daba cuenta de lo que pasaba en gran medida. No creas que era visible, las cosas no sucedían en las calles abiertamente como mucha gente lo dice. Las detenciones no se hacían públicas. Te enterabas de una que otra cosa cuando eran muy directas, cuando era el hijo de un amigo al que le pasaba algo pero no de la mayoría no te enterabas. Todo eso se pasa viendo después.*

* * * *

Interview in Buenos Aires, October 13, 1988

J.K. I plan on doing an intertextual examination of your poetry in relation to that of T. S. Eliot, Oliverio Girondo, and Alejandra Pizarnik in my study. I wonder what relation you see between your work and that of these other poets?

O.O. I don't think there is any. I was linked to Oliverio Girondo by a long and intimate friendship, and perhaps he might have influenced in some way my restrained behavior when faced with outside requests (I never was anxious about publishing, I didn't accept invitations from the media but was discriminating, including rejecting prizes when they came from entities I considered objectionable). With T. S. Eliot, whom I always admired, there is some correspondence in the sense of time, in the fact that each one of us includes others, and in our love of cats. Alejandra Pizarnik, who was a friend of mine, was substantially younger then I, so that if there is some similarity in themes ("the children I was," the childhood escapades, the masks in every face, etc.) look at the book she published after we met and come to your own conclusions.

J.K. *And what about the negativity in Pizarnik's poems? Do you share this theme?*

O.O. *My poetry is not about negation, neither is the work of Oliverio, no, no not at all.*

J.K. *And Pizarnik's poetry, is it about "negation"?*

O.O. *I don't think it is about negation. I think it is about abandonment, including a lack of enjoyment of life. I think it's the poetry of a lost person, it's a poetry that calls out for help. If you want to sum it up easily, you say "I am alone, I am hungry, I am thirsty, help me, I am cold. . . ." She says, "Speak you cowards" as if she were courageous but she is the weakest and most timid person in the world.*

J.K. *I have problems with the word "negation" in terms of your poetry too. Maybe a better word would be "rejection. . . ."*

O.O. *Yes, it refuses some things but does so in order to affirm others, while I think that what Alejandra rejects is life itself and she hangs on to the word as if it were a lifesaver and evidently words cannot take the place of life itself. A time arrives when one cannot sustain words because your life has become arid, loveless, dry, and words are not enough to sustain it.*

J.K. How would you qualify your influence on other poets of younger generations? Do you participate in poetry workshops or something similar?

O.O. Oliverio had a relative influence on the younger people in the literary field; they followed his attitudes and spirit more. Alejandra's influence was more overwhelming, since they adopted her style like a simple recipe: two or three images, a sharp cut or another disconnected, surprising image. Mine, if it exists, I don't see in anyone, just as it is difficult to recognize your face in that of others. I don't participate in poetry workshops; I don't teach or profession-ally practice poetry.

J.K. *Then there isn't anyone who follows in your poetic footsteps?*

O.O. *I don't really recognize it. I don't know . . . there are people who tell me, "oh, So-and-So really shows your influence!" or "How this other person follows you"; they tell me thousands of times but I don't spot it. For the same reason I'm telling you, [. . .] you don't meet someone in the street and think how much she looks like you, right? It could be that her face looks like a friend of yours but not your own. Even the woman who recently won the Nacion's poetry prize, the other day Enrique Molina said to me, "Of course she would interest you" (he voted for her enthusiastically); she would have to* *interest me because "she had a lot of things in common with me." But I said to him, "she doesn't have anything to do with my tone, with anything I do," and he began to show me things . . . in spite of this, I don't see it.*

J.K. *Does this seem common to you, for an author not to see relationships between his or her work and that of others?*

O.O. *No, it doesn't seem common; it seems exactly the opposite. It appears that in general they are very interested in seeing themselves reflected, so much so that they have the illusion that they influence everyone.*

J.K. In a number of other interviews the influence of authors such as Dostoyevsky, Poe, Cernuda, and Baudelaire has been mentioned . . . I noticed a lack of Latin American authors on the list. Who do you qualify as an aesthetic influence (and I don't mean to confine this to authors)?

O.O. I think there is a general tendency to confuse "preferences" or "admirations" with "influences." I never said that the writers you mention influenced me; I said that I greatly admired them. It was also enough that I said this about Luis Cernuda so that two or three commentators said he was my model. Absolutely false. Naturally I have people I admire, including in Latin America, but now it seems dangerous to me to mention them. Literary influences are felt inside as a great agreement, a blessed brotherhood, a tribal flavor. But from the outside they sound like an accusation of plagiarism, of usurpation, or at least a lack of originality when in reality it's very legitimate that we all come from someone.

J.K. Also you are spoken of in some places as a "poet from the pampas." How would you say this appears in your poetry and what brought you to Buenos Aires?

O.O. I am a "poet from the pampas" simply because I was born in La Pampa. I don't know how this would appear in the poetry or what you mean by this; as I see it, I can tell you that there are many allusions to this landscape in my poetry, to that infinite vision, toward that high vertigo which the dry plains produce. My childhood also was passed there, the childhood I continue to carry with me, which is always present, like all my times, such that this region entered completely in my childhood in my book of short stories *La oscuridad es otro sol* [The darkness is another sun] and it continues to enter in the book I am writing which will be titled *También la luz es un abismo* [The light is also an abyss]. What brought me to Buenos Aires? My parents, naturally. I came to live here when I was scarcely an adolescent, after spending a few years in Bahía Blanca.

J.K. *What I meant to say is that it seems to me that characterizing someone* *only by where they come from creates a problem. For example, would you say that there is a movement in your poetry toward the city, that the most recent work is more urban?*

O.O. *I don't know. I think it comes from anywhere, my later work; I don't think there are many traits of the area, taking away the childhood landscape.*

J.K. Also you have generally been situated as a member of the forties generation. What did it mean to be a member of that generation? I have seen two versions: one that describes it as an attempt at immersion in a subjective lyricism and another that says that there was concern with the "human condition" against the playful position of the martinfierrist generation. What was the intellectual outlook of that time like?

O.O. I always denied the existence of such a generation. If by generation we understand only a contemporaneous grouping of people, linked by a common vocation, who employ the same scarce means of diffusion and unite to found others, I would say that there is a compact and defined forties generation. But I don't think that these elements are enough to justify the use of such a label, just as it is not enough to have the same color wrapping, or the place and time of the song in order to classify a zoological species. Aesthetic criteria, ages, the general formation, tendencies, loves, hates, and even the attitudes toward life of the poets who have been named as part of this group were so varied that there is only one example of some types. The fact is that painstaking critics have registered them in general as neoromantics and have given them the same concern for showing the same geographical accidents with the same lyricism, crying the same woes with identical nostalgia. One only has to run through their names and works to prove that only with force, cutting off an arm, mixing feathers, and adding legs, can they be enclosed in a single cage.

The intellectual field at that time was much more exciting than it is today, more turbulent, livelier. Writers from another generation, such as Macedonio Fernández, Oliverio Girondo, Norah Lange, Ricardo Molinari, Jorge Luis Borges, Martínez Estrada, Francisco Luis Bernárdez, Leopoldo Marechal, Raúl González Tuñón, and many others were still active. There was the contingent of refugees from the Spanish Civil War, foreign visitors, the journal, *Sur,* which at times brought extraordinary artists and thinkers and published the latest cultural happenings simultaneously with Europe. There were also polemical meetings in cafes and group gatherings which lasted until dawn.

J.K. *In reality, your work transcends a generation as you are still producing.*

O.O. *Yes. This matter of generations—if a generation does or doesn't exist or if a women's writing exists—it can go on for years and not arrive at any conclusion, right?*

J.K. *It's a mad desire to categorize.*

O.O. *Yes, everything's much easier if you can put it all together under one label.*

J.K. Broadening our vision, What would you say is the function of poetry in our society?

O.O. The function of poetry in our society is that which it has always had, in all societies. I'll transcribe for you here something I've said about the role of the poet in the world: "Greatly reducing his mission in this world, omitting his personal destiny and his own ends, and limiting his destiny to the role of intermediary which he performs as opposed to the rest, even without proposing it and no matter how antisocial he may seem, the poet facilitates great catharsis, helps us to look into the depth of the night, to illuminate the unity in a world fragmented by separation and isolation, to denounce appearances and artifice, to know that we are not alone in our longings and in bad weather, to discover the 'you' through the 'I' and the 'we' through the 'them,' to catch a glimpse of other underlying realities in the here and now and to incite us so that we don't comfortably fall asleep, to celebrate the world's gifts and stretch meaning—why not?—when exaggeration contains truth." [This quote is from the "Discurso pronunciado con ocasión del Gran Premio del Fondo Nacional de las Artes," December 16, 1980].

J.K. *This definition appears to be atemporal.*

O.O. *Of course, to me the function of poetry in the world is atemporal—it attempts to change life but it is so difficult to change life. I don't think life can be improved through language, unfortunately. Unless we convinced everyone to write poetry; if everyone wrote poetry we would all be better off.*

J.K. There is an organic unity in your poetry, a return to and expansion of themes, but do you see any stages in your production as well?

O.O. Of course there are. I won't delineate for you here the limits of each because I can't mark them off with a drawing pen, since one stage foreshadows glimmers of another, but exactly each expansion of themes, each immersion in a deeper zone of the unconscious, each advance within language's territory, doesn't this constitute a stage in what you call the organic unity of my poetic experience?

J.K. In her recent book, Elba Peralta treated *La oscuridad es otro sol* in detail but she didn't mention the photomontages of Enrique Molina that I find fascinating. How did these occur and how would you define their role in the text?

O.O. Sometimes I find your questions unsettling because the answers are obvious. The function of Enrique Molina's collages is that of all illustrations:

to complete, to expand, to enrich through visual images the world which language projects onto the imagination. It does not have to do with submission to the letter, of course, but with creations within a determined scope. Enrique Molina, as well as a poet, is a painter and has worked a lot with collages made from old prints, a material the surrealists always used. I suggested that in this case he use photographs with a real child, a real grandmother, a real landscape and some other elements, with which he could make representations to parallel the moods suggested in the stories.

J.K. *Yes, I also could have said that they complement the text but what you say about the source of these photos is interesting . . . is it important that they are collages?*

O.O. *He made collages with prints, with old nature books, like Max Ernst and the surrealist group in general, no? Since Enrique always worked with books from the last century, he even used a lot of the illustrations from Jules Verne's books; the collage with these elements produced something more general, more fundamental about who each one was.*

J.K. *And the repetition of the child is one of the elements with the most impact.*

O.O. *Yes indeed, that closed and frightened child is so in keeping with the uneasiness of the book, no?*

J.K. *But you've never used illustrations in your books of poetry; do you think they are more useful in a narrative?*

O.O. *I don't know, maybe . . . it never occurred to me with a book of poetry. Maybe because the stories have a unity of characters and place, it all happens in the same place. While in poetry there is an internal unity but the issues are very different each time and less representable. There is more abstraction, things that are metaphysical, enclosed in emotion.*

J.K. Also in *La oscuridad es otro sol* we see many important female figures: Laura, Queen Guinevere, the "Virgin Mary," Nanni Fittipaldi, and we find the grandmother figure repeated in your poetry and that beautiful poem dedicated to Josefina Susana Fragueiro.

O.O. My house was a house of women. One brother dead at five years old; another half-brother in Europe; Papa, fifteen days with us and two months in the countryside, and mother, my grandmother, my aunt, my two sisters, and I at home. I suppose when you say the "Virgin María" you mean the Parrot, a protégée of my grandmother. But Nanni Fittipaldi is a man; he's the crazy singer who hides out in the barn. What can I explain to you? I have deep ties to the women of my family (I also have a poem to Emilio, another to Francesco, my brothers; one to E.V.L., my cousin; I mention my father in several), as I have great ties to Josefina Susana Fragueiro, who was a great friend. My inclination toward Queen Guinevere and the Parrot can be explained by the extravagance of their figures and their pathetic stories. I also had it [sympathy] for Nanni.

J.K. Much is said these days about women's writing, if there is such a thing, the differences between the man and the woman who writes. In your opinion, is there a difference? Can you see it in the genre chosen by women, in their style, in what they expect from their readers?

O.O. In the first place I don't understand this division, since I don't see "masculine writing" anywhere, just "writing," just as there isn't "women's painting" or "women's sculpture" or "women's science," etc. I don't believe in it. I think it is another discrimination to which I don't ascribe. I accept it only in a pejorative sense, when it is used to indicate a careless form, expression that lacks rigor, structure, measure, the style of women who didn't view writing as a mission or a destiny but as a release or entertainment. As there are elements in prose that can be better mastered by women (certain work, fabric, domestic matters, child-rearing, etc.) and others by men (the labor market, military issues, politics, etc.) this does not constitute a rule which justifies differentiation, since it concerns the materials of the writer and not style. I believe that poetic creation does not have a sex. I write *with* all of humanity and *for* no one in particular. I could talk to you for hours about all I experience from the first call to arms which stirs me to the poem to the final wave which returns me once more to the well-known coast, but I can assure you that in no moment of the trip have I ever touched the "isle of women" nor has my language undergone any genetic [*sic*] categorization.

J.K. Does the idea of anthologies of women's writing seem valid to you?

O.O. No, it doesn't. I refuse to participate. I do not want to be excluded from legitimate "Poetry" to enter the fallacy of "female poetry."

J.K. Do you think women in Argentina have the same opportunities to publish, to win prizes?

O.O. Yes, they have the same chances; this is not so in the field of jobs, the professions, and public offices.

J.K. Other figures or images that seem to fascinate you in your work are the Sphinx, the statue, the caryatid, Lot's wife—all semi-animate objects, mute but not mute at the same time. Can you comment on this process of "immobilization" in your poetry?

O.O. Yes, objects trouble me, as if they were waiting, witnessing me, ready to come to life. Why wouldn't they disturb me: statues, figurations of people, animals, or emissaries of the other world, whose purpose is unknown to me and who, in their immobility, appear to be awaiting an unknown signal to enter in this life, maybe only for a moment or for only one act. But I think your list isn't correct. The Sphinx does not disturb me because of her immobility but because of her secret knowledge and the sanction with which my ignorance is answered. Lot's wife, or the salt statue, is present more because of her looking backward than as a statue. The "blue statue" is another thing; it is like a tracing that a soul leaves in eternity and that it must reanimate; the soul left it at birth and will return upon its death.

J.K. And the image of the bowl? It frequently seems to be a balancing point in your poems; it is a humble object waiting to contain something.

O.O. As I said, whatever the object, no matter how graceless, can in a particular moment become charged with meaning and intention. On the other hand, I don't think that I often mention the bowl—no more than the cup, the vessel, or any other receptacle which might contain water, tears, memories or forgetfulness, or whatever—the bowl is smooth, smooth and in its own lack of expression it has something of a blind fatality [or destiny].

J.K. *What does "blind fatality" mean?*

O.O. *What happens is that at times I have dreamed about people who have faces without any features.*

J.K. *As if they were concave?*

O.O. *As if concave; so that they were also like bowls, do you see? Then, I don't know, there is no reference point on these things and it seems as if they might take one anywhere. A face like a bowl could bring you any kind of tremendous, fatal surprise, more than the most horrible faces.*

J.K. *It would be because of its lack of definition.*

O.O. *Exactly, because of its total lack of reference.*

J.K. Can you tell me a little about the relation you see between the fine arts and poetry? You have poems to Hieronymus Bosch, van Gogh, several references to the process of sculpting and terminology associated with this—"the quarry of meaning," for example.

O.O. All arts are complementary and function in an interchangeable way in relation to the different senses (music becomes color, word touch, etc.), but above all they retain deficiencies: literature cannot produce the simultaneity of painting, instead it provides me with a temporal succession which becomes the privileged quintessence in music. The quarry does not refer to sculpture but to a stone depository. For me stones have an interior life. Therefore as chipping away stone, "sculpting" produces a statue that was already present in the unformed material, so it is that chipping away words from language reveals a poem that already existed in the Verb, and chipping away this world reveals God, whom I cover over.

J.K. Another image or, better yet, an activity which recurs in your work is that of the witness ("Esbozos frente a un modelo" [Sketches in front of a model] "Al pie de la letra" [To the letter of the law]) which suggests a specific relation to reality (witnessing is different than contemplating, for example). How do you see this relation?

O.O. I don't think anything is indifferent. People and things are animated by affirmative and oppositional forces. There are allies and enemies which accompany some acts, some memories, and which bear witness for or against you. The beings and the objects that are indissolubly tied to your life will be your witnesses until the last day, until the final judgment.

J.K. In *Museo Salvaje* [Savage museum, 1974] the body is the main theme. Why this theme in that moment?

O.O. Throughout my life I've passed through times of extreme anguish, the motifs and themes—absorbing even disorder, alienating even danger and the imminence of the abyss—varied. But one of the most frequently recurring ones was the sudden strangeness of my own body, every part of my anatomy, and the impossibility of its containing me, representing me, expressing me. Yes the body, so close and so remote at the same time; so unknown and yet our only intermediary with the ineffable, the soul, with God. The body enables life and limits it at the same time; its dense form obstructs the possibility of extending oneself farther than sensorial reality. The body, to which I am attached and love, so that I cannot relinquish the body's resurrection (in spite of the fact that the weapon that will kill me grows in one of its parts).

Although all of this strangeness that I've spoken about is present in various moments in my different books, at the time when I wrote *Museo salvaje* I was going through a more objective stage which enabled me to submerge myself to the depth of my tissues, my viscera, my eyes, etc., and extract this handful of poems. Of course this almost entomological observation was interrupted every so often, altered by a progressive tension [which rose] to an almost intolerable point.

J.K. *This technique seems even more interesting to me after reading your latest book,* En el revés del cielo *[The other side of the sky] which has a lot to do with the body's limitations as well.*

O.O. *Yes, that's true, including the poem called "Catecismo animal" [Animal catechism], which is my resistance to leaving my body, my protest because the soul leaves the body—this poem is completely a petition for the body's* *resurrection. I also see this relation in many other moments of my work; although they are not centralized poems there are references to this estrangement or alienation produced by a contemplative look at the body in one poem or another in my different books. And above all it is present from the beginning of* La oscuridad es otro sol.

J.K. *Yes, I would say that it's a constant theme.*

O.O. *Yes, yes, because it's something that has always happened to me.*

J.K. *But there are books which take up this theme with more force, right?*

O.O. *Oh, well of course. I explained to you there [in the written text] exactly how when I obtained perhaps a little respite, the permanence of my anguish stimulated me to transfer it to that book that forms* Museo salvaje *which I later had to write in pieces because when I started a bit deeply in the subject, I immediately had a shift and once more I was submerged in anguish. Moreover and curiously, my body began to deteriorate. I wrote the poem about the eye, for example, and it produced something strange in me, I went to the oculist and I had pressure in an eye. I wrote the poem "Sangre" [Blood], and I had diabetes.*

J.K. *It was like a foreshadowing.*

O.O. *I wrote the poem to the skeleton—arthrosis, different things in succession. I decided to finish at once because there was this call of alarm through my body which was deteriorating. I don't know what it was before.*

J.K. You work on *Vuelta,* I've heard that you have ties with the University of Buenos Aires, do you have other jobs? Can anyone earn a living writing poetry?

O.O. I don't work on *Vuelta;* I am only on the editorial board. I don't have any ties with the university other than my literary studies. I don't have a job. In other times I worked as a newspaper reporter in the Abril publishing house and I was a technical secretary at Fabril Editors. No one can earn a living as a poet, except a very few privileged people whose talent, prestige, and luck supplies them with conferences and international prizes.

J.K. Where have you published? In which journals and why?

O.O. The list of magazines and newspapers in which I have published is long. I will mention some: *Sur* [see original Spanish version for the complete list].

Why? Because they asked me to collaborate, because I was in agreement with their general lines.

J.K. *And what would these general lines be?*

O.O. *Well, in an aesthetic sense, or that they weren't journals that were at some time . . . who knows?, franquist, let's say if one were publishing in Spain* or if I were not in agreement with the staff of contributors. For that reason I say general lines, without specifying.

J.K. Does it depend on the magazine or. . . ? Because it seems to me that you are calling attention to political rather than aesthetic traits.

O.O. It depends on everything . . . on the quality of the journal, although sometimes I have published in younger people's journals solely to help them— they don't pay you a cent, of course, and they don't even send you the magazine. But, I've collaborated with them sometimes when I saw that it was worthwhile helping them. But on the contrary, of course I've paid attention to the aesthetic quality of the journal itself.

J.K. A question a little off the theme but since I've been here in Buenos Aires I've noticed the influence of psychoanalytic theory here. Have you read much of this, does your work have anything to do with it? Where do you think this interest in psychoanalysis, in Lacan, comes from?

O.O. Yes, I've read quite a bit. It's not strange that people might want to look into their interior zones in order to better know themselves, but it's inadmissible for them to convert their inner life into a causal machine and try to fit their neighbor into a superficial, improvised cubicle. [. . .]

J.K. You are against its formulaic way of working.

O.O. I am against all stereotypes, naturally, and general classifications. I think each thing is very particular; that one can come to know oneself a little better but not try to catalog your neighbor and force him to fit under a certain heading. . . . So-and-So is compulsive for this reason and for this other he is anguished.

J.K. And do these psychoanalytic theories seem to you to be a valid approach to literature?

O.O. I don't know. I think that everything ends up in such a generalized formulation that it becomes almost conventional. I think the elements are good but without the classification.

J.K. The last thing that I'd like to know is if you think that during the years of the dictatorship, or as it's called here "el proceso" [the process/trial] . . . Why is it called "el proceso"?

O.O. I've never known; it gives the impression that they guessed it was going to end in a trial, no?

J.K. Yes. At first I thought people were talking about the end of the dictatorship as "el proceso" but now I understand that it's the whole period.

O.O. Yes, yes.

J.K. But do you think there was a change in poetic production, in the type of book published, fewer readers, things like that?

O.O. *During the "proceso"? No, one would suppose that there would be tons of books about exile, etc., etc., which is what was produced.*

J.K. *And this happened?*

O.O. *It continues to happen, no?*

J.K. *Yes, now but during the "proceso"?*

O.O. *Ah, no, during the "proceso" no one dared to speak of anything.*

J.K. *What I'd like to know then, according to what you know about this time, is if there were fewer books published here in Buenos Aires, perhaps for lack of interest, or lack of spirit, or the lack of other things, or something like this?*

O.O. *I think that many poets left. Many publishing houses closed; in the center of this is also the economic question which paralleled the thing and even culture began to be a little solitary.*

J.K. *Yes, because there are people who say, for example, that more poetry was written during the dictatorship, others say less was written.*

O.O. *I think the same amount was written. What changed in some respects were the themes for those who were far away and for those who were here.*

J.K. *And how would you characterize this change for those who were here?*

O.O. *Well, in those who were here one finds perhaps something more oppressive in those who did not have the courage to speak openly. I mean in the people who write social poetry. I don't know, I've never written it.*

J.K. *They say that in Chile, for example, the poet Enrique Lihn, upon finding that he could not speak openly, used the sonnet form (anachronic, restrained) to demonstrate the confines of his situation. Could one see something similar in Argentina?*

O.O. *No, I'm not aware of any of this. No, here the people were not moved to speak during the "proceso." What are we going to speak for? I don't know, later everyone talks, of course; moreover I understand very well why no one would speak because he who spoke disappeared. The ones that left reproached those that stayed for not having spoken. Speaking from outside is much easier than to speak when one is here. But everything is hard; it is not only hard to go, it is also hard to stay. But they also speak to you as if one had countenanced the emptying out of the country. It is not simple. One isn't twenty years old anymore either. They also accuse us of having {juggled/been suspicious} and of collaborating.*

J.K. *No, no, the whole thing seems very difficult to me. For example the other night they showed the film "La noche de los lápices" [The night of the pencils] on television, and it really impressed me.*

O.O. *Yes, yes, of course. But you know those who left, everyone believes that they were heroic, and they weren't heroic either. Then when they returned they thought they had to have extraordinary positions . . . well I don't know, not for one group nor for another; we've all suffered the same things. Moreover one didn't realize to a great degree what was going on. Don't think that it was visible, things didn't happen openly in the streets as many people say. The detentions weren't carried out in public. You found out one thing or another when they were very direct, when it happened to the child of a friend but the majority of things you didn't find out. Everything was seen afterward.*

Notes

Chapter 1. Defining the Subject

1. All translations are my own unless otherwise noted.

2. In her aforementioned book on modernism, Gwen Kirkpatrick offers an insightful and detailed account of Lugones's poetry and its relation to *modernismo*. Importantly, Kirkpatrick's reading demonstrates how Lugones's work formed a bridge (rather than a rupture) to the *vanguardia* while showing how his formal experimentation also textualized social changes of the twenties.

3. "Cosmopolitan" not in the sense of the early modernist's admiration of others' "Kulture" but, in this case, cosmopolitan in terms of the desire for a place in the world literary community.

4. The Yrigoyen government represented the liberal perspective; the governing "Partido Radical" was actually more reformist than radical. Historian Melcíades Peña argues that Yrigoyen achieved stability largely by maintaining the status quo, a theory which helps to explain the government's downfall in spite of its apparent successes (Peña 83).

5. Juan Carlos Ghiano describes the situation of Argentina in the forties as resulting from the failure to recover from the economic crisis of 1931, combined with an attack against democratic institutions symbolized by the Spanish Republican defeat — both conditions that affected all of South America. These economic and antidemocratic factors were increased in Argentina by the "consecuencias desastrosas en la vida económica y política de un país cuyos gobernantes tardaron en definir la política exterior sin aclarar la interna" [disastrous consequences in the economic and political life of a country whose governing agents delayed defining exterior policy without clarifying internal policy] (Ghiano 59).

6. Luis Soler Cañas (*La generación poética del 40*), like Benarós, shows the diversity of this generation, the variety of relations between texts and politics

evidenced in this decade, reminding us of the very artificial nature of the generational construct.

7. Easthope is elaborating the ideas of Louis Althusser who argues that poetry is a specific instance of an ideological practice defined by its relative autonomy. Althusser says that poetry participates in both base and superstructure, is both a material *and* an ideological process. Althusser's proposal helps to explain the dialectical relation between a general definition of poetry and a specific poetic practice.

8. It would be convenient if this correspondence worked as neatly as Jameson proposes but in Lacanian theory the Real is not simply the opposite of the Imaginary realm, and unlike most notions of history, it is unknowable, not in direct contact with the symbolic realm (Smith 20). This distinction does not, however, undo Jameson's relation of Marxism and psychoanalysis as "master texts."

9. Andreas Huyssen provides an excellent discussion of the shift in the relation between economy and culture that takes place in the transition from liberal capitalism to monopoly capitalism. According to Huyssen the commodification of culture, the existence of a mass culture valued almost exclusively in terms of exchange, is a sign of late monopoly capitalism.

10. In a 1987 roundtable discussion entitled "El psicoanálisis argentino: Un cuestionamiento," Silvia Bleichmar describes Argentina as saturated with psychoanalytic theory: "Tenemos la sensación de una hipertrofia mostruosa de esta actividad en la Argentina, que se ha convertido en el país con más pacientes y analistas del mundo, no sólo en términos relativos sino también absolutos" [We have the feeling of a monstrous hypertrophy of this activity in Argentina, which has been converted into the country with the most patients and analysts in the world, not only in relative but in absolute terms] (*Vuelta* 28). This entire article provides an insightful consideration of the psychoanalytic phenomena in Argentina.

11. But even Kristeva's work must be historicized—her (and my) attention to the feminine, to gender differences, is specific to this moment's concerns and our attention to the feminine can be construed as participation in the existing hierarchical system. Page duBois, in the introduction to *Sowing the Body*, responds to this problem by suggesting that "the issue of gender—this form of ideological, metaphysical difference—has assumed great importance for women, perhaps because it has reached the limits of its significance. . . . The penis as analogous to the commodity is being superseded" (duBois 15). Our attention to the issue is a sign of the challenge posed to the traditional process of gendering.

12. Kristeva is, of course, also linked to Bakhtin as an early translator of his work into French; in 1967 she published "Bakhtine, le mot le dialogue et le roman" (*Critique* 239), and in 1970, Kristeva wrote the Foreword to *La Poétique de Dostoïevski*.

13. In her introduction to *Feminism, Bakhtin and the Dialogic*, Dale M. Bauer suggests that Bakhtinian dialogism can be generalized as a description of women's speech in patriarchal society. She says, "If we use Bakhtin's definition of dialogism 'another's speech in another's language, serving to express authorial intention but in a refracted way' (*Dialogic Imagination* 324) we can see that feminine language could be described as a woman speaking a man's language, expressing her intentions, but in a refracted masculine-defined way" (16).

14. Although John King, in his recent book, *Sur*, informs us that poetry was not Ocampo's preferred genre, T. S. Eliot is still continually cited as an influence and presence in the magazine both as poet and as editor of *The Criterion*. In this context and others, Eliot is almost always mentioned as an influence or inspiration in the work of Alberto Girri, another prominent poet of Orozco's generation.

Chapter 2. From a Distance

1. This can be seen in the poet's direct references in which she regrets the solitude of her voice, a position possibly related to Orozco's interest in gnosticism—a nostalgia for a lost spiritual unity. Her intertextual references also express her desire to blend her literary voice with others.

2. This is not a characterization Eliot would approve of, having continually defined himself as antiromantic. He is antiromantic in many respects but inevitably has poetic moments that reflect his debt to romanticism. In his essay "Baudelaire" (*Selected Essays* 376), Eliot praises the French poet while he describes Baudelaire's contradictory position as "the offspring of romanticism, and by his nature the first counter-romantic in poetry." As George Bornstein observes, this may be read as an indirect reference to Eliot's own position. "Four Quartets," one of his later poems, provides one of the strongest examples of this shadow of romanticism.

3. "Olga Orozco," a poem that memorializes the still-living author, is surprisingly similar to an earlier poem by Argentine Alfonsina Storni, "Epitafio para mi tumba" [Epitaph for my tomb] (from her 1925 collection *Ocre*). One way to interpret this coincidence is in terms of these poets' shared anxiety of authorship, as Svetlana Boym explains in her book, *Death in Quotation Marks: Cultural Myths of the Modern Poet*. Boym proposes that "killing off" a poetic persona which incorporates societal expectations can be a freeing experience for female poets, permitting them to continue to write.

Chapter 3. The Limits of Poetic Discourse

1. This figure is from estimates given by a representative of "Las Madres de la Plaza de Mayo," obtained in an oral interview in November, 1988.

2. *En la masmédula*, the most radical of Girondo's experiments with language, includes a neologism in its title, a foreshadowing of many more to come. I will attempt to translate these by combining the suggested denotations; *En la masmédula*

would be "In the most or deepest marrow," perhaps, but of course this means of translating does not account for the sonorous play so essential to the original.

3. Delfina Muschetti, in an interview in Buenos Aires (October, 1988), noted two resurgences of interest in Girondo's poetry: one in the sixties, when more attention was paid to his earlier work with its more "democratic" traits, and now, in the eighties when his later, more avant-garde production is in synch with critical concerns.

4. Indicative of this perspective is the recent book by Jorge Schwartz, *Homenaje a Oliverio Girondo* (1987), which includes Girondo's more explicitly political articles, poems that other South Americans wrote to Girondo, situating him as a farsighted, nationalistic literary innovator.

5. It is also present, for example, in the poems "Canes más que finales" [Dogs more than ends], "Islas sólo de sangre" [Islands only of blood], "El pentotal a qué" [The "pentotal" towards what], and others. In her perceptive study of the Argentine vanguard, *Lenguaje e ideología,* Francine Masiello also observes the fragmentation and self-cancellation of speaking subjects in Girondo's poetry. Examining these speakers' relation to the city and foreign places, Masiello proposes that they in fact gain authority through their displacement, in their confrontation with the "other" (126).

6. Stella Maris Colombo's study, "Metáfora y cosmovisión en la poesía de Olga Orozco" presents a detailed description of the function of the metaphor in Orozco's poetry. Colombo also observes that Orozco's images are usually composed of "conjuntos metafóricos" (metaphoric groups) and she classifies the poet's figures according to different existential themes.

7. Sculpture and its associated terms recur consistently in Orozco's poetry. In *Mutaciones de la realidad,* for example, she uses terms like *cantera, lápidas, estatua, modelo, cariátide, bloques, moldear, esculpir* (quarry, stone tablets, statue, model, caryatid, blocks, to mold, to sculpt), often as metaphors for the creative process. I am proposing that the way the metaphor functions in "Esbozos" is an extension of its role in other situations in Orozco's work.

8. Jaqueline Rose, speaking of the semiotic and the chora in *Sexuality in the Field of Vision,* explains the origin of the term "which Kristeva calls 'chora' or receptacle after Plato's cosmology (*The Timaeus*), where it stands for the mediating instance in which the copies of the eternal model receive their shape" (Rose 153).

9. Muriel Ruckeyer's poem "Myth" recalls the Sphinx's question and contemporary responses to Oedipus's query about where he went wrong. Orozco does not repeat Oedipus's error but differentiates herself from the unspoken term "man."

10. In a later poem, "Al pie de la letra" [To the letter of the law], she is alternately judge, witness, and criminal in a trial, reminding us of Kristeva's "sujet en procès." Paul Smith points out the legal resonances of this term, which is meant

to evoke the liberties and the limitations of the relation between the symbolic and the semiotic. Speaking of Kristeva, Smith says, "She claims that in the 'subject' there is always a 'heterogeneous contradiction between two irreconcilable things' (*La Révolution du langage poétique* 80) which will allow her to talk about a 'sujet en procès': the subject not only in process, but also as it were on trial, put to the test as to its ability to negotiate this contradictory term" (121).

Chapter 4. The Struggle of Imagination

1. In the recent collection published by Centro Editores (*Extracción de la piedra de locura y otros poemas*, 1988), the poems from *Arbol de Diana* are numbered; this is a change from the original edition, a change that I will follow, not only to facilitate references but because this ordering allows us to observe the numbered progression of silence in this collection.

2. This strategy is very similar to the "doubleness" that Alicia Ostriker observes in her study of North American women's poetry. In her chapter entitled "I'm Nobody: Women's Poetry, 1650–1960," taken from the Emily Dickinson poem of the same name, she observes that although duplicity is a strategy employed by both male and female poets, it dominates the poetry of the nineteenth- and early twentieth-century women writers she studies. It is a strategy that serves them well, she argues, as one device "which makes possible the secret transmission of opposed messages within a single poem" (43). Pizarnik, as we will see, uses it in much the same way: to both assert her presence and retract it.

3. Pizarnik mentions this connection to surrealism in her interview with Marta Moia, as do Francisco Lasarte in "Más allá del surrealismo: la poesía de Alejandra Pizarnik," and Alfredo Roggiano in "Alejandra Pizarnik: persona y poesía" (noteworthy especially for his contextualization of Pizarnik's work).

4. Coincidentally, *Los juegos peligrosos* was published in 1962—the same year as Pizarnik's *Arbol de Diana*, from which I chose the previous example of a double subject.

5. Again there is an interesting coincidence with history in this gesture. *En el revés del cielo* was published in 1987, making it the first entirely postseventies dictatorship collection of Orozco's; in this period silence takes on different symbolic import as speaking, remembering, recording, and judging the crimes committed during the "Dirty War" become a primary concern of the Argentine people. Speaking in defiance of an imposed silence can be read in this case, then, as not only a theoretical concern but as a proposal having a direct link to social and historical anxieties.

6. See Moia interview (*Deseo* 251).

7. The poem, "Tiempo," which Pizarnik dedicates to Orozco, speaks of the shared nostalgia for and import given to childhood by these two poets.

8. In *The Madwoman in the Attic*, these authors argue that "the 'anxiety of influence' that a male poet experiences is felt by a female poet as an even more

primary 'anxiety of authorship'—a radical fear that she cannot create, that because she can never become a 'precursor' the act of writing will isolate or destroy her. . . . Her battle . . . is not against her (male) precursor's reading of the world but against his reading of *her*. In order to define herself as an author she must redefine the terms of her socialization" (48–49).

9. As do Orozco's critics, particularly Cristina Piña in her "Estudio preliminar" to *Páginas de Olga Orozco* and Elba Torres de Peralta, as evidenced in the subtitle to her book, *La poética de Olga Orozco: Desdoblamiento de Dios en máscara de todos*.

10. The most prominent members of the group, according to Katra, are Jitrik, Prieto, Sebreli, and Viñas (17). Katra provides an excellent overview of the social and political situation which formed this group: the lack of a leftist tradition in Argentina, a brief history of the Communist party in twentieth-century Argentina. Katra argues that what appeared to be differences earlier, i.e., earlier leftist literature which was not truly proletariat but "proletarianized," in the 1950s after Perón really become *different* (95).

11. We see a clear example of his philosophy in his poem, "Arte poética," from the 1979 collection, *Hechos* [Deeds]. The poem begins: "como un martillo la realidad / bate [/] las telitas del alma o corazón..." (98) [like a hammer reality / hits / the soul or heart's membrane].

12. In "Las mujeres que escriben: aquel reino anhelado, el reino del amor," Delfina Muschetti explores the circumscribed themes considered "appropriate" for early twentieth-century female poets in Argentina (1916–30). Muschetti's work provides pertinent evidence of the ideological constraints and the tradition of female silence through a valuable exploration of the popular media's construction of women's "proper realm." Orozco, one of the few female forties poets, writes in the generation following Alfonsina Storni's pioneering rupture of thematic spaces socially designated as "feminine."

Chapter 5. Succeeding Silence

1. I am grateful to David Lagmanovich's paper read at the 1991 MLA for bringing the work of Lukin and Aráoz to my attention.

2. Suzanne Chavez-Silverman's dissertation, "The Ex-centric Self: The Poetry of Alejandra Pizarnik," provides an excellent and much needed discussion of the limitations of reading Pizarnik's work in terms of her life or death; see particularly her last chapter, "Silence, Madness, and Death: Three Central Obsessions" (176–231).

3. Piña, like Orozco, also situates her work in terms of other authors and artists; in this volume she dedicates poems to or uses epigraphs from Dylan Thomas, Djuna Barnes, François Truffaut, San Juan de la Cruz, Gustave Mahler, and Roberto Juarroz, as well as Orozco and Pizarnik.

4. In her recent article, "La poesía de las argentinas frente al patriarcado" [The

poetry of Argentine women confronted with the patriarchy], Gwen Kirkpatrick contrasts Argentine and North American poetries: "no se ve en la poesía de las mujeres argentinas esa insistencia sobre el cuerpo femenino que se da, por ejemplo, en la poesía norteamericana, donde se destaca ese tema por encima de cualquier otro" [in Argentine women's poetry one doesn't see this insistence on the female body which is found, for example, in North American poetry, where this theme stands out more than any other] (131). The difference is one of degree, for the body regularly appears as a theme in Argentina; Kirkpatrick is correct when she asserts (earlier in this article) that the language theme is more prominent; however, the frequent association between the body and language has suggestive implications I will take up later.

5. I employ this term thinking of Adrienne Rich's important essay, "When We Dead Awaken: Writing as Re-Vision." Rich explains that "Re-vision—the act of looking back, of seeing with fresh eyes, of entering an old text from a new critical direction—" is crucial for "until we can understand the assumptions in which we are drenched we cannot know ourselves" (35). Whether or not Piña is familiar with Rich's writings, what she proposes in *Para que el ojo cante* is a process of re-visioning.

6. The intervening volume, *Malasartes,* was published in 1981 and more closely resembles *Abracadabra* (stylistically and thematically) than *Descomposición,* which will follow. However, *Malasartes* does include some poems (such as "Procedimiento" 42) that anticipate the next book focusing on the body and suggesting unseen violence.

7. In 1987, the first year an openly lesbian contingent marched in the International Women's Day parade, gay women in Buenos Aires still expressed fear about the periodic raids on bars (evidenced in interviews with women at Lugar de la Mujer in 1988).

Chapter 6. The Author as Subject

1. Anthony Easthope demonstrates the connections between Althusser's explanation of ideology and Lacan's utilization of the mirror stage to explain how identity is "produced in a structure of alienation," linking the two through the idea of "misrecognition" (40). Looking in the mirror, the child can only be present to him- or herself through a reflection. In a similar fashion, subjects in society always misrecognize themselves, taking their ideological "reflections" as themselves. As we will see, Therborn argues that we misrecognize ourselves in multiple ideological "reflections" in our various societies.

2. This is not true *only* in the specific context of a dictatorial regime but, as Bakhtin reminds us, in all texts for the word is always "permeated with the interpretations of others"; it can never be completely separated from its context (*Problems of Dostoevsky's Poetics* 202).

3. Alicia Ostriker observes many of these same traits in modern North Ameri-

can women's poetry and reads them as indications that "women writers have been imprisoned in an 'oppressor's language' which denies them access to authoritative expression" (11). Ostriker notes that many of the writers she examines revise myths and make formal decisions that are meant to "disrupt and alter our sense of literary norms" (11–12).

Conclusion

1. In his article entitled "La poesía argentina antes y después de 1950," Raúl Aguirre points out that in an anthology of *justicialista* poetry published in the midfifties the sonnet form predominates. At first glance it seems surprising that the poetry of a populist movement such as Peronism should revive classical forms, but not when we take into account the fact that poetry was not *peronismo's* preferred genre. In the case of this anthology, it appears to be the aesthetic space relegated to an older elite and is notable for its lack of influence on the movement. In contrast to this poetry, Aguirre qualifies Orozco as one of a number of poets who "denotaban actitudes disidentes con la poética del endecasílabo" [demonstrated dissident attitudes with the poetics of the hendecasyllabic verse] (59).

2. A term I use to distinguish writers of the "mainstream" vanguard from those of another, more local, vanguard tradition (exemplified by writers such as Raúl Gonzalez Tuñón in Argentina).

Bibliography

Adorno, Theodor. "Lyric Poetry and Society." *Telos* 20 (1974): 56–71.

Agustini, Delmira. *Poesías completas* [Complete poetry]. Buenos Aires: Editorial Losada, S.S., 1944.

Alonso, Fernando P., Sergio D. Povenzano, and Hector René La Fleur. *Las revistas literarias argentinas 1893–1967* [Argentine literary journals 1893–1967]. Buenos Aires: Centro Editores, 1962.

Althusser, Louis. "Ideology and Ideological State Apparatuses." *Lenin and Philosophy and Other Essays.* New York: Monthly Review, 1971: 127–86.

———. *Positions.* Paris: Editions Sociales, 1976.

Amar Sánchez, Ana María. *El relato de los hechos: Rodolfo Walsh, testimonio y escritura* [Telling the facts: Rodolfo Walsh, testimony and writing]. Buenos Aires: Beatriz Viterbo Editora, 1992.

Aráoz, Inés. *Ciudades* [Cities]. Tucumán: Ediciones de la Hoja, 1981.

———. *La ecuación y la gracia* [The equation and the grace]. Buenos Aires: Ediciones de la Hoja, 1971.

———. *Los intersticiales* [The intersticies]. Buenos Aires: El Imaginero, 1986.

Azubel, Alicia, et al. "El psicoanálisis argentino: un cuestionamiento" [Argentine psychoanalysis: an examination]. *Vuelta Sudamericana* 16 (1987): 25–40.

Bakhtin, M. M. *The Dialogic Imagination.* Trans. Caryl Emerson and Michael Holquist. Austin: University of Texas Press, 1981.

Bassnet, Susan, ed. *Knives and Angels: Women Writers in Latin America.* London: Zed Books, 1990.

Bauer, Dale M., and Susan Jaret McKinstry, eds. *Feminism, Bakhtin and the Dialogic.* New York: SUNY Press, 1991.

Becco, Horacio J., Carlos R. Giordano, and Eduardo Romano. *El 40* [The 40s]. Buenos Aires: Colección Biblioteca, Editores Dos, 1969.

Bellessi, Diana. *Danzante de doble máscara* [Double-masked dancer]. Buenos Aires: Ediciones Ultimo Reino, 1985.

———. *Destino y propagaciones* [Destiny and propagations]. Guayaquil: Casa de la Cultura de Guayaquil, 1972.

———. *El jardín* [The garden]. Buenos Aires: Bajo la Luna Nueva, 1992.

———. *Eroíca*. Buenos Aires: Ediciones Ultimo Reino, 1988.

———. "La diferencia viva: El poema eres tú" [The lively difference: you are the poem]. *Nuevo texto crítico* 4 (otoño 1989): 7–9.

———. "Mes de la Historia y el Orgullo Gay y Lesbiano" [Lesbian and gay pride and history month]. *Feminaria* 3, no. 6 (1990): 38.

Benarós, León. "La generación de 1940" [The generation of 1940]. *El 40* 1 (1951).

Benedetti, Mario. *Los poetas comunicantes* [The communicating poets]. Montevideo: Biblioteca de Marcha, 1981.

Beneyto, Antonio. "Alejandra Pizarnik: Ocultándose en el lenguaje" [Alejandra Pizarnik: hiding oneself in language]. *Quimera* 34 (1983): 23–27.

Blanchot, Maurice. "The Igitur Experience." Ed. Harold Bloom. *Stéphane Mallarmé*. New York: Chelsea House Publishers, 1987: 5–15.

Bonzini, Silvia, and Laura Klein. "Un no de claridad" [A clear no]. *Punto de Vista* (1984): 32–38.

Bornstein, George. *Transformations of Romanticism in Yeats, Eliot and Stevens*. Chicago: University of Chicago Press, 1976.

Boym, Svetlana. *Death in Quotation Marks: Cultural Myths of the Modern Poet*. Boston: Harvard University Press, 1991.

Bürger, Peter. *Theory of the Avant-Garde*. Minneapolis: University of Minnesota Press, 1984.

Campanella, Hebe. "La voz de la mujer en la joven poesía argentina: cuatro registros" [Women's voice in younger Argentine poetry: four registers]. *Cuadernos Hispanoamericanos* (June, 1975): 543–64.

Campbell, Joseph. *The Hero with a Thousand Faces*. Princeton, N.J.: Princeton University Press, 1968.

Chávez-Silverman, Suzanne. "The Ex-centric Self: The Poetry of Alejandra Pizarnik." Diss. U. of Cal.-Davis, 1990.

Cobo-Borda, J. G. "Olga Orozco." *Poesía* (January-March 1985): 35–37.

Collazos, Oscar, ed. *Los vanguardismos en América Latina* [The vanguards in Latin America]. Barcelona: Península, 1977.

Colombo, Stella Maris. *Metáfora y cosmovisión en la poesía de Olga Orozco* [Metaphor and cosmovision in the poetry of Olga Orozco]. Rosario, Argentina: Cuadernos Aletheia, Grupo de Estudios Semánticos, 1985.

Córdova Iturburu, Cayatano. *La revolución martinfierrista* [The martinfierrist revolution]. Buenos Aires: Dirección General de Cultura, 1962.

Corro, Gaspar Pío del. *Oliverio Girondo: los límites del signo* [Oliverio Girondo: the limits of the sign]. Buenos Aires: Fernando García Cambeiro, 1976.

Cortázar, Julio. *Argentina, años de alambradas culturales* [Argentina, years of cultural fencing]. Buenos Aires: Muchnik Editores, 1984.

Coward, Rosalind, and John Ellis. *Language and Materialism*. London: Routledge and Kegan Paul, 1977.

Culler, Jonathan. "Presuppositions and Intertextuality." *MLN* 91, no.6 (December, 1976): 1380–96.

———. *The Pursuit of Signs: Semiotics, Literature, Deconstruction*. Ithaca, N.Y.: Cornell University Press, 1981.

David-Menard, Monique. "Lacanians Against Lacan." *Social Text* 6 (1982): 88–111.

deMan, Paul. *Allegories of Reading*. New Haven, Conn.: Yale University Press, 1979.

de Nobile, Beatriz. *El acto experimental* [The experimental act]. Buenos Aires: Editorial Losada, 1972.

de Torre, Guillermo. *Historia de las literaturas de vanguardia* [History of the vanguard literatures]. Madrid: Ediciones Guadarrama, 1965.

des Pres, Terrence. *Praises and Dispraises: Poetry and Politics in the Twentieth Century*. New York: Viking, 1988.

du Bois, Page. *Sowing the Body: Psychoanalysis and Ancient Representations of Women*. Chicago: University of Chicago Press, 1988.

Easthope, Anthony. *Poetry as Discourse*. London and New York: Methuen, 1983.

Eliot, T. S. *Collected Poems 1909–1962*. New York: Harcourt, Brace and World, Inc., 1963.

———. *Selected Essays*. New York: Harcourt, Brace and World, 1964.

———. "The Social Function of Poetry." *Poetry and Politics*. Ed. Richard Jones. New York: William Morrow and Co., Inc., 1985: 17–28.

Fish, Stanley. "How to Do Things with Austin and Searle: Speech Act Theory and Literary Criticism." *MLN* 91 (1976): 983–1025.

Foucault, Michel. *Discipline and Punish: The Birth of the Prison*. Trans. Alan Sheridan. New York: Vintage Books, 1977.

Fuss, Diana. *Essentially Speaking: Feminism, Nature and Difference*. London: Routledge, Chapman and Hall, 1989.

Ghiano, Juan Carlos. *Poesía argentina del siglo veinte* [Twentieth-century Argentine poetry]. México–Buenos Aires: Fondo de Cultura Económica, 1957.

Gil-Montero, Martha, and María Gowland de Gallo. "Beyond the Metaphors of Life." *Américas* 42, no. 5 (1990): 43–46.

Gilbert, Sandra, and Susan Gubar. *The Madwoman in the Attic: The Woman Writer and the Nineteenth-Century Imagination.* New Haven, Conn.: Yale University Press, 1979.

Girondo, Oliverio. *Oliverio Girondo: Espantapájaros y otros poemas* [Oliverio Girondo: Scarecrow and other poems]. Buenos Aires: Centro Editores, 1987.

Gomez de la Serna, Ramón. *Retratos contemporáneos* [Contemporary portraits]. Buenos Aires: Sudamericana, 1941.

Gomez Paz, Julieta. *Cuatro actitudes poéticas* [Four poetic attitudes]. Buenos Aires: Conjunta Editores, 1977.

———. *Dos textos sobre la poesía de Olga Orozco* [Two texts about Olga Orozco's poetry]. Buenos Aires: Tekhné, 1980.

Gray, Nancy. *Language Unbound: On Experimental Writing by Women.* Urbana: University of Illinois Press, 1992.

Graziano, Frank. *Divine Violence: Spectacle, Psychosexuality, and Radical Christianity in the Argentine "Dirty War."* Boulder, Col.: Westview Press, 1992.

Harlow, Barbara. *Resistance Literature.* New York and London: Methuen, 1987.

Herrera, Ricardo. "La poesía de los límites y los límites de la poesía" [The poetry of limits and the limits of poetry]. *Usos de la imaginación.* J. G. Cobo Borda, R. Herrera, and M. J. de Ruschi Crespo, eds. Buenos Aires: El Imaginario, 1984, 95–106.

Hodges, Donald. *Argentina 1943–76.* Albuquerque: University of New Mexico Press, 1976.

Hollander, John. *Melodious Guile: Fictive Pattern in Poetic Language.* New Haven, Conn.: Yale University Press, 1988.

Huyssen, Andreas. *After the Great Divide: Modernism, Mass Culture, Postmodernism.* Bloomington: Indiana University Press, 1986.

Jameson, Fredric. "Imaginary and Symbolic in Lacan: Marxism, Psychoanalytic Criticism, and the Problem of the Subject." *Literature and Psychoanalysis, the Question of Reading: Otherwise.* Shoshana Felman, ed. Baltimore, Md.: Johns Hopkins University Press, 1982: 338–95.

Jitrik, Noe. *Ensayos y estudios de literatura argentina* [Essays and studies of Argentine literature]. Buenos Aires: Editorial Galerna, 1970.

———. *Escritores argentinos: dependencia o libertad* [Argentine writers: dependency or freedom]. Buenos Aires: Ediciones del Candil, 1967.

Kamenszain, Tamara. *El texto silencioso: tradición y vanguardia en la poesía sudamericana* [The silent text: tradition and vanguard in South American poetry]. México: Universidad Nacional Autónoma de México, 1983.

———. *La casa grande* [The big house]. Buenos Aires: Sudamericana, 1986.

———. *Los no* [The no]. Buenos Aires: Sudamericana, 1977.

———. *Vida de living* [Life of living]. Buenos Aires: Sudamericana, 1991.

Katra, William H. "The Argentine Generation of 1955: Politics, the Essay and Literary Criticism." Diss. University of Mich., 1977.

King, John. *Sur: A Study of the Argentine Literary Journal and Its Role in the Development of a Culture, 1931–70*. Cambridge: Cambridge University Press, 1986.

Kirkpatrick, Gwen. "La poesía de las argentinas frente al patriarcado" [The poetry of Argentine women confronted with patriarchy]. *Nuevo texto crítico* 4 (1991): 129–35.

———. *The Dissonant Legacy of Modernismo: Lugones, Herrera y Reissig, and the Voices of Modern Spanish American Poetry*. Berkeley: University of California Press, 1989.

Kristeva, Julia. *Revolution in Poetic Language*. Trans. Margaret Waller. New York: Columbia University Press, 1984.

———. *The Kristeva Reader*. Ed. Toril Moi. New York: Columbia University Press, 1986.

Lagmanovitch, David. "La poesía de Alejandra Pizarnik" [Alejandra Pizarnik's poetry]. *Literatura Hispanoamericana 2*. Proc. of *El Congreso del Instituto Internacional de Literatura Iberoamericana*. Ediciones Cultura Hispánica del Centro Iberoamericana de Cooperación, 1978: 885–97.

Lange, Norah. *Estimados congeneres* [Esteemed members]. Buenos Aires: Editorial Losada, 1968.

Lasarte, Francisco. "Más allá del surrealismo: La poesía de Alejandra Pizarnik" [Beyond surrealism: Alejandra Pizarnik's poetry]. *Revista Iberoamericana* 125 (1983): 868–78.

Lindstrom, Naomi. "Olga Orozco: La voz poética que llama entre mundos" [Olga Orozco: the poetic voice that calls between worlds]. *Revista Iberoamericana* 132–33 (1985): 765–76.

Liscano, Juan. *Descripciones* [Descriptions]. Buenos Aires: Ediciones de la Flor S.R.L., 1983.

———. Introduction. "Olga Orozco y su trascendente juego poético" [Olga Orozco and her transcendent poetic game]. *Veintinueve poema*. by Orozco. Caracas, Venezuela: Monte Avila Editores, 1975: 9–35.

Lojo, María Rosa. Introduction. "Olga Orozco: la poesía como viaje heroico" [Olga Orozco: poetry as heroic journey]. *Olga Orozco* by Orozco. Buenos Aires: Centro Editores, 1989: 2–6.

———. "La poesía de Olga Orozco: música de la memoria" [Olga Orozco's poetry: memory's music]. *Cultura de la Argentina contemporanea* (Spring 1988): 38.

Lopez de Espinosa, Susana B. "Retórica de la máscara y el rostro en la poesía de Olga Orozco" [The rhetoric of mask and face in Olga Orozco's poetry]. *Estudios de Literatura Argentina* 8 (1987): 37–45.

Lotman, Yuri. *Analysis of the Poetic Text*. Ann Arbor, Mich.: Ardis, 1976.

——. *La structure du texte artistique* [The structure of the artistic text]. Trans. Anne Fournier. Paris: Gallimard, 1973.

Loubet, Jorgelina. "Tres miradas en trascendencia" [Three transcending gazes]. *BAAL* 51 (1986): 343–58.

Ludmer, Josefina. *El género gauchesco: Un tratado sobre la patria* [The gaucho genre: a treatise on the country]. Buenos Aires: Sudamericana, 1988.

Lukin, Liliana. *Abracadabra*. Buenos Aires: Editorial Plus Ultra, 1978.

——. *Cortar por lo sano* [Cut to the quick]. Buenos Aires: Ediciones Culturales Argentinas, 1987.

——. *Descomposición* [Decomposition]. Buenos Aires: Ediciones de la Flor, 1986.

Mangieri, José Luis, ed. *Antología Ultimo Reino* [Anthology of *Ultimo Reino*]. Buenos Aires: Libros de Tierra Firme, 1987.

Masiello, Francine. *Between Civilization and Barbarism: Women, Nation, and Literary Culture in Modern Argentina*. Lincoln: University of Nebraska Press, 1992.

——. *Lenguaje e ideología: Las escuelas argentinas de vanguardia* [Language and ideology: schools of the Argentine vanguard]. Buenos Aires: Librería Hachette S.A., 1986.

Medina, Enrique. "Oliverio Girondo en la médula del lenguaje" [Oliverio Girondo in the marrow of language]. *Xul: revista de poesía* (mayo, 1984): 16–24.

Milosz, Czeslaw. *The Witness of Poetry*. Cambridge, Mass.: Harvard University Press, 1983.

Molina, Enrique. Prologue. *Obras Completas, 1891–1967* [Complete works, 1891–1967], by Oliverio Girondo. Buenos Aires: Editorial Losada, 1968.

Muschietti, Delfina. "La fractura ideológica en los primeros textos de Oliverio Girondo" [The ideological fracture in the early texts of Oliverio Girondo]. *Filología* 20.1 (1985): 153–69.

——. "Las mujeres que escriben: Aquel reino anhelado, el reino del amor" [Women who write: that desired realm, the realm of love]. *Nuevo texto crítico* 4 (1989): 79–102.

Orozco, Olga. *Con esta boca en este mundo* [With this mouth in this world]. Buenos Aires: Sudamericana, 1994.

——. "Diálogo con Luis Martínez Cuitiño" [Dialogue with Luis Martínez Cuitiño]. *La tabla redonda* 1 (December, 1983): 29–30.

——. *En el revés del cielo* [The other side of the sky]. Buenos Aires: Editorial Sudamericana, 1987.

——. "*En la masmédula* por Oliverio Girondo" [Oliverio Girondo's *En la masmédula*]. *Macedonio* 1, no. 3 (1969): 69–73.

——. "Entrevista" [Interview]. *Clarín,* sección Cultura y Nación (20 noviembre, 1980).

——. *La noche a la deriva* [Night adrift]. México: Fondo de Cultura Económica, 1983.

——. *Mutaciones de la realidad* [Reality's mutations]. Buenos Aires: Editorial Sudamericana, 1979.

——. *Obra poética* [Poetic works]. Buenos Aires: Ediciones Corregidor, 1985.

——. *Páginas de Olga Orozco seleccionadas por la autora* [Pages from Olga Orozco, selected by the author]. Buenos Aires: Editorial Celtia, 1984.

——. *Poesía antología* [Poetic anthology]. Buenos Aires: Capítulo, Biblioteca Argentina Fundamental, 1982.

——. "Poesía y verdad" [Poetry and truth]. *Clarín* 11, no. 120 (1967): 42–43.

Ostriker, Alicia S. *Stealing the Language: The Emergence of Women's Poetry in America.* Boston: Beacon Press, 1986.

Pasini, Delia. *Un decir que se repite entre mujeres* [A saying repeated among women]. Buenos Aires: Editorial Calidon, 1979.

Paulson, William R. *The Noise of Culture: Literary Texts in a World of Information.* Ithaca: Cornell University Press, 1988.

Pellarolo, Silvia. "La imagen de la estatua de sal: síntesis y clave de Olga Orozco" [The image of the statue of salt: synthesis and key to Olga Orozco]. *Mester* 1 (Spring, 1989): 41–49.

Pellegrini, Aldo. *Oliverio Girondo.* Buenos Aires: Ediciones Culturales Argentinas, 1964.

Peña, Melcíades. *Masas, caudillos y élites* [Masses, leaders and elites]. Buenos Aires: Ediciones Fichas, 1973.

Perloff, Marjorie. *Radical Artifice: Writing Poetry in the Age of Media.* Chicago: University of Chicago Press, 1991.

Pezzoni, Enrique. *El texto y sus voces* [The text and its voices]. Buenos Aires: Sudamericana, 1986.

Piglia, Ricardo. *Respiración Artificial* [Artificial respiration]. Buenos Aires: Sudamericana, 1988.

Piña, Cristina. "'Carina,' de Olga Orozco: Un análisis estilístico" [Olga Orozco's "Carina": a stylistic analysis]. *Explicación de textos literarios* 12, no. 2 (1983–84): 59–78.

——. *Extracción de la piedra de locura y otros poemas* [Extraction from the stone of madness and other poems]. Buenos Aires: Centro Editor, 1988.

——. *Oficio de máscaras* [Employment of masks]. Buenos Aires: Botella al Mar, 1978.

——. *Para que el ojo cante* [So that the eye might sing]. Buenos Aires: Torres Agüero Editor, 1983.

————. Prologue. *Extracción,* by Pizarnik: 2–6.

————. Prologue. *Páginas de Olga Orozco,* by Orozco. Buenos Aires: Celtia, 1984.

————. *Puesta en escena* [Performed]. Buenos Aires: GEL, 1993.

Pizarnik, Alejandra. *El deseo de la palabra* [The word's desire/desire of the word]. Spain: OCNOS, Barral, 1975.

————. *Extracción de la piedra de locura.* Buenos Aires: Editorial sudamericana, 1968.

————. "Olga Orozco o la poesía como juego peligroso" [Olga Orozco or poetry as a dangerous game]. *Zona Franca* 7–8 (1964).

————. *Poemas.* Buenos Aires: Centro Editor de América Latina, 1987.

Poblete-Araya, Kira Inés. "Trayectoria del surrealismo en las revistas literarias argentinas" [Surrealism's trajectory in Argentine literary magazines]. Diss. University of Texas, Austin, 1983.

Ponce, Liliana. *Composición: poesía 1976–1979* [Composition: poetry 1976–1979]. Buenos Aires: Ediciones Ultimo Reino, 1984.

Prieto, Adolfo. *El discurso criollista en la formación de la argentina moderna* [Creole discourse in the formation of modern Argentina]. Buenos Aires: Sudamericana, 1988.

Rabell, Carmen R. "El gato como sujeto-objeto poético en *Cantos a Berenice* de Olga Orozco, y 'Oda al gato,' de Neruda" [The cat as poetic subject-object in Olga Orozco's "Songs to Berenice," and "Ode to the cat" by Neruda]. *Extremos* 2 (1986): 119–27.

Rebok, Maria Gabriela. "Finitud, creación poética y sacralidad en la obra de Olga Orozco" [Finality, poetic creation and sacredness in Olga Orozco's work]. *Revista de la Sociedad Argentina de Filosofía* 5, no. 3 (1985).

Reibetanz, Julia Maniates. *A Reading of Eliot's Four Quartets.* Ann Arbor, Mich.: U.M.I. Research Press, 1983.

Rich, Adrienne. "When We Dead Awaken: Writing as Revision." *On Lies, Secrets, and Silence: Selected Prose 1966–1978.* New York: W.W. Norton and Co., 1979: 33–49.

Richard, Nelly. *La estratificación de los márgenes* [The stratification of the margins]. Santiago: Zegers Editor S.A., 1989.

Roggiano, Alfredo A. "Alejandra Pizarnik: persona y poesía" [Alejandra Pizarnik: person and poetry]. *Letras de Buenos Aires* 1, no. 2 (1981): 49–58.

Romano, Eduardo. "Qué es eso de una generación del 40" [What is this about a 40s generation]. *Cuadernos de poesía* 1, no. 1 (1966): 50–56.

Rose, Jaqueline. *Sexuality in the Field of Vision.* London: Verso, 1986.

Rossler, Oswaldo. *Cantores y trágicos de Buenos Aires* [Buenos Aires' singers and tragic cases]. Buenos Aires: Ediciones Tres Tiempos, 1981.

Royer, Jean. "De l'entretien" [On the interview]. *Etudes françaises* 22, no. 3 (1987): 117–23.

Running, Thorpe. *Borges' Ultraist Movement and Its Poets.* Michigan: International Book Publishers, 1981.

———. "Imagen y creación en la poesía de Olga Orozco" [Image and creation in Olga Orozco's work]. *Letras Femeninas* 13, no. 1–2 (1987): 12–20.

Russell, Charles. *Poets, Prophets, and Revolutionaries: The Literary Avant-garde from Rimbaud through Postmodernism.* New York: Oxford University Press, 1985.

Salvador, Nélida. "Actitud creadora de la mujer en la poesía argentina" [Women's creative attitude in Argentine poetry]. *Letras de Buenos Aires* 2, no. 8 (1983): 25–32.

Sarlo, Beatriz. *Una modernidad periférica: Buenos Aires 1920 y 1930* [A peripheral modernity: Buenos Aires 1920 and 1930]. Buenos Aires: Ediciones Nueva Visión, 1988.

Schwartz, Jorge. *Homenaje a Oliverio Girondo* [Homage to Oliverio Girondo]. Buenos Aires: Corregidor, 1987.

Scrimaglio, Marta. *Oliverio Girondo.* Santa Fe: Cuadernos del Instituto de Letras, Facultad de Filosofía y Letras, Universidad Nacional del Litoral, 1964.

Serra, Edelweis. "Exploración de la realidad y estrategia textual en la poesía de Olga Orozco" [Exploration of reality and textual strategy in Olga Orozco's poetry]. *Anales de Literatura Hispanoamericana* 14 (1985): 93–101.

Shumway, Nicolas. *The Invention of Argentina.* Berkeley: University of California Press, 1991.

Sirimarco, María Cristina, and Héctor Roque-Pitt. "Primera antología española de Olga Orozco" [First Spanish anthology of Olga Orozco]. *Cuadernos Hispanoamericanos* 445 (julio 1987): 65–70.

Smith, Paul. *Discerning the Subject.* Minneapolis: University of Minnesota Press, 1988.

Sola, Graciela de. *Proyecciones del surrealismo en la literatura argentina* [Surrealism's projections in Argentine literature]. Buenos Aires: Ediciones Culturales Argentinas, 1967.

Sontag, Susan. "Approaching Artaud." *Under the Sign of Saturn.* New York: Farrar, Strauss and Giroux, 1980: 13–70.

Storni, Alfonsina. *Antología poética* [Poetic anthology]. Buenos Aires: Editorial Losada S.A., 1988.

Sucre, Guillermo. *La máscara, la transparencia* [The mask, the transparency]. Caracas, Venezuela: Monte Avila Editores, 1975.

———. "Olga Orozco: Los juegos peligrosos" [Olga Orozco: the dangerous games]. *Revista Nacional de Cultura* 158–59 (1963): 174–76.

Tacconi, María del Carmen. "Para una lectura simbólica de Olga Orozco" [Toward a symbolic reading of Olga Orozco]. *Sur* 348 (1981): 115–23.

Therborn, Goran. *The Ideology of Power and the Power of Ideology.* London: Verso, 1980.

Todorov, Tzvetan. *Mikhail Bakhtin: The Dialogical Principle.* Trans. Walad Godzich. Minneapolis: University of Minnesota Press, 1984.

Torres de Peralta, Elba. "Algunas consideraciones sobre la poética de Olga

Orozco" [Some considerations of Olga Orozco's poetics]. *Rio de la Plata: Culturas* 7 (1988): 31–40.

——. *La poética de Olga Orozco: desdoblamiento de Dios en máscara de todos* [Olga Orozco's poetics: the unfolding of God in the mask of everyone]. Madrid: Nova-Scholar, 1988.

Veiravé, Alfredo. "La poesía: generación del 40" [Poetry: the 40s generation]. *La historia de la literatura argentina,* 49. Buenos Aires: Capítulo, 1967.

——. "La poesía social después del Boedo" [Social poetry after the Boedo group]. *La historia de la literatura argentina,* 50. Buenos Aires: Capítulo, 1967.

Yurkievich, Saúl. *Fundadores de la nueva poesía latinoamericana* [Founders of the new Latin American poetry]. Barcelona: Ariel, 1984.

——. "Sobre la Generación argentina de los 40: Girri/Orozco: la persuasión y el rapto" [About the Argentine generation of the 40s: Girri/Orozco: persuasion and rapture]. *Las vanguardias tardías en la poesía hispanoamericana.* Rome: Bulzoni Editore, 1993: 237–43.

Zapata, Miguel Angel. "Liliana Lukin: El cuerpo del deseo en la escritura" [Liliana Lukin: The body of desire in writing]. *Inti* 26–27 (otoño 1987–primavera 1988): 235–39.

Zolezzi, Emilio. "Olga Orozco o la creación incesante" [Olga Orozco or uninterrupted creation]. *Clarín* (May 1975).

Index

147, 171–72 [160–61]; as "el
proceso," 171 [160]; and torture, 140
"Dirty war, the": and Orozco's poetry,
3; and *los desaparecidos,* 103–4
Discourse: Easthope on, 14; limits of, 25;
in the literary interview, 18; and
postmodernism, 109; and the subject,
15–16
Disunity: in Eliot's poetry, 34; and the
feminine, 91; in Orozco's poetry, 20,
30–31, 32–33, 44, 61–62, 63, 71; and
the semiotic, 42. *See also* Divided
subject; Fragmentation
Divided subject: in Girondo's poetry,
55–56; in Orozco's poetry, 17, 71, 73,
140–41; in Pizarnik's poetry, 17, 68–
70, 73; as trait shared by Orozco and
Pizarnik, 86–87. *See also* Disunity;
Fragmentation; Poetic Subject;
Subjectivity
duBois, Page, *Sowing the Body,* 176n.11

Easthope, Anthony: and Althusser,
176n.7; on discourse, 14; on reading
poetry, 10
Elegy: in Orozco's poetry, 33, 81–86
El 40 (generation). *See* Forties generation.
El 40 (periodical), 4
Eliot, T. S.: on Baudelaire, 177n.2; and
enlightenment, 40–41; and the hero,
65–66; and language, 26, 39, 42, 43;
modernism, as representative of, 6,
25, 64, 65–66; and Orozco, 16, 25–
26, 64, 65, 130, 161 [149], 177n.14;
poetic subject, in poetry of, 65–66, 87;
and romanticism, 177n.2; and
tradition, 34; mentioned, 21, 57, 107
—"Burnt Norton," 40; "Dry Salvages,"
40; "Four Quartets," 25, 34, 39–40,
65–66, 177n.2; "Little Gidding," 25,
34–36, 38–39, 41, 42, 43, 64; "The
Social Function of Poetry," 43
Ernst, Max, 166 [154]

Faulkner, William, *Light in August,* 37
Feminine, the: in Aráoz's poetry, 109; in
Bellessi's poetry, 113; in Girondo's
poetry, 52, 54; images of, 86, 97,
141–42; and lesbian desire, 115, 116–

19; objectification of, 92; Orozco's
relation to, 89; as poetic subject, 1,
90, 91, 97, 121–22; and self-
alienation, 86–87; and the social
relation of poetry, 147; and the
traditional heroine, 92; and "women's
writing," 89, 122, 137–38
Forties generation: and Argentine literary
tradition, 2–3, 4, 6–7, 8–9, 145; and
the avant-garde, 9; concept of, 4, 175–
76n.6; and elegy, 8; and
neoromanticism, 4; Orozco, included
in, 4, 132, 164 [152]; poet's role, ideas
on, 2–3; and the social relation of
poetry, 8–9, 87; stylistic disunity
within, 6, 7; mentioned, 10, 147
Foucault, Michel: *Discipline and Punish,*
140; and the poetic subject, 1; "What
Is an Author?" 124
Fragmentation: in Aráoz's poetry, 110–
12; and the body, 101–2; and
language, 120–21; in Lukin's poetry,
101–2; in Orozco's poetry, 59–60; in
Pizarnik's poetry, 79–80; and the
social relation of poetry, 2. *See also*
Disunity; Divided Subject
Fragueiro, Josefina Susana, 82
Fuss, Diana, 12

García Lorca, Federico, 99
Gelman, Juan: Generation of '55,
representative of, 88; and objectifica-
tion, 89; mentioned, 101
Gender: in Agustini's poetry, 23–24; in
Aráoz's poetry, 105–6, 109; in
Bellessi's poetry, 116–17; construction
of, 91; and language, 114, 119–21; in
Lukin's poetry, 98, 105; in Orozco's
poetry, 137, 140–41; and the poetic
subject, 36, 44, 62, 91, 98, 112–13,
114, 121–22. *See also* Feminine, the
Generación del 40. See Forties generation
Generación del 60: Pizarnik as member
of, 17
Generation of '55, 88
Ghiano, Juan Carlos, 175n.5
Gilbert, Sandra, and Susan Gubar, 79;
Madwoman in the Attic, 179–80n.8
Giordano, Carlos, 8; *El 40* (book), 4
Girondo, Oliverio: and the anti-hero, 66;

WITHDRAWN